D0862031

Governance Series

Governance is the process of effective coordination whereby an organization or a system guides itself when resources, power and information are widely distributed. Studying governance means probing the pattern of rights and obligations that underpins organizations and social systems, understanding how they coordinate their parallel activities and maintain their coherence, exploring the sources of dysfunction, and suggesting ways to redesign organizations whose governance is in need of repair.

The series welcomes a range of contributions—from conceptual and theoretical reflections, ethnographic and case studies, and proceedings of conferences and symposia, to works of a very practical nature—that deal with problems or issues on the governance front. The series publishes works both in French and in English.

The Governance Series is part of the publications division of the Centre on Governance and of the Graduate School of Public and International Affairs at the University of Ottawa. This is the 26th volume published in the series. The Centre on Governance and the Graduate School of Public and International Affairs also publish a quarterly electronic journal, www.optimumonline.ca.

Editorial Committee

Caroline Andrew
Linda Cardinal
Monica Gattinger
Luc Juillet
Daniel Lane
Gilles Paquet (Director)

The published titles in the series are listed at the end of this book.

The Case for Centralized Federalism

edited by
Gord DiGiacomo &
Maryantonett Flumian

UNIVERSITY OF OTTAWA PRESS
OTTAWA

University of Ottawa Press
542 King Edward Avenue
Ottawa, ON K1N 6N5
www.press.uottawa.ca

uOttawa

The University of Ottawa Press acknowledges with gratitude the support extended to its publishing list by Heritage Canada through its Book Publishing Industry Development Program, by the Canada Council for the Arts, by the Canadian Federation for the Humanities and Social Sciences through its Aid to Scholarly Publications Program, by the Social Sciences and Humanities Research Council, and by the University of Ottawa.

We also gratefully acknowledge the Centre on Governance at the University of Ottawa and the Institute on Governance, whose financial support has contributed to the publication of this book.

LIBRARY AND ARCHIVES CANADA CATALOGUING IN PUBLICATION

The case for centralized federalism /
edited by Gordon DiGiacomo & Maryantonett Flumian.

(Governance series, ISSN 1487-3052; 26)
Includes bibliographical references and index.
ISBN 978-0-7766-0744-3

1. Decentralization in government—Canada. 2. Federal government—Canada. I. DiGiacomo, Gordon II. Flumian, Maryantonett III. Series: Governance series (Ottawa, Ont.) ; 26

JL86.D39C37 2010   352.2'830971   C2010-902835-X

Table of Contents

Contributors

Behiels, Michael D.
Michael Behiels is Professor in the Department of History at the University of Ottawa.

Collier, Cheryl N.
Cheryl Collier is Assistant Professor in the Department of Political Science, University of Windsor.

DiGiacomo, Gordon
Gordon DiGiacomo is a public policy research consultant and a Sessional Lecturer in Political Science with Carleton University and the University of Ottawa.

Flumian, Maryantonett
Maryantonett Flumian is President of the Institute on Governance, Ottawa, Ontario.

Jeffrey, Brooke
Brooke Jeffrey is associated with the Department of Political Science, Concordia University.

Weibust, Inger
Inger Weibust is Assistant Professor at the Norman Paterson School of International Affairs, Carleton University.

Foreword

This volume is one of a pair of books published in its Governance Series by the University of Ottawa Press that have been the outcome of the Federalism Redux Project that was undertaken in 2008. These two books are designed to provide the requisite vocabulary and schemes of arguments likely to be useful for those who would like to articulate the best case that can be made for centralized and decentralized federalism respectively.

This particular volume makes the case for centralization while the companion volume, edited by Ruth Hubbard and Gilles Paquet, makes the case for decentralization.

The Federalism Redux Project is aimed at presenting the best case for each position in the most analytically sound way. It is for the reader to determine whether the books have delivered on their promises, and whether, as a result, someone who has worked carefully through both books is likely to be persuaded more effectively by one or the other.

Our main objective is to enrich the debate about federalism in Canada. Our intent is to get away from the continuous whining about petty grievances or the doldrums of institutional plumbing, and to stimulate a serious discussion about the best way to initiate an important and useful conversation on federalism in Canada, and on how it might best serve Canada going forward. We invite readers to communicate with authors and editors in order to make their views and criticisms known.

It is the intention of the Editor in Chief of *Optimumonline* at www.optimumonline.ca to provide a forum for a broad range of views on these books in forthcoming issues.

We would like to thank the Centre on Governance at the University of Ottawa and the Institute on Governance; their various forms of support for the Federalism Redux Project are gratefully acknowledged.

Gordon DiGiacomo and Maryantonett Flumian
Ruth Hubbard and Gilles Paquet

Introduction

Gordon DiGiacomo and
Maryantonett Flumian

In the 2008 federal election, the Conservative party won 21.7 percent of the popular vote in Quebec, which gave it 10 seats. In the previous election, in 2006, the party also won 10 seats but its popular vote total in the province was 24.6 percent (Elections Canada 2009). What is interesting about these figures is that between 2006 and 2008 the Conservative party declared the Quebecois to be a nation, gave the government of the province a seat at UNESCO (United Nations Educational, Scientific and Cultural Organization), responded to Quebec's concerns about the so-called "fiscal imbalance", and generally articulated a highly provincialist vision of Canadian federalism. Apparently, the voters in the province were not impressed.

Going back a little further, the Liberal party won 21 seats and 33.9 percent of the vote in Quebec in the 2004 federal election, down from 36 seats and 44.2 percent of the vote in the 2000 election (Elections Canada 2009). The reason for the drastic decline in the fortunes of the Liberal party in Quebec, of course, was the sponsorship scandal. In an effort to stem the party's hemorrhaging, shortly before the 2004 election, then Prime Minister Paul Martin agreed to devolve responsibility for parental benefits to the government of the province—even before the Supreme Court handed down its decision on the constitutionality of the federal parental benefits initiative. Not surprisingly, the devolution move was not able to dissipate the stench of corruption that hung over the Liberal party.

What the above electoral comparisons contain is the germ of a proposition. Maybe, just maybe, the citizens of the Province of Quebec have become more interested in clean, progressive government than in seeing the provincial political elite acquire more power from the federal government. If this is the case, then the traditional tactic of federal parties trying to win votes in Quebec by diminishing the role of Ottawa in the province has run its course. It is a possibility devoutly to be wished not only in the case of Quebec but of all provinces.

Over the past several years, Ottawa has demonstrated an extraordinary degree of subservience to the provinces, repeatedly backing off from playing a leadership role on several issues, even when the issue falls squarely within its jurisdiction. In general, the six readings in this book condemn this jurisdictional timidity and call for a new federal assertiveness. The arguments presented in the readings make a convincing case that the absence of federal policy leadership has led to abysmal national performance. As a result, to paraphrase Theda Skocpol, it is time to bring Ottawa back in.

The federal government's diminished status has prompted one veteran political scientist to conclude that there is no government of Canada! Richard Simeon has written:

> It is important to get away from the rhetoric that says, "We are the government of Canada." The federal government is one government, with specific responsibilities, in a system of multi-level governance. "Government" in Canada is the combined actions, individually and collectively, of federal, provincial, and increasingly municipal and aboriginal governments. We do not have the hierarchy implied by "levels" of government; we have equal "orders" of government (Simeon et al. 2006: 3).[1]

Simeon's view is becoming the common view among politicians, bureaucrats and scholars. It is distressing that it is.

It is difficult to imagine a scholar in the United States or Australia (or any other advanced federal country for that matter, aside from Belgium and Switzerland) presenting such a view. It is also difficult to imagine that Canadian citizens want their federal government to be considered just one of the many governments in Canada, on the same level as, say, the governments of the cities of Charlottetown, Prince Edward Island and Windsor, Ontario, and the government of the Yukon territory. It is particularly disturbing that this transformation of Ottawa's role appears to have the support of all federal political parties.

Simeon makes another observation that merits a reaction. He contends that the argument that "decentralization inevitably leads to a 'rush to the bottom' in terms of social justice or environmental standards, simply has no empirical support. The image that national standards must be defined and enforced by Ottawa, in Ottawa, to stave off provincial regression is not sustainable" (Ibid., 4).

Simeon may be right here. Canadian federalism is not so backward that blatant races to the bottom are a regular feature in the various policy domains.[2] However, as the readings in this book and in others show, when Ottawa does not make full use of its valid constitutional powers bad things happen. Consider the environment. No one would seriously suggest that Canada's performance in this area has been stellar, or even mediocre. Indeed, the OECD (Organisation for Economic Co-operation and Development) has ranked Canada near the bottom in terms of environmental stewardship. The reason, as Inger Weibust argues in this book, has to do with the federal government's reticence to be the dominant government actor. For many years, it even refused to enforce its own laws.

Gordon DiGiacomo's chapter on internal trade demonstrates the inadequacy of the federal-provincial Agreement on Internal Trade (AIT). Ottawa's refusal to use its valid interprovincial trade power, strengthened by several Supreme Court decisions, resulted in an agreement that has been glaringly ineffective and has almost no defenders. Even the public servant who negotiated on behalf of the federal government has issued a scathing indictment of the agreement (Knox and

Karabegović 2009). One would have to look far and wide to find someone who would say that the AIT represents a model of how to do public policy in this country.

In labour market training, evidence suggests that Ottawa's decision to devolve responsibility to provinces and territories was not prudent. This is the conclusion one must draw from Table 0.1. It shows Canada's ranking among about fifty countries (depending on the year) on the availability of skilled labour and it was compiled from the *World Competitiveness Yearbooks*.

Table 0.1

1996	2000	2001	2002	2003	2004	2005	2006	2007	2008
15th	11th	18th	14th	24th	26th	25th	31st	21st	19th

Source: International Institute for Management Development, *World Competitiveness Yearbook*, selected years, (Lausanne, Switzerland).

Only twice since 2000 was Canada's ranking higher than it was in 1996, the year that Parliament passed the legislation allowing for the negotiation of devolution agreements with the sub-national units.[3]

In a number of social policy areas, such as child care, health care,[4] and housing,[5] advocacy groups regularly plead for federal engagement because they know that, without the national leadership that only the federal government can provide, national programs will not emerge.

The editors' conception of federalism

The editors' conception of federalism can be briefly stated. First, we do not accept that the federal government is just another government in the country. We, therefore, subscribe to what Rocher and Smith call the nationalizing vision of federalism in which the federal government is the dominant government actor. Notable proponents of this view throughout Canadian history were Sir John A.

Macdonald, F. R. Scott, and the Rt. Hon. Pierre Trudeau. Further, as set out in the Calgary Declaration, we believe in the equality of the provinces with each other. Secondly, it is in Canada's interest to have provinces with a substantial range of autonomy, as well as adequate taxing powers to make that autonomy meaningful. This does not mean, however, that provincial autonomy should reach the point where it threatens federal dominance or where the provinces are able to dictate to Ottawa what powers they will let it use. Thirdly, in general, a federal arrangement is superior to a confederal arrangement, at least for Canada. We do not accept that national policy must always be formulated jointly by the federal level of government and the provincial governments. Among other things, this method of policy making demeans Parliament. Finally, contrary to the view of some politicians, the federal government does have the right (and obligation) to determine the national interest. This does not imply that it ought to do so in isolation from the provinces or citizens. It does mean that the definition of the national interest is legitimately and ultimately a responsibility of federal political institutions, not the responsibility of the Council of the Federation or of a federal-provincial conference.

These general features of a federal arrangement for Canada are based on five principles: democracy, equality, efficiency, national solidarity and diversity.

Federalism is to be valued because it supports democracy. It does so by diffusing political power. Thus, absolutist government is more difficult to achieve in a polity with multiple levels of governance. Federalism enables one level to act as a counterweight to another and, if there is a degree of competition among governments, citizens experience more responsive government. Daniel Weinstock makes the additional point that federalism "increases the number of political levers available to citizens, and thus increases the likelihood of the development of active citizenship..." (Weinstock 2001: 76). Related to this point is Weinstock's observation that democracy is advanced under federalism because it situates "certain political decisions at a level that is cognitively more accessible to the average citizen" (Ibid., 77). This argument, however, should not be exaggerated as sub-national governments, too, can be difficult to access, particularly those like the governments of, say, Ontario, Quebec, California and New York, that have seen huge growth in their public bureaucracies. Indeed, Samuel LaSelva notes that, for communitarians "the problem with federalism...is not that it fails to secure justice, but that the provinces have become too large" (LaSelva 1996: 71). Still, most Canadian provinces have small populations and most are long distances from Ottawa. Thus, the local and provincial governments may perhaps be more easily accessed. As well, more centres of power mean more citizens actively working those centres.

For these reasons and because in federalism there can be an unmediated relationship between citizens and the central government, we are of the view that federalism is superior to unitary government and to collaborative federalism in the democracy dimension.

A second principle that shapes our view of federalism is equality. A federal arrangement characterized by a dominant central government is valued because it is better able to ensure that citizens are treated equally regardless of their province of residence. For the editors, it is unacceptable that the residents of one province have available to them the latest cancer-fighting drugs while the residents of another do not. Consider, also, pay equity. A couple of provinces have progressive pay equity legislation; others provide some legislative support to pay equity; and yet others give no legislative protection for the principle of equal pay for work of equal value. As a result, the degree of protection that a woman at work receives is dependent on where she works. The inequity is obvious. Why should a woman in one province have to settle for inferior protection simply because she works in the "wrong" part of the country? For the editors, equality rights trump provincial autonomy.

Another important principle is efficiency. National governments are obliged, not only to advance the general interest, but also to formulate and execute policies as efficiently as possible. A federal system is more likely than collaborative federalism or a confederal arrangement to provide efficient government. Collaborative federalism requires lengthy decision-making processes but, more importantly, it frequently produces lowest-common-denominator decisions. Unable to reach agreement on difficult issues, governments settle for vague agreements that require little commitment on the part of the participants.

The fourth principle is national solidarity. Our view is that, because of the peculiar way the country was established and the strains on the country's cohesion, the federal government must have the institutional wherewithal to create a positive sense of attachment to Canada. If the federal government is nowhere to be seen, unsupportive of citizen striving, it will disappear from citizen consciousness. Conversely, when the federal government has legislative capacity on issues of importance to Canadians, it "brings itself closer to the people and gains more visibility" (Leclair 1998: 377). For this reason, legal scholar, Jean Leclair, supported the Supreme Court's rulings in Imperial Tobacco and Hydro-Québec. In his view, the importance of the Supreme Court's decision in R. v Hydro-Québec is not the broad interpretation given to the federal criminal law power but rather:

> ...the fact that the Court reinforces the legitimacy of the central government by authorizing it to encroach extensively on provincial jurisdictions for the sake of protecting matters which are considered vitally important to all Canadians wherever they live, whatever language they speak. In other words, these encroachments are justified because they are aimed at protection of the "fundamental values of our society." In identifying and defining those fundamental values, the Court actively participates in the construction of a "Canadian identity" (Ibid., 378).

What Leclair is saying is that the Court, in the two decisions, not only identified fundamental values of importance to all

Canadians, it also gave the federal government the opportunity to be involved in the lives of all citizens, in all parts of the country, in a meaningful way. Of course, the federal government cannot always rely on the Supreme Court to provide it with opportunities; it must not only take advantage of those opportunities but also create its own opportunities to become known to, accessible to, and valued by citizens.

Finally, we support federalism because it is better able to accommodate the country's diversity than a unitary system. However, a word must be said on the notion of diversity. Undoubtedly, the country is big and diverse and, undoubtedly, the francophone population and Aboriginal citizens, among others, have legitimate concerns, needs and interests that must be accommodated. Federalism, therefore, is highly desirable for Canada. But the degree of the country's diversity has been vastly exaggerated, sometimes for political reasons. At the same time, the commonalities among Canadians have been seriously downplayed. Consider, for example, the issue of Quebec's civil law tradition. This is often cited as one of the differences that distinguish Quebec from the other provinces. But the comment of the Rt. Hon. Pierre Trudeau on the civil law tradition is highly instructive:

> Much is made of the fact, for example, that the civil law is the law in Quebec, whereas common law applies in other provinces. Yet, however important the Civil Code may be, in reality it occupies a very small place in the total picture of provincial laws by which we in Quebec are governed. Just like the other provinces, Quebec has enacted a vast number of statutory laws; they apply to all aspects of our collective lives and are the product of a juridical culture far more closely related to that of the other provinces than to the laws of New France or the Napoleonic Code (Trudeau 1996: 266–267).

Quebec journalist Lysiane Gagnon also commented on the supposed differences between Quebec and the rest of Canada. She has written:

There is also that all-too-common perception that there are fundamental differences between Québec and the rest of Canada. That is not true....Québec and the 'ROC' have much more in common than not....The basic values of the two societies are the same, and in fact are shared by all liberal democracies....In reality, it is social status and urbanization, not residence in one province or another, that determine the differences (Gagnon 2007: 3).

While federalism is to be preferred because of its capacity to accommodate diversity, Canada's sub-national units are not so diverse that the nation needs further provincialization.

Some federal provincializing measures since the defeat of the Charlottetown Accord

For many Canadians outside of Quebec, the whole Meech Lake Accord/Charlottetown Accord debacle was a searing experience. The spectacle of Canada's elite attempting to manipulate a transformation of the Constitution lit a fire under Canadians that was arguably unprecedented. As a result, the Meech Lake Accord made it to the ash can of the country's political history. The Charlottetown Constitutional Accord, with slightly more legitimacy, made it to the referendum stage. But it, too, was a provincializing document. For instance, the accord:

- states that labour market development and training should be identified as "a matter of exclusive provincial jurisdiction";
- calls for limitations on the federal spending power;
- recommends that the following be recognized as areas of exclusive provincial jurisdiction: housing, forestry, tourism, recreation and urban affairs;
- calls for the recognition of Quebec as "a distinct society, which includes a French-speaking majority, a unique culture and a civil law tradition"; it affirmed the role of the government of the province to preserve and promote the distinct society of Quebec; and

- suggests that the economic union is a shared responsibility.

On October 26, 1992, the citizens of Canada rejected the agreement.

Ottawa, however, was unwilling to take no for an answer. Thus, shortly after the referendum on the accord, it began to implement the very measures that were rejected by Canadians, and then some. The federal government agreed to these provincializing measures, among others:

- the limitation of the federal spending power;
- the devolution of labour force training; in the labour market development agreements that Ottawa signed with each province and territory, Ottawa agreed to the insertion of a clause which states that labour force training is a matter of provincial jurisdiction;[6]
- the reduction of federal involvement in housing and other policy areas;
- the refusal to use its internal trade power and instead negotiate a federal-provincial agreement on internal trade;
- the willingness to use the confederal Canadian Council of Ministers of the Environment in its environmental policy development; as a result, the federal government signed the Canada-Wide Accord on Environmental Harmonization under which Ottawa largely agreed to let the provinces take the lead on environmental issues;
- the adoption by the House of Commons of a resolution in December 1995 recognizing Quebec as a distinct society in Canada that includes a French-speaking majority, a unique culture and a civil law tradition; the resolution committed the House and the government to be guided by the resolution;
- the adoption by the House of Commons of a motion in November 2006 recognizing that Quebecers form a nation within a united Canada;

- the devolution of parental benefits to the provinces;
- federal agreement to give the government of Quebec a seat at UNESCO and to let it speak on behalf of the province at UNESCO meetings;
- federal willingness to allow some provinces to have their own systems of securities regulation;
- the reduction of conditionality and accountability in federal transfers to the provincial governments;
- federal acceptance of *de facto* asymmetry for Quebec; and
- the heightened involvement of the provincial governments in the formation of international trade policy and in international trade negotiations.

To be sure, none of the above was constitutionalized but the practical effect is the same.

The six chapters

The editors did not establish a set of criteria to use in the selection of topics for this book. Rather, we simply looked for scholars who shared our concern about the jurisdictional retrenchment of the federal government from the economic and social life of the country. After we found an author, we left it to him/her to determine what to write about. We did hope that we would get a mix of philosophical reflection and policy discussion and, as it turned out, that is pretty much what we got.

The first chapter, by Gordon DiGiacomo, offers an explanation of why Ottawa routinely refuses to fully use its valid constitutional powers. The explanation, the chapter argues, goes back to the ambivalence of the country's founders regarding Canadian sovereignty and nationhood. The theory is tested by an exploration of the federal government's approach to internal trade barriers and is found to be valid.

In chapter two, Michael Behiels analyzes the concept of asymmetrical federalism. Accepting that all federal societies display a range of asymmetries, Behiels is

nevertheless impelled to ask whether it is "wise and necessary to expand the existing range of well-defined, yet
limited asymmetries that are formally recognized within
the Canadian Constitution." Behiels thinks not and rejects
constitutionally entrenched asymmetry. He proposes significant reforms to Canada's central political institutions
to ensure the full participation of Canada's minorities in
national and regional politics.

Behiels's chapter critiques asymmetrical federalism.
DiGiacomo's chapter looks at collaborative federalism. In
the third chapter, Brooke Jeffrey investigates "open federalism", the model advanced by the current government led
by Prime Minister Stephen Harper. She is particularly concerned about the impact of open federalism on the future
of the welfare state in Canada. She points out that Harper's
rationale for open federalism was the need "to return to the
original principles of the constitution" and "revert" to the
practice of federalism "at the time of Confederation." The
problem with this argument, Jeffrey makes clear, is that it is
historically inaccurate. Indeed, classical federalism with its
watertight compartments and two separate but equal levels of government has never existed in this country. Jeffrey
argues further that in the absence of a strong federal presence and a national framework, the likelihood of developing new social architecture in Canada, or even of maintaining current programs, is slim.

The fourth chapter, by Cheryl Collier, agrees with Jeffrey. Collier compares the development of Medicare in
Canada with the arrested development of child care and
concludes:

> Decentralizing movement away from cooperative federal-
> ism to collaborative and perhaps open federalism is partic-
> ularly distressing in that the federal government appears
> to have all but abandoned its ability to use the federal
> spending power to take a leadership role in policy areas
> of provincial responsibility. Recent cuts to the federal GST
> also indicate a willingness to abandon federal tax room
> that facilitates the use of the federal spending power.

Collier's exhaustive analysis shows how child-care advocacy groups have had little influence on federal child-care
policy because of the combined effect of ideology and institutions. She writes:

> ...advocacy influence is likely lessened further by the
> presence of a more right-wing Conservative govern-
> ing party that has traditionally been less open to child
> care advocacy both provincially and federally over the
> years. The fact that the intergovernmental process has
> remained the same or is even further decentralized,
> would help to solidify this situation. Thus, the pres-
> ent political landscape suggests that national child care
> interests will continue to be shut out of the child care
> policy community.

Collier's discussion resurrects a question that political scientists going back at least to Donald Smiley have asked: to what
extent are intergovernmental processes about accommodating government interests rather than citizen interests?

In the fifth chapter, Maryantonett Flumian, a former
senior public servant in the federal government, takes a
practitioner's perspective to the analysis of Canadian federalism. Clearly affirming that Canada was intended "to be
greater than the sum of its parts," and that, while the traditional lines of jurisdiction have become blurred, "the need
for strong national leadership has not," Flumian goes on to
argue that there must be greater attention to a "new paradigm of governance in a federal state." In this paradigm,
coherence and collaboration are the watchwords, and they
are made possible by strong leadership. This kind of leadership must come from the central government. Looking back
over the past twenty years, Flumian is critical of the federal government for failing to articulate a "common coherent vision that will power the Canadian journey in the 21st
century." This is a responsibility of the federal government.
"Strong leadership speaking on behalf of all Canadians
must provide a common context and values for interpretation and belonging."

The subject of the final chapter is environmental policy. If there is an area where the federal approach has been an utter failure, it is the environment. Inger Weibust offers a devastating critique of Ottawa's hands-off policy on the environment. She describes how Ottawa's abandonment of environmental policy to the provinces and the confederal Canadian Council of Ministers of the Environment has left the country with an incoherent and spectacularly ineffective policy on environmental protection.[7] Weibust emphasizes that "lack of constitutional authority is not a sufficient explanation for federal timidity." She then identifies the considerable powers that the federal government does have but does not use for fear of upsetting the provinces.

Avoiding a death by a thousand cuts

Neither the editors nor the contributors want to see Canada turned into a unitary state or see its provinces reduced to administrative units. But neither do we wish to see the federal government suffer a death by a thousand cuts. Contrary to Simeon, we believe there is a Government of Canada—the federal government—not a system of several governments of comparable status. Canada is the envied country that it is, in large part, because the federal government had the wherewithal—and used the wherewithal—to involve itself in areas that are important to citizens—social policy, economic development policy, labour and employment policy, human rights, etc. When the federal government, on a consistent basis, sacrifices citizen concerns on the altar of intergovernmental peace or of provincial autonomy, both citizen well-being and national solidarity suffer.

The spoken or unspoken reaction to demands for a more assertive federal government usually has to do with the possible consequences, for example, the secession of Quebec. Thus do the advocates of a muscular federal authority become paralyzed and lose their voice. Our deep hope is that this small book will make a modest contribution toward the recovery of that voice.

Endnotes

1   There seems to be a contradiction in Simeon's comment. On the one hand, he does not like the term "levels of government" but, on the other, he says that Canada has a system of multi-level governance.

2   See, in endnote 11 of DiGiacomo's chapter, the comment of Véronique Marleau, a labour law scholar and former member of the Canada Industrial Relations Board. See also the April 2007 report of the House of Commons Standing Committee on Environment and Sustainable Development, which stated, in reference to the establishment of national environmental standards, "The trick is to avoid a race to the bottom, which does seem to be what is happening. The federal government should show leadership at the CCME [Canadian Council of Ministers of the Environment] in an effort to prevent this from happening (Canada 2007: 4).

3   In a recent paper on the federal spending power, Tom Kent, who was one of the key designers of federal training policy in the 1960s, called for a return to the system whereby Ottawa "purchased" training courses from industry, private agencies or provincial departments. Such a program, Kent wrote, "is a major part of the 'investment in human capital' now recognized to be crucial to a productive economy" (Kent 2007: 5).

4   For instance, on health care, the president of the Canadian Healthcare Association, Pam Fralick, told a House of Commons committee in 2008:

> Canadians legitimately expect to have access to comparable services, regardless of the jurisdiction in which they reside, and the *Canada Health Act* commits to this. Since jurisdiction over health delivery is a provincial-territorial responsibility, some argue that the federal government should only provide the funding, without linking it to conditions or objectives. However, the federal government has a constitutional right— some would say duty—to use its spending power to achieve health objectives for the good of all Canadians (Fralick 2008).

5   In her chapter, Brooke Jeffrey references the comments of four national housing groups—the National Housing and Homelessness Network (NHHN), Federation of Canadian Municipalities, the Canadian Housing and Renewal Association, and the Co-operative Housing Federation of Canada—all of whom participated in a joint press event on April 15, 2003, and then the NHHN reported in a press release on April 16 that "it is astonishing that the provinces and territories, most of whom have failed to even meet the minimal commitments of the

[federal-provincial] Affordable Housing Framework Agreement, continue to insist that provinces should have the primary role in the design and delivery of programs..." (NHHN 2003).

6 This federal concession was not supported by the Supreme Court. In Confédération des syndicats nationaux v Canada, which came down in December 2008, the Court held that federal training programs have their justification in the federal unemployment insurance power.

7 Even the highly respected scholar, Thomas Courchene, as strong an advocate of provincial autonomy as this country is likely to see, in a paper he co-authored for *Policy Options*, called upon the federal government to assume the mantle of leadership on climate change (Courchene and Allan 2008–09: 66).

References

Canada 2007. House of Commons Standing Committee on Environment and Sustainable Development. *The Canadian Environmental Protection Act, 1999.* "Five-Year Review: Closing the Gaps." Report. Ottawa: 5: 44.

Courchene, Thomas J. and John Allan 2008–09 (December–January). "The Provinces and Carbon Pricing: Three Inconvenient Truths." *Policy Options*, 60–67.

Elections Canada. http://enr.elections.ca/Provinces_e.apsx [retrieved March 22, 2009].

Fralick, Pam 2008 (May 13). *Remarks to the House of Commons Standing Committee on Health on its Review of the 10-Year Plan to Strengthen Health Care.* Canadian Healthcare Association. www.cha.ca/index [retrieved January 22, 2009].

Gagnon, Lysiane 2007 (Spring) "Quelling Stereotypes." *Tabaret: The Magazine of the University of Ottawa.* www.tabaret.uottawa.ca/article_e_335.html [accessed April 29, 2010].

Kent, Tom 2007. "The Federal Spending Power Is Now Chiefly for People, not Provinces." Working papers. Institute of Intergovernmental Relations (IIGR). www.queensu.ca/iigr/working/spendingPower.KentT.pdf.

Knox, Robert and Amela Karabegović 2009 (February 12). *Myths and Realities of TILMA.* Fraser Institute. www.fraserinstitute.org/researchandpublications/6501.aspx [retrieved March 3, 2010].

LaSelva, Samuel V. 1996. *The Moral Foundations of Canadian Federalism: Paradoxes, Achievements, and Tragedies of Nationhood.* Montreal and Kingston: McGill-Queen's University Press.

Leclair, Jean 1998. "The Supreme Court, the Environment, and the Construction of a National Identity: R. v Hydro-Québec." *Review of Constitutional Studies*, 4: 2: 372–378.

NHHN 2003 (April 16). *NHHN Letter to Housing Ministers*. Toronto: National Housing and Homelessness Network.

Simeon, Richard et al. 2006. *Open Federalism: Interpretations, Significance*. Kingston, ON: Institute of Intergovernmental Relations.

Trudeau, Pierre Elliott 1996. *Against the Current: Selected Writings 1939-1996*. Toronto: McClelland & Stewart Inc.

Weinstock, Daniel 2001. "Towards a Normative Theory of Federalism." *International Social Science Journal*, 53: 166: 75–83.

Chapter 1

Ottawa's Deferential Approach to Intergovernmental Relations[1]

Gordon DiGiacomo

Introduction

In his 2009 budget, the federal Minister of Finance announced his intention to establish a single Canadian securities regulator to improve the regulation of capital markets. But rather than make clear that the regulator would operate for ALL of Canada, the Minister indicated that he would work with "willing provinces and territories" to establish the regulator (Canada 2009a: 88). Although virtually every constitutional scholar in the country, save those with a secessionist orientation, would probably agree that securities regulation is a federal responsibility, Ottawa intends to allow some provinces, presumably Alberta and Quebec, to maintain their own systems of securities regulation.[2]

This announcement from the current government led by Prime Minister Stephen Harper is the latest example of federal reluctance to fully assert its valid constitutional powers. Even though the economic union is one of the areas cited by Prime Minister Harper as clearly being a federal responsibility, he still could not bring himself to confront Alberta and Quebec on the issue. Other examples of federal submissiveness in the Harper years, so far, include Ottawa's intention to legislatively restrain its own spending power, and Ottawa's agreement to let Quebec have a seat and to speak at meetings of the UNESCO (United

Nations Educational, Scientific and Cultural Organization), even though international affairs is an exclusively federal responsibility.

The Harper government has not been the first to display an extraordinary willingness to restrict or devolve its powers. Among the policy areas where other federal governments accepted or proposed an attenuated role for Ottawa are: labour force training policy; environmental policy; parental benefits policy; and as we will see, internal trade (Haddow 2003; Harrison 2003; DiGiacomo 2009). And, of course, we cannot forget former Prime Minister Brian Mulroney's efforts to 'constitutionalize' the weakening of the federal government.

We can go back further. In a paper originally published in 1931, Frank R. Scott attributed the diminution of federal authority to "the attitude of the leaders of the Dominion parties of recent years. They seem to have wished to hand over as much as possible to the local legislatures" (Scott 1977: 47). This does not mean that there have not been politicians who recognized the importance and value of a strong central government. Nor does it mean that there have not been periods of confident federal activism. It does suggest that the federal impulse towards deference based on jurisdiction is a constant theme in Canadian political history.

This deference is the subject of this chapter. It hypothesizes that federal reticence stems from serious omissions in the Constitution that the founders crafted, omissions that are related to a major constitutional abeyance, in Michael Foley's terminology, having to do with the very idea of Canadian sovereignty and nationhood. Because of that abeyance, and the particular constitutional exclusions that resulted, the Government of Canada routinely backs away from a leadership role even when the issue in question appears to fall squarely within its jurisdiction. In recent years, those constitutional omissions have led to the development of a type of elite accommodation that some have labeled, 'collaborative federalism,' which, under Prime Minister Harper, has been supplemented by its weaker cousin, 'open federalism', (discussed by Brooke Jeffrey in this book). Both types represent what former Supreme Court Chief Justice Bora Laskin would have called "a limping federalism under which the central government will be one with dependent status, whether in respect of one Province or all of the Provinces" (Laskin 1968: 139).

The task of the chapter, therefore, is to determine if federal deference to the provinces can be explained by the chapter's theoretical framework. It opens with a discussion on the meaning of federalism and then moves to an explanation of the theory, the main pillars of which are historical institutionalism and the theory of constitutional abeyances. This framework is tested by an analysis of the federal approach to interprovincial trade barriers.

The essence of federalism

Federalism is a system of governance characterized by a division of law-making powers between a central government and constituent governments, applied on a territorial basis. That said, several other points ought to be made.

Essentially, federalism is a mechanism for unification. Colonies and states enter into a federal arrangement in order to come together; they do not do so in order to maintain their previous independence. They recognize that, because federalism is above all a means for effecting a union of some sort, they will have to surrender some of their autonomy to a central authority. They rightly expect to receive something—protection, financial aid—in return.

The founders of the nation[3] envisaged Canada as a federation, not a confederation. Even though the sub-national governments have jurisdiction over several specific areas, they are not independent or semi-independent states. They are the constituent units of a sovereign state—Canada. And the central government in a federation, unlike that in a confederation, is more than a kind of secretariat or cheque-clearing entity. These seemingly banal statements are, nevertheless, contrary to the views of Marc-Antoine Adam. In a recent paper he made this astonishing comment: "Hence, under Canadian federalism, both orders of government are said to be sovereign in their own areas of jurisdiction, in the same manner and to the same extent as independent states" (Adam 2009: 304).

Another point that should be made about federalism is that there is no one type of federal arrangement common to all states. Although they are characterized by a sharing of power, federal states differ in institutional configurations and distributions of powers. As a result, Scott argued that Canadian federalism was never meant to conform to a pre-conceived notion of federalism.

> ...the Canadian constitution was never expected to oper-ate on strictly federal principles as the political scientist understands them; we adopted, for what seemed good reasons, a constitution leaning toward a strong central authority whose power might offset in some degree the centrifugal forces which are always present in the body politic (Scott 1977: 298).

Scott cautions against being misled "by the word 'federal', which has a meaning in political theory that it does not have in Canadian constitutional law" (Ibid., 189). The definition of Canadian federalism should be based on what the Canadian Constitution provides, not on some accepted meaning of federalism. In Scott's view we should not say, 'A federal state requires such and such relationships between the governments, therefore we will find them in the Canadian constitution.' We should say, 'This is what the Canadian constitution provides: what kind of federalism is it?' (Ibid., 177).

Federal states differ in their institutional configurations because they differ in the values they privilege and support. Diversity, equality, efficiency, harmony and democracy are among the values a federal system may at any one point in time either privilege or undermine (Rocher and Smith 2003a: 23). In Canada, one of the important tasks of the federal government has long been to ensure that individuals receive rel-atively equal treatment regardless of where they live in the country. However, in recent years, the salience of the equality value has receded, while the desire to accommodate diversity has heightened.

Writing in the context of a discussion on the federal spending power, Gaudreault-Desbiens has also commented on the values that federalism reflects. He posits that not only is autonomy inherent in federalism, so also is national solidarity. He draws a conclusion about the Canadian arrangement: *"being what it is, and considering what it is not—that is, a confederation*—a federation can hardly tolerate blatant discrepancies in the delivery and accessibility of basic social services" (Gaudreault-Desbiens 2006: 195–196, italics added for emphasis).

Types of federalism

Several types of federalism compete for preeminence in Canada and political scientists have labeled or categorized them in various ways. One type has already been mentioned, collaborative federalism, defined by Cameron and Simeon as "the process by which national goals are achieved, not by the federal government acting alone or by the federal government shaping provincial behaviour through the exercise of its spending power, but by some or all of the 11 governments and territories acting collectively" (Cameron and Simeon 2002: 54). The governance of Canada is seen by the proponents of collaborative federalism *"as a partnership between two equal, autonomous and interdependent orders of government that jointly decide national policy"* (Ibid., 49, italics added for emphasis). While the federal and provincial governments have always worked together to formulate policies and programs, collaborative federalism is distinguished by the willingness of the federal government to accept a diminished role for itself in national policy making and to acknowledge that it is but one of fourteen governments in the country. This degree of federal submissiveness is a somewhat new development, emerging most visibly around the early 1990s.

Collaborative federalism seems like a concept that one would have a hard time opposing. After all, who could be against collaboration? The problem arises when collaboration becomes collusion—that is, when governments collude to achieve their own interests rather than citizen interests, or, as Gerald Baier put it, "when governments co-operate too well" (Baier 2002: 35).

Martin Painter illustrated the negative and positive features of collaborative federalism and its opposite, competitive federalism, in figure 1.1 (Painter 1991: 270). For Painter, the latter occurs when governments keep their distance from each other and provide separate bundles of services as they compete for public support. Collaborative federalism is practiced when governments come together to cooperate in the provision of public services, "with the provincial governments seeking a close involvement in spheres of federal policy that are perceived to intrude on provincial jurisdiction" (Ibid., 269).

Figure 1.1

Mode	Negative Features	Positive Features
Competition	Confrontation	Responsiveness
Collaboration	Collusion	Coordination

Competitive federalism, it is argued, leads to confrontation and deadlock; to federal intervention in provincial affairs; and to contradictory policies. Collaborative federalism "produces better co-ordinated outcomes that achieve a more satisfactory balance of provincial and federal perspectives" (Ibid., 270). While collaboration is said to also produce barriers to public access, to provincial vetoes and to cartel-like behaviour, competition is said to yield more diverse, more responsive policies. "[S]o long as the competitive dynamic operates, governments will remain answerable to their own electorates rather than merely to each other in the deals that they strike" (Ibid.).

Painter concludes that collaborative federalism is a flawed model and argues against two possible institutional reforms that are advanced by advocates of collaborative federalism. One, a re-designed Senate modeled on the German Bundesrat—with members appointed by the provincial governments—"would clearly 'hobble Ottawa' in spheres of action where the constitution has assigned it the capacity to act unilaterally" (Ibid., 286). Secondly, permanent first ministers' conferences "would afford additional temptations for political executives to engage in collusive forms of collaboration" (Ibid., 287).

In their categorization of Canadian visions of federalism, Rocher and Smith include a type similar to collaborative federalism (or confederalism), which they call the equality of the provinces vision—that is, the equality of the provinces with the federal government. It sees Ottawa and the provinces as being sovereign in their areas of jurisdiction and able to act independently of each other. Their use of the phrase, 'orders of government', is meant to convey a non-hierarchical relationship between the federal and provincial governments. The implications of this view are profound. As Rocher and Smith point out, "in this view, the provincial premiers have as much right to represent citizens as does the Prime Minister of Canada." The central government "is not in a position to speak for provincial interests" (Rocher and Smith 2003a: 24). Thus, the federal government is just another government in the country.

Other visions of Canadian federalism identified by Rocher and Smith are the equality of the provinces with each other, a vision reflected in the Calgary Declaration (an agreement on how to approach future amendments to the Constitution); asymmetrical federalism (discussed in this book by Michael Behiels); the rights-based vision of federalism; and the nationalizing vision of federalism.

In the nationalizing vision, the basis of political identity is Canada itself, not a province and not one of Canada's national minorities. Since it privileges the federal level of government, it "tends to be centralizing". The main proponents of the nationalizing vision throughout Canadian history have been Sir John A. Macdonald; the Depression-era social democrats such as F. R. Scott; and the Rt. Hon. Pierre Trudeau. In describing this vision, Rocher and Smith make an interesting observation: "Taken to its extreme, this centralizing dynamic permits the federal government to appropriate the authority to define a 'national interest'" (Rocher and Smith 2003b: 9–10). That a federal government power to define the national interest could be described as "extreme" demonstrates how far the provincial autonomy advocates have taken their argument.

Rocher and Smith's nationalizing vision has been described in a more disparaging way by Alain Noël. In his analysis of the Social Union Framework Agreement, Noël describes the federal government's approach to the negotiations as an example of 'hegemonic cooperation,' a term borrowed from international affairs scholar, Robert Keohane. This type of cooperation, Keohane writes, "relies on a dominant power making rules and providing incentives for others to conform with those rules" (Noël 2000: 6).

Noël's use of the word "hegemonic" is pejorative, intended to draw a parallel between the aggressive behaviour of the United States in the world and the approach of the federal government to intergovernmental relations. But—apparently it needs to be said—the relationship between the United States and other countries is not at all like the relationship between the federal and provincial governments. And, as we will see, the phrase certainly does not describe the way Ottawa went about negotiating the Agreement on Internal Trade,[4] among other intergovernmental agreements. Noël is clearly unhappy when Ottawa acts like any self-respecting central government in a federal system, determining the rules in accord with what it deems to be the national interest and willing to use whatever tools and incentives it possesses to move the sub-national units in a certain direction. Indeed, it would be difficult to find an advanced federal country where the central government is not dominant.

That said, I am able to find an area of agreement with Noël. He accuses Ottawa of failing "to enunciate a clear overarching view or a well-defined set of principles" and he agrees with Harvey Lazar in that "the federal government's behaviour is difficult to predict, making it an uncertain, and at times, unreliable partner for the provinces" (Ibid.). I concur. The centralism of the founders' Constitution was undermined by the Judicial Committee of the Privy Council (JCPC), leaving Canadian decision makers at the federal level confused and conflicted, to this day, over which vision of the country to take seriously.

Consequences

Federal restraint in its use of its valid powers raises a number of questions. For instance, what is the effect on the relationship between Ottawa and citizens? In collaborative federalism, relations between the government of the country and citizens are mediated by provinces and territories. What would be the impact on citizens' positive sense of attachment to Canada? How would the federal government be perceived by citizens? Secondly, is Ottawa's reliance on intergovernmental agreements (IGAs) rather than the application of its own policy-making authority conducive to democratic decision making? It was perhaps this concern that impelled the Rt. Hon. Lester B. Pearson to write: "The federal government must remain responsible to Parliament, and the provincial governments to their legislatures: federal-provincial conferences must, it seems to us, occupy themselves with the art of influence rather than the power of decision-making" (Pearson 1968: 191). Thirdly, Johanne Poirier legitimately wonders: what is the effect of reliance on IGAs on citizen respect for the constitutional order? She suggests that IGAs enable governments to decide on "who does what" regardless of "who is constitutionally competent to do what".[5] The result, she says, can be "a marginalization" of the division of powers sections of the constitution (Poirier 2004: 453). In this regard, one also has to wonder about the eventual fate of an unused federal power. Finally, what is the impact of federal submissiveness on policy making? It is arguable that the impact has been significant. In a number of policy domains, most especially internal trade and the environment, federal willingness to let the provinces lead has resulted in abysmal national performance.

Theoretical framework

The theoretical framework has been constructed with two theories, historical institutionalism and the theory of constitutional abeyances.

Historical institutionalism

Historical institutionalists argue that institutions shape action. They influence the strategies that actors adopt and help to determine the goals that they will pursue. Generally, historical institutionalism (HI) theorists define institutions as formal rules and structures as well as informal rules and norms and would include electoral rules, party systems, public policies, corporatist structures and constitutions. Particularly important from the perspective of this chapter is Thelen and Steinmo's inclusion of "the relations among various branches of government" within the definition of institution (Thelen and Steinmo 1992: 2). In this chapter, the concern is with the enduring influence of the judiciary, that is, the Judicial Committee of the Privy Council, on the federal executive branch of government.

Historical institutionalists agree that institutions not only shape and channel interests they also possess and defend certain interests. As March and Olsen point out: "The bureaucratic agency, the legislative committee, and the appellate court are arenas for contending social forces, but they are also collections of standard operating procedures and structures that define and defend interests. They are political actors in their own right" (March and Olsen 1984: 738).

A concept central to HI is path dependency. Margaret Levi describes it this way:

> Path dependence has to mean, if it is to mean anything,
> that once a country or region has started down a track,

> the costs of reversal are very high. There will be other choice points, but the entrenchments of certain institutional arrangements obstruct an easy reversal of the initial choice. Perhaps the better metaphor is a tree, rather than a path. From the same trunk, there are many different branches and smaller branches. Although it is possible to turn around or to clamber from one to the other—and essential if the chosen branch dies—the branch on which a climber begins is the one she tends to follow (Pierson 2004: 20).

In other words, what comes before conditions what comes next.

Given that the paper's independent variable is the judiciary, which is guided by the doctrine of *stare decisis* or precedent, it is not surprising that path dependence would be a central concept herein. The doctrine refers to the influence of previous decisions on the court's deliberations on a current case. That influence can be weak or powerful depending on the attitude of the judges to the doctrine. It appears that, in the case of the JCPC, the influence was relatively strong during the years when it was Canada's final court of appeal.

The judiciary, it must be stressed, is often a veto player, defined by George Tsebelis as an individual or collective actor "whose agreement is necessary for a change of the status quo" (Tsebelis 2002: 19). The probability that a course of action will unfold is frequently dependent on what the courts have to say about it. Obviously, path dependence is reinforced when the judiciary sanctions a course of action or rules out certain alternatives.

Path dependence happens not only because the judiciary is a veto player and because of the influence of precedent. Paul Pierson asserts that the crucial path dependent process is positive feedback and, in his work, he discusses how this process occurs. One mechanism has to do with self-reinforcing norms. To illustrate his point, Pierson employs a metaphor: "Every time we shake hands, the strength of that norm is reinforced." Conversely, we can say that every time we do not shake hands, that norm is reinforced. Further,

political values, orientations, ideologies and understandings of how government should work are generally 'tena-
cious' once established.

A second positive feedback mechanism at work has to do
with the reactions of political actors to government actions.
Political actors, whether individuals, groups or the public service, "make important commitments in response to
certain types of government action. These commitments,
in turn, may vastly increase the disruption caused by new
policies, effectively 'locking in' previous decisions" (Pierson
1993: 608).

Pierson stresses that the analyst must take note of the
timing of political events. When an event occurs may be as
important as the event itself. An "event that happens 'too
late' may have no effect, although it might have been of great
consequence if the timing had been different" (Pierson 2004:
45). Again Pierson uses a metaphor, borrowed from Ray-
mond Aron, to make his point: "A man takes the same walk
every day. On one occasion, a heavy tile becomes dislodged
from a building along his route. Depending upon the particular of these two streams of activity (strolling man, fall-
ing tile), the observed outcome will be radically different"
(Ibid., 57). As we will see, the timing of a number of Supreme
Court of Canada decisions turned out to be crucial.

For some HI analysts, the concept of critical junctures is
central to HI. In John Hogan's view, critical junctures are
characterized by the adoption of a particular institutional
arrangement. They "establish pathways that funnel units
in particular directions" (Hogan 2006: 660). A critical juncture, Hogan argues, is identified by two requirements. One
is that the critical juncture must come from an important
social cleavage, the tensions from which generate a mandate for change. The manifestations of a social cleavage
range from violent wars and revolutions to economic crises
and electoral landslides to class differences and urban–rural
disputes. The second requirement is that the critical juncture must produce change that is significant; that occurs
relatively swiftly; and that affects a sizable segment of the
population or an important sector of the population. The

critical juncture featured in this paper, namely, the era of Confederation, would seem to satisfy Hogan's criteria.

The law endures
In his work on the shaping power of American labour law, specifically judge-made law, the legal historian, William Forbath, offered some reflections that are pertinent to this discussion. He prefaces his book by pointing out that scholars in the United States have ignored the impact of the law and the courts on the goals, strategies and overall effectiveness of American labour unions. For them, the law made no big difference in labour history. Judge-made law was a reflection of fundamental social conflicts; it was, they said, 'derivative'. As Forbath found:

> Among historians and social and political scientists as with law professors, scholarship about law and society has emphasized the ways that the interests of social groups shape the law; it has slighted the ways that law shapes the very interests that play upon it (Forbath 1991: x).

In words that sound eerily similar to those written by Alan Cairns in another context, Forbath summed up the view of traditional labour historians as being "what happened would have happened, whatever the courts had done" (Ibid.).

But, as Forbath goes on to show, American labour law was anything but derivative. As interpreted by judges, it was decisive in fashioning the labour movement's strategies and capacity for collective action. The argument that American unions have not been as effective as others in Canada and Europe because US workers are more conservative and individualistic has little merit. American unionism is relatively weak, Forbath demonstrates, because of the impact of judge-made law. He writes: "Nowhere else among industrial nations did the judiciary hold such sway over labor relations as in nineteenth- and early-twentieth-century America. Nowhere else did trade unionists contend so constantly with judge-made law" (Ibid., 6).

Since the period covered by Forbath, 1880–1930, legislation and court decisions have frequently been more favourable to organized labour. But, as Forbath argues, American labour unions never recovered from the court decisions rendered in those years. "The old common law concepts rule from the grave," Forbath declares. Labour remains a commodity and labour protest continues to be denied constitutional protection. So, Forbath concludes with a warning:

> In the past, the institutional framework and policies of labor law played a substantial part in shaping the character of the labor movement. We deceive ourselves if we attribute too much of that character to "deeper" forces. Thus the imagining and scrutinizing of possible new institutions and new laws should be done with all the canniness labor and its friends can muster; for these institutions and laws may go a long way toward shaping the identity and the capacities for collective action of the labor movement of the future (Ibid., 172–173).

The point of this short discussion on Forbath's book is simply to emphasize the shaping influence of judicial decisions. It was not the 'deeper forces' that framed the goals and strategies of organized labour in the United States but rather the courts. Thus, the Cairns' thesis, that the JCPC's decisions did not take Canada in a direction it would not otherwise have gone, must be treated very cautiously. It is also noteworthy that the effects of the court decisions on labour made in the period covered by Forbath endure, despite the favourable legislation and court decisions of the New Deal and afterwards.

Constitutional abeyance theory

The second pillar of my theoretical framework comes from the work of Michael Foley. In *The Silence of Constitutions*, Foley uses the term constitutional 'abeyances' to refer to those issues that are either omitted from constitutions or mentioned in only the vaguest terms because, were they to be clearly articulated and set out, they could become sources

of conflict, or worse. They are the constitutional and political issues that receive 'studied inattention'.

Abeyances "may include contradictions, tensions, anoma-
lies and inequities, but the fragility and, at times, total illogi-
cality of such packages are kept intact through a convention
of non-exposure, of strategic oversight and of complicity in
delusion..." (Foley 1989: 9).

Foley describes abeyances as the continuing flaws, the
half-answers and the partial truths that are "endemic in the
sub-structure of constitutional forms." C-haracterized by
ambiguity in meaning, abeyances are further described by
Foley as "obscurities" and "gaping holes of constitutional
unsettlement". They are uncertain understandings, and
they stay undefined and un-clarified because to attempt
to define and clarify would be to threaten the Constitution
itself. Through various forms of evasion and obfuscation,
the unsettled questions, "the gaps and fissures" are kept in
a state of irresolution. By remaining obscure they are able
to accommodate conflicting interpretations and, therefore,
Foley sees abeyances in positive terms.

Clearly Foley does not see constitutional development as
a process of continual clarification. It can mean that, but it
can also mean the maintenance of gaps; the avoidance of
'hard' issues; and the tolerance of contradictions. In the case
of Canadian sovereignty, it took the country's politicians
well over a century to settle the issue.

The founders' ambivalence

The *Constitution Act, 1867* does not proclaim Canada as a
fully sovereign, independent nation. A number of serious
omissions in the Constitution ensured that Canada would
remain subordinate to Britain. From the perspective of this
paper, the most important was the absence of any provision
for the establishment of an indigenous final court of appeal.
As a result, Canada's final court of appeal, until 1949, was
the Judicial Committee of the Privy Council, a committee of
Britain's House of Lords.[6]

Why did the founders not seek full sovereignty and
speak frankly and fully about their limited self-government

objective? One reason is that Prime Minister Macdonald believed that the British monarchy would be a unifying force in the new country, while George-Étienne Cartier, Quebec's major political leader, and others believed that the rights of French Canadians would receive better protection from British institutions than they would from the institutions of a completely independent Canada. For instance, Jean-Thomas Taschereau stated in an 1865 speech in the Legislative Assembly of the Province of Canada, "Lower Canadians will assuredly be less satisfied with the decisions of a Federal Court of Appeals than those of Her Majesty's Privy Council" (Canada 1865: 896–897). This warm view of the British connection endured well into the 20th century. In 1907, Rodolphe Lemieux, a Laurier minister, told a crowd in Aurora, Ontario: "Bear in mind that the British institutions that happily govern us are, when applied in their true spirit, the only safeguard of the French-Canadians as a race. We cling to them, because we feel that under them, and with them, our rights, our franchise, our liberties are secured to us" (Lemieux 1907: 3).

As a result, Canada's founders avoided pressing the issue of independence and sovereignty. David Thomas has written that the founders saw sovereignty and other issues as "intractable, volatile, injurious to our constitutional health, and better left alone" (Thomas 1997: 76–77). He notes that as late as 1925 the federal Cabinet decided not to 'Canadianize' the Constitution because such a step "was too dangerous an issue to raise, since it was likely to unite in opposition the imperialistic Ferguson [premier of Ontario] with Taschereau [premier of Quebec], who considered that Britain could still provide significant protection for French-Canadian rights" (Ibid., 118).

Another reason why the founders did not seek full sovereignty has to do with the colonies' political economy. To put it less delicately, it has to do with the influence of British finance capital on the thinking of the founders and of the British government. In a recent volume, the historian, Andrew Smith, showed how British investors came to believe that a political union of the British North American colonies would work to their advantage, and they lobbied for this development. They did not support complete independence.

> The British financiers who supported Confederation did so because they thought that the union of the colonies would solidify their connection to Britain. They did not see Confederation as some sort of stepping stone to Canadian independence. ... The financiers who supported Confederation valued the constitutional bond linking them to their fellow subjects in North America because colonial status made Canadian securities easier to sell to individual investors in Britain. Many British investors distinguished investments in self-governing colonies from those in sovereign countries such as the United States. Because the distinction was widespread, those who marketed Canadian investments in Britain had a compelling reason to dislike the proposal for colonial independence... (Smith 2008: 129).

In advancing their ideas, British financiers had a supportive audience in the colonies, for "many of the Fathers of Confederation were personally involved in projects that were dependent on the continued inflow of British capital" (Ibid., 18).

Notwithstanding the limited objective of the founders, the language that they used to describe their project was often the language of sovereignty. Consider, for instance, the words of Macdonald himself: in his view, he and his colleagues were "trying to form a great nation", "joining these five peoples into one nation...to take our position among the nations of the world." Cartier stated, "*Nous avons a faire en sorte que cinq colonies...forment une seule et grande nation... Le temps est venu pour nous de former une grande nation...Lorsque nous serons unis...nous formerons une nationalité politique indépendante de l'origine nationale.*" Cartier's colleague, Hector Langevin, declared: "*La mesure actuelle est destinée à nous faire prendre rang dans la grande famille des nations...former une*

*puissante nation...Nous ne formerions qu'une seule nation...Je
parle de nation grande et forte...une grande nation...une nationalité nouvelle...une grande et puissante nation."* Sir Étienne-
Paschal Taché said the Confederation project would create
*"une puissante nation une nation prospère...une nation indé-
pendante."* Sir Narcisse Belleau similarly stated, *"Tous les
éléments qui sont nécessaires pour faire une nation puissante se
trouvent dans les colonies réunies....La réunion de ces éléments
ferait de la confédération une grande puissance parmi les autres
nations du globe,...une peuple nouveau et puissant"* (Forsey
1974: 253–254).

These expressions of the founders belied the actual nature
of the state they were creating. They certainly misrepre-
sented the contents of the Constitution. In Foley's language,
they exercised the tactic of obfuscation.

It should be noted that the correspondence of Alexander T. Galt indicates that full sovereignty for Canada may
indeed have been on the minds of the founders. In a May
1869 letter to the Governor-General, barely two years after
union, Galt wrote: "I regard the Confederation of the British North American provinces as a measure which must
ultimately led to their separation from Great Britain"
(Skelton 1966: 221). In the same year, he wrote to Britain's
Secretary of State for War: "I therefore think the wisest
policy will be to commence a discussion of our possible
future as an independent country, so as to prepare for the
time when the trial will have to be made" (Ibid., 223). Galt
went so far as to advocate the acquisition of an independent treaty power for Canada for commercial agreements.
Why would Galt make these comments so soon after Confederation? He may have realized how difficult it would
be to create a country while urging its citizens to direct
their allegiance elsewhere. In any event, it suggests that
full sovereignty for Canada was an option of which the
founders were aware and which they may have seriously
debated in private.

Thomas concludes that, while the obfuscation tactic
may have served the founders' political purposes, Canadians have paid a high price. He writes: "The irony is that

Macdonald's very 'Britishness', Cartier's and Quebec's
acceptance of British institutions, and the success of a court-
statist patronage approach sowed the seeds for one of our
now most problematic questions, the lack of an overarching
agreement on national identity and community" (Thomas
1997: 70). He adds that the absence of a clear statement of
national sovereignty may have undermined "the arsenal of
federal powers" right from the start. He does not get precise
here but it is clear that the founders' decision to maintain
the JCPC as Canada's final appellate court did, in fact, result
in a federal arsenal with far fewer powers.

In the vast majority of division of powers cases, the JCPC
favoured provincial autonomy. "Between 1880 and 1896
the Judicial Committee decided eighteen cases involving
twenty issues relating to the division of powers. Fifteen of
these issues (75 percent) it decided in favour of the provinces" (Russell 2004: 42). This trend continued throughout
the JCPC's time as Canada's final appeal court. The federal
trade and commerce power, the federal residual power and
the federal treaty-making power are among those that fell
victim to the 'provincialist' bias of the JCPC. Notable also
is the 1925 JCPC decision to strike down an eighteen-year-
old federal labour relations law and assign the power to the
provinces, with some exceptions. In addition, provincial
taxing powers were interpreted very broadly to the point
where there is little difference between what the federal
government can tax and what the provinces can tax.

To some degree, the decisions of the Supreme Court
have reclaimed the jurisdiction that the federal government lost, particularly its trade and commerce power. But
in no sense could one argue that it overturned the decisions of the JCPC. In addition, the Court has demonstrated
a deep reluctance to tamper with the overall federal–provincial balance.

If, then, a constitutional abeyance can be said to be (a)
a constitutional contradiction or inconsistency or obscu-
rity or gap, that (b) if pressed for clarity has the potential to
produce serious constitutional crisis, and that (c) endures
for a substantial period of time since it tends to be avoided

by political leaders or, when it is addressed, it is with the use obfuscation tactics, for example, vague terminology or mixed messaging, then we can say that the failure of Canada's founders to constitutionally assert Canada's full sovereignty qualifies as a constitutional abeyance.

The basic argument

So, this chapter's theoretical argument runs as follows: a particular constitutional abeyance pertaining to the founders' views of Canadian sovereignty left Canada incomplete in terms of its political institutions. This resulted in a continuing role for the JCPC. Indeed, it became a veto player. Its rulings demonstrated a view of Canadian federalism that was highly provincialist in orientation, an orientation that was very much at odds with the type of federalism envisaged by the founders. They also set the committee and its successor institution, the Supreme Court of Canada, on a path from which deviation would have been very problematic. In the language of HI, the judiciary became path dependent. As it is required to do in a democratic political system characterized by the rule of law, the executive branch of the federal government fashions its approach to intergovernmental relations to conform with the judiciary's decisions. The executive's decisions also became path dependent. More precisely, the judiciary defined the direction of the path, and it was clearly away from federal assertiveness. As a result, the executive branch has sought out a confederal relationship with the provinces—that is, a relationship based on collaborative federalism—on several issues rather than ask Parliament to enact the necessary legislation. In so doing, it has opted to play a secondary role in the development and implementation of policy, sometimes even in areas that appear to fall within its own jurisdiction. With the rise of 'open federalism', Ottawa has displayed even less willingness to take a leadership role in several areas, including most notably, internal trade and the environment.

Internal trade barriers and the Agreement on Internal Trade (AIT)

Internal trade barriers refer to policies that impede the flow of goods, labour, services and capital among the provinces and territories. Section 121 of the Constitution requires that "All Articles of the Growth, Produce, or Manufacture of any one of the Provinces shall, from and after the Union, be admitted free into each of the other Provinces." The power to ensure that commerce flowed freely was given by the country's founders to the federal government. Section 91 (2) of the Constitution sets out "The Regulation of Trade and Commerce" as being among the powers of the federal government.

The section clearly reflects the wishes of the founders, which they expressed on several occasions. For instance, Charles Fisher, one of the framers of the *Constitution Act, 1867*, who became a justice on the Supreme Court of New Brunswick, stated: "It was clearly the intention of the framers of the Act that Parliament should have the power to regulate the trade between the several Provinces, and the internal trade of each Province as well as the foreign trade of the whole Dominion" (Saywell 2002: 26)

Notwithstanding the founders' intent to establish a Canadian economic union, and to equip the central government with the authority to ensure that union, internal trade barriers emerged as a concern by the 1930s and since then at least three formal inquiries into the issue have been undertaken. Among other things, the inquiries noted the political importance of strengthening the economic union.

No federal government took the issue of interprovincial trade barriers seriously until Prime Minister Pierre Trudeau made the Canadian economic union a constitutional priority. But he had limited success. The provinces resisted encroachments on their powers, and the insertion of citizens' mobility rights into the Canadian Charter of Rights and Freedoms was the best that could be done. Former Prime Minister Brian Mulroney, too, tried to broaden Section 121 but could not overcome provincial opposition.

That the federal government has exhibited diffident behaviour on the issue of economic union and internal trade barriers has been a contention of McGill University legal scholar, Armand de Mestral. In a forceful attack on the Agreement on Internal Trade (AIT), de Mestral declared:

> The text [of the AIT] is drafted in a style reminiscent of the Canada-US Free Trade Agreement, the North American Free Trade Agreement (NAFTA), or the GATT. The underlying assumption appears to be that the provinces are totally independent sovereign actors and that it is appropriate for them to make mutual concessions on interprovincial trade barriers comparable to concessions made by governments in the GATT or the NAFTA. I find this truly extraordinary, and *it is all the more extraordinary that the federal government should be aiding and abetting the process.* This, in my view, can only legitimate the view of the federal government's role that is widely held in nationalist circles in Quebec. It is a view that I consider to be in the broad sense unconstitutional (de Mestral 1995: 97, italics added for emphasis).

Here, de Mestral makes two critically important points: first, that the sub-national units were assumed to be "totally independent sovereign actors", and secondly, that, to his amazement, the federal government refused to avail itself of Section 91 (2) or Section 121 of the Constitution.

One of the concerns of the Royal Commission on Dominion–Provincial Relations (the Rowell–Sirois Commission), established in the late 1930s, was the growing demand for provincial protectionism. Its report identified six types of interprovincial trade barriers. One had to do with taxation. For instance, British Columbia imposed a tax on fuel oil, which served to protect the province's coal industry. A second type was provincial legislation aimed at fixing prices, such as Manitoba's fixing of the price of beer sold but not brewed in the province above that of beer brewed locally under authority of provincial legislation. A third consisted of inspection and grading laws that discriminated against goods made outside of the province. Special licensing provisions were a fourth type. A fifth type consisted of provincial government procurement policies, and the sixth was 'propaganda' to encourage the purchase of provincial products. While decrying the creation of these barriers and coming down in support of free trade within Canada, the commission refrained from making a recommendation on the elimination of those barriers, preferring instead to identify options for policy makers.

By the 1960s internal trade issues became part of the national unity discourse. Interestingly, concerns about internal trade barriers emerged initially from the provinces. In 1968 the government of Quebec proposed that the free mobility of persons and goods be entrenched in the Constitution (Howse 1992: 62). In 1979 a report from the Ontario Advisory Committee on Confederation argued that the federal government "must act as the protector and guarantor of the Canadian national market...." (Government of Ontario 1979: 13). It recommended that 'serious consideration' be given "to entrenching a 'freedom of movement of people, capital, goods and information' provision in the constitution" (Ibid., 15).

The 1979 Task Force on Canadian Unity (Pépin–Robarts Task Force) also commented on internal trade. The report is considered to be supportive of provincial autonomy generally and special status for Quebec specifically, but it is critical of the provinces for erecting a multitude of interprovincial trade barriers, arguing that "these provincial barriers contradict the spirit of economic union and should be prevented as far as possible..." (Canada 1979: 71). It recommended that Section 121 of the Constitution be "clarified in order to guarantee more effectively free trade between the provinces for all produce and manufactured goods, and be extended to include services" (Ibid., 123). It also recommended that interprovincial barriers to the movement of capital be constitutionally prohibited. Impediments to the mobility of professionals and trades people should be reduced through interprovincial cooperation, a proposal that would obviously minimize the role of the federal government in promoting the economic union.

During the federal-provincial constitutional negotiations that preceded patriation in 1982, Ottawa endeav-
oured to make the case for enhanced economic mobility
in Canada. It argued that Section 121 did not adequately
safeguard the economic union and that court decisions
had rendered Section 91 (2) ineffective in preventing the
rise of provincial protectionism. It clearly perceived that
its power to secure the economic union was weak. It, therefore, proposed a three-pronged constitutional methodol-
ogy to ensure economic mobility in the country. One was
the constitutional entrenching of citizens' mobility rights.
A second was a broadening of Section 121 to limit governments' powers "to impede economic mobility." A third
was a broadening of federal trade and commerce powers to encompass "all matters that are necessary for economic integration" (Chrétien 1980: 29). As it turned out,
Ottawa was unable to convince the provinces and could
get agreement only on citizens' mobility rights, which
now comprise Section 6 of the Canadian Charter of Rights
and Freedoms.

The report of the Royal Commission on the Economic
Union and Development Prospects for Canada (Macdonald
Commission) stressed the political dimension of the concept
of economic union. It states:

> The objective of building a Canadian economic union has
> meaning because we are first a national political com-
> munity. Threats to the economic union are threats to the
> national community because they erode the ties of affin-
> ity and interest that bind Canadians together (Canada
> 1985: vol. 2, 100).

Elaborating further, the report says:

> Political opposition to [economic] fragmentation has sev-
> eral dimensions. It is derived, in part, from a sense of com-
> mon citizenship....A political view argues that building
> economic linkages among Canadians is of value in itself,
> and that it increases personal contacts and relationships

> among Canadians which contribute to a sense of shared
> identity and common citizenship (Ibid., 113).

For the commissioners, the Canadian economic union is
related to perceptions of political identity and political community, and citizens' sense of attachment to that community.
Thus, "barriers that may be trivial in economic terms may
be politically significant if they offend against our sense of
Canadian citizenship" (Ibid., 114). However, the commissioners were quick to add that federalism allows for a diversity of preferences and an attempt to eradicate all internal
trade barriers would probably mean the end of Canadian
federalism.

Perhaps the main recommendation of the Macdonald
Commission pertaining to internal trade, although it was
not stated as such, has to do with the pre-eminent role that it
said the federal government should play. This role involves
"safeguarding the economic union" but it did not say how
Ottawa was to do this. In the commission's view, the "development of the federal power over interprovincial trade and
commerce could help to ensure the effective operation of
the economic union" (Ibid., 140), although, again, it did not
say how the "development of the federal power" was supposed to be accomplished. Consistent with its comments
on the political value of removing internal trade barriers,
the commission's report stated: "[The federal government's]
role as the national government means that its primary
focus must be on the health of the whole, and that it must
continually foster the development of positive linkages of
all kinds among Canadians" (Ibid.).

By the time that the Macdonald Commission reported, a
new government, led by the Rt. Hon. Brian Mulroney, was in
office in Ottawa. Having pledged to get Quebec to sign the
Constitution Act, 1982, he made two attempts at constitutional
reform, neither of which was successful. The first attempt,
the 1987 Meech Lake Constitutional Accord, concentrated on
meeting Quebec's conditions and did not deal with the economic union. The second effort, the Charlottetown Constitutional Accord, signed in 1992, addressed the issue.

The road to the Charlottetown accord began with a discussion paper issued in 1991 by the federal government entitled, "Shaping Canada's Future Together: Proposals". Here, the Mulroney government proposed that the Constitution be amended to give Parliament "a new power to make laws for the efficient functioning of the economic union" (Canada 1991: 30–31). However, in a statement that the country's founders may have disputed, the paper says "the management of the economic union is an area of shared responsibility." Thus, even though it proposed giving itself a 'new' power, Ottawa also proposed that federal legislation under the new power "could not be enacted without the approval of at least seven of the provinces representing 50 percent of the population." In addition, three provinces could opt out of the federal law for three years if sixty percent of the members of the provincial legislature supported opting out.[7]

The discussion paper also recommended a broadening of Section 121, proposing that it be:

> ...modernized to enhance the mobility of persons, capital, services and goods within Canada by prohibiting any laws, programs or practices of the federal or provincial governments that constitute barriers or restrictions to such mobility. This would provide all Canadians with the right to pursue the livelihood of their choice and economic opportunities wherever they choose to do so in Canada (Ibid.).

But even these modest attempts at promoting the economic union were too much for the provinces to take. Reform of Section 121 was dropped and the accord deals with the economic union in only the vaguest and most general of terms. With respect to the federal–provincial negotiations on Section 121, Peter Russell wrote: "In the multilateral meetings the provincial premiers pressed for so many exemptions that they might have ended up with a clause that weakened rather than strengthened the existing constitutional protection of internal free trade" (Russell 2004: 200). The commitments of the political actors of which Pierson spoke were no doubt in the minds of the provincial premiers.

Judicial decisions

Very early in the life of Canada the courts were asked to make decisions about the economic union. In the first two cases, which were not appealed to the JCPC, the Supreme Court of Canada upheld the federal trade and commerce power. The third case, however, was the decisive case, and it was followed by a number of others that confirmed its outcome. In Citizens Insurance Company v Parsons, the JCPC ruled that the federal government had the authority to regulate only in the areas of interprovincial trade and international trade, (the so-called first branch or limb), but it may also provide for the "general regulation of trade affecting the whole dominion", (the so-called second branch or limb, which was rarely invoked or referred to until the 1970s). The JCPC ruling undermined the interprovincial aspect of the first branch when it declared that the federal power "does not comprehend the power to regulate by legislation the contracts of a particular business or trade...in a single province" (Citizens Insurance Company v Parsons 1881: 113). The critics of the decision vigorously condemned it because of its blanket prohibition against federal regulation of an intra-provincial trade or business, regardless of its size or importance.

In other decisions, the JCPC ruled that companies established in one province could operate in any other province if granted permission by the other province. For some reason, the Law Lords did not think that the incorporation of companies seeking to do business in more than one province might more suitably be a federal responsibility.[8] In yet another ruling, the JCPC held that a federal law providing for the setting up of marketing schemes for natural products whose principal market was outside of the province of production, or some part of which was intended for export, was invalid. The judicial committee seemed to want to restrict the federal trade and commerce power to regulating the actual movement—the flow—of goods from one province to another. In a case known as the Board of Commerce case, the committee even ruled that the federal trade and commerce power was merely an ancillary power; that is, it was valid only when it supplemented another federal power. This view of the power was set out again in the decision in Toronto Electric Commissioners v Snider, which struck down an eighteen-year-old federal labour relations law and held that labour was a provincial responsibility. A later JCPC ruling repudiated the ancillary interpretation but not before the JCPC had dismissed the trade and commerce power as a justification for federal assumption of responsibility for labour policy.[9]

The story of the Toronto Electric Commissioners case is revealing. In 1923, the members of the Canadian Electrical Trades Union became involved in a dispute over wages and working conditions with the Toronto Electric Commission (TEC), which was responsible for the city's electric power transmission and distribution. The union, as was its right under the federal *Industrial Disputes Investigation Act* (IDIA), applied for the establishment of a board of conciliation and investigation. The TEC refused to recognize the authority of the board and sought an injunction from the Supreme Court of Ontario to stop the board from proceeding on the grounds that the federal act was unconstitutional. Justice Orde of the High Court Division of the Supreme Court of Ontario granted the injunction, arguing that the IDIA interfered with the civil rights of employers and employees, as well as with the operation of a municipal institution, and that both issues were the responsibility of the provincial government.

The TEC then applied for a permanent injunction. This time the case was heard by Justice Herbert Mowat. He refused to grant the injunction and referred the matter to the Appellate Division of the Supreme Court of Ontario. In a four-to-one decision, the justices ruled that the IDIA did indeed fall within the jurisdiction of the federal government. They determined that, in its 'pith and substance', the federal act was not about civil rights or municipal institutions but about providing machinery to investigate industrial disputes, disputes which could affect the national interest. Justice Ferguson, writing for the majority, stated: "It cannot be disputed that to deprive the city of Toronto of electric power on which it depends for light, heat and power is to disturb and hinder the national trade and commerce and to endanger public peace, order and safety" (Canada 1925: 21). Bypassing the Supreme Court of Canada, the TEC brought the case before the JCPC, which reversed the Supreme Court of Ontario decision and held that the act was *ultra vires* of the Parliament of Canada.

The case was very similar to a 1913 case involving the Montreal Street Railway Company and its workers. (Montreal Street Railway Company v Board of Conciliation and Investigation [1913]). As with the Snider case, the workers were engaged in a dispute with the company and had requested the establishment of a board of conciliation. And, as in the Snider case, the company sought and obtained an injunction from a judge and the board was ordered to stop doing its work. The company then sought a prohibition order to permanently prevent the board from proceeding. However, Justice Lafontaine of the Quebec Superior Court dismissed the request and upheld the constitutionality of the federal IDIA. The company appealed his decision to the Quebec Court of Review. The three judges on the court ruled that the act "is constitutional and *intra vires* of the Dominion Parliament, and its enactment is within the legislative powers of the Dominion Parliament".[10]

As a result of the two cases, a total of twelve Canadian judges considered the constitutionality of the federal IDIA. Ten upheld the validity of the act, (including four from Quebec), and only two thought it *ultra vires*. What is interesting and significant about these two cases is that judges of two provincial courts upheld the constitutionality of a federal law. For the Supreme Court of Ontario—the province that gave Canada Oliver Mowat—national trade and commerce was legitimate grounds for the enactment of a federal labour relations law, even if the law applied to a municipal organization.

The Snider decision is interesting, too, because, like the JCPC ruling in the Citizens Insurance case, it is an example of the JCPC going to the extreme in its determinations. In the latter case, it issued a blanket prohibition against federal regulation of intra-provincial trade or business, regardless of the size or dimensions of the trade or business. In the Snider case, it determined that labour was not a federal matter unless the trade, business or industry was specifically identi- fied in the Constitution as being under federal jurisdiction, again regardless of the size of the organization. A reasonable alternative would have been to provide for provincial regu- lation of labour for organizations confined to a province but to allow for federal regulation when an organization: creates a subsidiary in another province; or when it exports most of its output outside one province; or imports most of its inputs from outside of the province. This arrangement would pro- tect provincial diversity while ensuring federal authority over organizations that take on significant or national dimen- sions.[11] It also might have facilitated the growth of strong, dynamic national labour unions.

Another JCPC decision, not directly related to the issue of trade and commerce, nevertheless had a profound impact on the exercise of federal power generally. Known as the Maritime Bank decision, it came down in 1892 and it clearly set out the Law Lords' view of Canadian federalism. Lord Watson, the president of the JCPC, wrote:

> The object of the [British North America] Act was neither to weld the provinces into one, nor to subordinate provin- cial governments to a central authority, but to create a fed- eral government in which they should all be represented, entrusted with the exclusive administration of affairs in which they had a common interest, each province retain- ing its independence and autonomy (Liquidators... 1892: 441–442).

In making this statement, the JCPC let it be known that it had no intention of upholding the express wish of the founders to create a dominant central government. In addition, the committee ruled that the position of provincial lieutenant- governor, now largely a ceremonial post, was equal in sta- tus to the Governor-General. Lord Watson determined that "a Lieutenant-Governor, when appointed, is as much the representative of Her Majesty for all purposes of provincial government as the Governor-General is for all purposes of Dominion government" (Ibid., 443). Robert Vipond argues that this decision helped to transform "provincial legislatures into fully self-governing and sovereign parliaments...." This enables both the federal and provincial governments to come to the bargaining table "as genuinely parliamentary governments, fully loaded as it were. This means they can negotiate as formal equals" (Vipond 1991: 73).

The consensus among constitutional scholars is that the Supreme Court has revived the federal trade and commerce power. But the revival took some time to become full-blown. Indeed, legal scholar, James MacPherson, in a 1980 paper analyzing a number of Supreme Court decisions rendered in the 1976–1980 period that failed to uphold the federal trade and commerce power, concluded that "the constitutional bases for federal economic legislation have never been shakier" (MacPherson 1980–81: 174). Not since the Depression, MacPherson wrote, "have federal economic laws been treated so harshly by the highest court" (Ibid., 217). Peter Hogg, who wrote a commentary on the MacPherson paper, supported his conclusion, arguing that the Supreme Court's decisions in Dominion Stores Ltd. v The Queen and Labatt Breweries v A.-G. Canada "seem to indicate a deliberate return to pre-1949 doctrine" (Hogg 1980–81: 223).

It was not until the late 1980s that the Supreme Court moved decisively away from the JCPC's trade and commerce rulings. The following comment by the Supreme Court—taken from Black v Law Society of Alberta, which struck down a rule of the Alberta Law Society prohibiting members of the society from entering into partnerships with non-residents of Alberta—indicates the court's new attitude.[12] Justice La Forest, writing for the majority, stated:

> A dominant intention of the drafters of the *British North America Act* (now the *Constitution Act, 1867*) was to establish "a new political nationality" and, as the counterpart

to national unity, the creation of a national economy.... The attainment of economic integration occupied a place of central importance in the scheme....The creation of a central government, the trade and commerce power, s. 121 and the building of a transcontinental railway were expected to help forge this economic union. The concept of Canada as a single country comprising what one would now call a common market was basic to the Confederation arrangements and the drafters of the *British North America Act* attempted to pull down the existing internal barriers that restricted movement within the country (Black v Law Society of Alberta 1989: 608–609).

Justice La Forest's unequivocal language suggests that the Supreme Court of Canada will not be reticent about supporting the economic union in its rulings. But that said, it must also be acknowledged that the Court's enthusiasm for the federal trade and commerce power was a long time coming.

Patrick Monahan, dean of the Osgoode Hall Law School, is convinced that recent judgments of the court have strengthened the federal authority to maintain the economic union to such an extent that Parliament could take a number of negative integration measures that would represent very strong assertions of federal authority. In Monahan's view, as a result of those decisions:

Parliament could legislate so as to give effect to a 'non-discrimination' principle...such that one province would not be permitted to impose discriminatory standards on the goods, services, investments, or persons of another province.

Ottawa "could legislate so as to prevent the establishment or maintenance of restrictions on the free movement of persons, goods, services, or investments across provincial boundaries....The free movement of factors of production across provincial boundaries is essential to the effective conduct of interprovincial trade, the regulation of which has always been clearly a matter of federal jurisdiction.

Parliament could legislate so as to prevent or eliminate obstacles to internal trade—measures that are more trade restrictive than necessary or are adopted as disguised restrictions on trade. In Hunt, La Forest stated that measures which are designed to discourage interprovincial commerce and the efficient allocation of resources (as opposed to the achievement of legitimate provincial objectives) offend the basic structure of the Canadian federation.

Parliament could legislate so as to provide a common set of rules for the mutual recognition of standards or regulations by provinces.

Parliament could provide for the enforcement of these requirements by private individuals and persons, either through a specialized tribunal or through the ordinary courts (Monahan 2006: 308–309).

Monahan's list suggests clearly that Parliament's trade and commerce and economic integration powers are now formidable. Monahan is not alone in his assessment. Legal scholar, Robert Howse, also notes the strengthened powers of the federal government as a result of case law. He writes:

Both Crown Zellerbach and General Motors clearly afford the federal government some scope to sustain constitutionally harmonizing regulation that impinges on areas of provincial jurisdiction, whether in consumer protection, environment, or financial services. Subsequently, *even in cases such as Hunt, where no federal statute has been at issue, the Supreme Court has emphasized the importance of federal jurisdiction to securing the economic union.* In Hunt, the Court even went so far as to suggest that the federal government could set rules for the recognition and enforcement of private law judgments by provincial courts where necessary to ensure order and fairness within the Canadian economic union. *I do not think one could ever expect a clearer statement by the Court on the link between the expanded scope of the federal government's general powers and the need for harmonization of provincial laws to secure the Canadian economic union* (Howse 1996: 12, italics added for emphasis).

Given Justice La Forest's strong language, as well as the consensus among legal scholars that the federal trade and commerce power has been 'rehabilitated', one could argue that Parliament could have used the power to strengthen the economic union on its terms, in which case there would have been no need for the Agreement on Internal Trade.

The agreement

The Agreement on Internal Trade (AIT) was signed on July 18, 1994, fifteen months after negotiations commenced and a year after the Liberal Party returned to power under the Rt. Hon. Jean Chrétien. It became effective on July 1, 1995.[13]

The agreement came about in the aftermath of the failed constitutional accords in the late 1980s and early 1990s. It was negotiated by actors who were keenly aware that, although Quebec was represented at the table by the purportedly non-secessionist Liberal government, in the not-too-distant future a second referendum on secession would be held in Quebec. This context, as Bruce Doern and Mark MacDonald state, "produced a need for success, or as federal negotiators frequently put it, 'Canada needs a win!'" (Doern and MacDonald 1999: 8). That Canada is among the most successful states on the planet, politically, economically and socially, apparently was not enough for the federal negotiators.

It is a truism among professional negotiators and dispute resolution scholars that the party most anxious to get a deal is the party most likely to get the least from the negotiations. Since Ottawa was the party to want a deal the most, it is arguable that its objective—a more integrated economic union—was the one that was advanced the least. Indeed,

MacDonald concludes that the exceedingly large number of omissions, exemptions and exceptions "to the intended philosophy of the Agreement" produced an accord "that is important in only a limited number of unimportant areas" (MacDonald 2002: 143).

In addition, the motivation to reduce or eliminate internal trade barriers was no doubt tranquilized by the willingness of each province to factor in the Quebec Liberal party's needs for the eventual referendum. Those needs probably served also as a convenient excuse for some provinces to maintain their own interprovincial trade impediments. Thus, as David Cohen argues, linking an internal trade agreement with Quebec secession "made the existence of an Agreement inevitable, but simultaneously assured that it could not accomplish the national economic integrative agenda which would have been expected in a trade agreement" (Cohen 1995: 275).

It appears, therefore, that, if the negotiation route was the federal government's preferred option, it would have been well-advised to pursue the talks under conditions more favourable to its agenda.

In their analysis of the AIT negotiations, Doern and MacDonald describe the overall approaches of the various actors. They refer to the federal government and the governments of Alberta and Manitoba as being "the most supportive of an agreement with a minimum number of exceptions". Quebec, too, was supportive, "and indeed the presence of both Alberta and Quebec as allies of the federal government was an interesting reversal of many of the normal recent configurations of federal-provincial politics...." (Doern and MacDonald 1999: 81) Since both of Quebec's political parties endorsed free trade in general and the North American Free Trade Agreement (NAFTA) and the Canada-US Free Trade Agreement (CANUSFTA) in particular, one wonders why Ottawa did not take advantage of this support and push harder for internal free trade. Since free trade with Canada is in Quebec's own interest, particularly if it were to secede, one could plausibly argue that the full application of the federal trade and commerce power to promote internal free trade would not have aroused the kind of reaction in the province that seems to so worry federal decision makers.

This line of argument is reinforced by the comments on internal free trade contained in the Quebec Liberal party report (Allaire Report), a highly provincialist document endorsed by the Quebec Liberal party in 1991. The report states, for instance: "One of the objectives of Canadian federalism is to create a common market, a strong national economy. Yet it is readily acknowledged that the integration of Canada's economy has yet to be achieved. Many barriers to trade remain and, each in its own way, harms our economic performance" (Quebec Liberal party 1991: 16). Sounding very much like a document issued by the Chamber of Commerce, the Allaire Report warned:

> Despite the existence of full economic integration for 123 years, inter-regional trade in Canada is hampered by barriers that limit trade in goods (government policies, standards and rules, discriminatory commercialization policies, etc.) or the free mobility of people (non-recognition of diplomas, difficulties in obtaining permits to facilitate the right to do business and freedom to provide services, etc.). The redefinition of the political system will have to avoid any further fragmentation of the Canadian market or the introduction of new trade barriers. In fact, this is a golden opportunity to further facilitate the free circulation of goods and services among the various regions of the country. The new political and economic order proposed by Quebec must recognize the benefits of increased trade between the regions. It must seek to maximize the existing potential by eliminating all obstacles to trade (Ibid.).

Quebec's interest in removing internal trade barriers was also reflected in the agreement that the Bloc Québécois, Parti Québécois, and the Action Démocratique du Québec came to in 1995, on the eve of the secession referendum. It stated that as a priority the treaty between Canada and the new state of Quebec would ensure that the new

partnership council, comprised of representatives of Canada
and Quebec, would have the authority to act on a customs
union, and the free movement of goods, individuals, services and capital. In addition, the two member states of the
Council would be free "to adapt and strengthen the provisions of the Agreement on Internal Trade" (*Montreal Gazette*,
1995: A6).

Le Devoir reported the reaction of the Parti Québécois
to the AIT. Jacques Parizeau, Bernard Landry and Richard
Le Hir were highly critical of the agreement for its many
exemptions and exclusions. Parizeau described it as an "*aveu
d'impuissance*", while Landry, according to the report, said it
reflected "*l'incapacité du système fédéral canadien de s'adapter
aux réalités contemporaine de la globalisation et de la mondialisa-
tion.*" Le Hir, according to the report, said the AIT showed
that "*la plus farouche résistance à l'ouverture des marchés vient
du Canada anglais*" (O'Neill 1994: A1).

Support for strong federal action on the economic union
would probably have been forthcoming from another
unlikely source: the West. The Canada West Foundation,
for instance, urged Ottawa to use its constitutional right to
maintain one common market (Brodie and Smith 1998: 89).
It was a view shared by the Reform party. Its spokesperson,
Ed Harper, told the House of Commons that the position of
his party was to support:

> ...the removal of interprovincial barriers to trade through
> agreements which include trade dispute settlement
> mechanisms among the provinces. Should the provinces
> fail to co-operate in the removal of interprovincial trade
> barriers, the Reform Party supports constitutional chal-
> lenges to such impediments wherever possible (Canada
> 1995: 12920)

Another Reform party MP and former Harper government minister the Hon. Monte Solberg argued in the
House of Commons that, while his party always favoured
decentralization, "on some issues, and I would say commerce is one of them, the authority more properly rests at

the federal level. That is why section 121 of the Constitution needs to reign supreme" (Canada 1995: 14134). In his estimation, there was "growing support that this should be challenged in the courts the next time the provinces try and assert their authority in this area" (Ibid.). In this manner, Ottawa would "be more in charge of interprovincial trade barriers" (Ibid., 14132).

Not to be outdone, the Progressive Conservative leader at the time, Jean Charest, pledged that if he was elected Prime Minister he would give the provinces one year in which to negotiate with Ottawa the establishment of an interprovincial trade commission "that would regulate and enforce interprovincial trade rules." It would include a binding dispute-resolution mechanism that could be used by both governments and businesses. According to the *Financial Post*, "If an agreement was not reached, Charest would be ready to use Ottawa's constitutional trade and commerce powers to establish the commission" (*Financial Post* 1997: 68).

The contextual factor that shaped the AIT the most was the negotiation of international trade agreements like NAFTA. They clearly supplied the motivation for governments to do something about the considerable number of internal trade barriers. Indeed, in a *Financial Post* piece, Monique Jérome-Forget wrote: "The deal was born of the recognition at both the federal and provincial level that it is ridiculous to negotiate free trade with the U.S. and Mexico and still maintain more than 500 barriers between the provinces" (Jérome-Forget 1995). At one point, a company in one province could bid on a contract tendered by the US government but could not bid on a contract issued by another province! Clearly, such a situation was unacceptable.

Douglas Brown, in his analysis of the AIT, observes that its "basic architecture bears strong similarities to the twenty chapters of the FTA [Free Trade Agreement] and the twenty-two chapters of NAFTA" (Brown 2002: 150). Doern and MacDonald go further. In their view, there was an implicit understanding that the rules for the AIT would "follow a similar path to those of the General Agreement on Tariffs and Trade (GATT), FTA, and later NAFTA" (Doern and

MacDonald 1999: 48). Thus, what we had were sub-national governments assuming the stance of sovereign states, with the full acquiescence of the national government, even though it is the national government that has the power to deal with interprovincial trade barriers.

While the emergence of international trade agreements may explain why Ottawa moved when it moved, it does not explain the way it moved. As intimated earlier, it may be argued that the explanation for federal meekness had to do with a perceived need to avoid antagonizing the provinces, especially Quebec. With the constitutional failures of the Mulroney government still lingering in people's memory, Ottawa was both 'gun shy' and desperate. And yet, as we have seen, the degree of support at the elite level across the country, including Quebec, for an end to interprovincial trade barriers was substantial. Thus, if a federal-provincial conflict was going to take place, the federal government was in a position of relative strength. Moreover, internal free trade is not an issue that has the potential to inspire mass public protests, let alone secession. It is an issue that causes consternation in the boardrooms of the nation, not in its living rooms. Given that the political and business elites in the country, including the nationalist and secessionist elite in Quebec, supported internal free trade, it seems reasonable to suggest that provincial opposition to strong federal action to do away with internal trade barriers would have had little credibility, sustainability or persuasive power. Of course, much would have depended on federal willingness to vigorously make its case to the provinces, in the courts if necessary, and in the media.

The AIT consists of eighteen chapters. It sets out definitions, operating principles and general rules and it deals with procurement; investments; labour mobility; consumer-related measures; agricultural products; alcoholic beverages; natural resource processing; communications; transportation; environmental protection; institutions to monitor implementation and adherence; and exemptions from the agreement.

Like most intergovernmental agreements, the AIT is not legally binding, despite the use of legalistic language in the text. Disputes are to be settled through non-binding arbitration and monitoring. Sanctions are allowed but only if negotiations and publicity fail to result in compliance from an offending party. Even then, there is no recourse to the courts to resolve disagreements between governments.

Also, since the agreement was the result of collaborative federalism, it begs the question: if the agreement fails to do what it is supposed to do, namely, efficiently eliminate or reduce barriers to trade among Canada's sub-national units, who do Canadians hold accountable?

Consistent with Cameron and Simeon's definition of collaborative federalism was the stance that the federal government adopted during both the negotiation of the AIT and its operation. Quite simply, Ottawa functioned and functions as one government among many. It could not even be described as first among equals since it no longer chairs the meetings of the Committee on Internal Trade. As of 2004, the chair of the meetings is rotated annually. Decisions are made by consensus, which, in effect, means the unanimity rule.

Douglas Brown has characterized the federal government's role during the negotiations as being "facilitating and non-aggressive" and suggests that this federal approach has been "one key to the success of the AIT" (Brown 2002: 171). He notes that, throughout the negotiations, Alberta, "in particular, sought to ensure that the federal role in the agreement would be as one party among the others, with no special role to enforce the agreement and no special privileges in its implementation and administration" (Ibid., 153). Federal agreement to assume the stance of just another government at the table speaks to its intensifying habit of self-diminution and increasing willingness to accept confederalism.

In assessing the AIT's impact on the federal–provincial balance, Brown contends that it has not been "perceived as a vehicle for centralization, and, indeed, the nature of its architecture and its institutional support exemplify a decentralized approach to economic union reform" (Ibid., 171). Rather than focus on the process, Doern and MacDonald look at the content of the agreement. First, they describe the opposing arguments: on the one hand, there are those who

fear that the AIT "has set limits around the [federal] powers, and that the courts, using doctrines of 'constitutional
convention,' may simply conclude that what is practiced
(namely, the internal agreement as a living document) is
what the constitutional trade-and-commerce power in fact
is" (Doern and MacDonald 1999: 162).

On the other hand, there is the argument, which Doern
and MacDonald endorse, that the federal trade and commerce power is strengthened by the agreement "because it
is the discriminatory power of provincial governments that
have been most reined in. In short, the range of available
provincial policy instruments has been narrowed. Many
actions that provinces previously did take are simply less
and less possible" (Ibid.).

While Doern and MacDonald are correct in saying that
some provincial actions are no longer permissible, this did
not come about because of the exercise of federal power.
The very modest restrictions on the provincial ability to
erect internal trade barriers were put in place by the provincial governments themselves. It was not the application of federal power, through federal legislative action or
otherwise, that set up the restrictions. Rather, it was done
through political negotiations by the parties. Admittedly,
Section 91(2) probably gave the federal government some
leverage in cajoling the provinces to reduce or eliminate the
barriers but one cannot infer, as Doern and MacDonald do,
that the AIT strengthened the federal government's trade
and commerce power.

It is obviously not clear what the agreement will lead to,
constitutionally, if anything. It may or may not produce a
constitutional convention, but it is arguable that, if the federal government continues to ignore its trade and commerce
power, it will probably go the way of the disallowance
power or, perhaps, the declaratory power. The adage about
'using it or losing it' seems particularly apt in this case.

In any event, one cannot conclude that the AIT has been
effective. Certainly, the absence of an energy chapter, fourteen years after the agreement became effective, does not
speak well of the AIT. And the fact that full labour mobility

has still not yet been achieved is a fairly clear demonstration that the AIT process is not a model of how to do public policy.[14] The agriculture chapter leaves most existing barriers in place but "says the introduction of new ones should be prevented. Governments were supposed to review and expand the coverage of the agriculture chapter by September 1997, but discussions continue more than 10 years later" (Knox and Karabegović 2009: 16).

Further, former Industry Minister James Prentice told the Senate Standing Committee on Banking, Trade and Commerce that "The examples of internal trade barriers in our country are legion" (Senate Standing Committee on Banking, Trade and Commerce 2008: 4). He went on to point out that "...it is easier for a truck to carry a heavy load of goods from Alberta to Mexico than to travel to British Columbia, because the weight and dimension restrictions for transport trucks vary from province to province" (Ibid.). And this after thirteen years of the AIT. The Minister also commented on the dispute resolution procedures. In his testimony to the Senate committee, he stated: "The essential criticism of the Agreement on Internal Trade process has been the absence of teeth in the dispute resolution clause. I read somewhere that, of the eight rulings made under the Agreement on Internal Trade, the provinces chose to disregard six rulings" (Ibid., 14).

In a recent paper, Robert Knox, who was the federal negotiator in the AIT talks, and Amela Karabegović were scathing in their condemnation of the AIT, describing it as "a limited and complex undertaking that is difficult to understand and apply. It is unenforceable and its obligations can be and are ignored by governments" (Knox and Karabegović 2009: 7).[15]

Perhaps the most persuasive indicators of the AIT's inadequacy are the Trade, Investment and Labour Market Agreement (TILMA) signed by the governments of Alberta and British Columbia which came into effect on April 1, 2007, and the internal trade negotiations that Ontario and Quebec are pursuing. TILMA is a trade agreement that is described by its supporters as going much further than the AIT in removing interprovincial trade barriers and it appears to have been the motivation behind the Ontario-Quebec negotiations.

If the AIT had accomplished what it was established to accomplish, TILMA would not exist and Ontario and Quebec would not now be negotiating.

The ineffectiveness of the AIT has to do with the model used to bring it about: collaborative federalism. This type of decision making, where the federal government plays the role of equal partner as opposed to guardian and protector of the national interest, is problematic because the provincial participants have little incentive to make anything other than painless, inconsequential demands on each other. The impulse to collude in keeping obligations and commitments to a minimum is irresistible. With Ottawa acting as though interprovincial trade was a provincial concern; appearing not to have a bottom line on internal trade barriers; surrendering the role of chair of the negotiations to a private citizen; forming its negotiation strategy on the basis of the upcoming Quebec election; and agreeing to a NAFTA-like negotiation format, there was no actor to vigorously make the case for the economic union and to insist on substantial concessions from the provinces. Moreover, in choosing not to engage the public on the issue, Ottawa missed an opportunity to garner support for its position. By explaining to citizens the link between trade barriers and national cohesion and the rationale for federal jurisdiction over interprovincial trade, the federal government might have been able to strengthen its negotiating position and to stiffen its resolve to get a more demanding agreement.

The AIT was negotiated while Jean Chrétien was Prime Minister. Neither of his two successors, Liberal Paul Martin nor Conservative Stephen Harper, repudiated the agreement. The Harper government has made the economic union a top concern but it has not been willing to fully use its constitutional powers to secure that union. In 2006, then Industry Minister Maxime Bernier told the Senate Standing Committee on Banking, Trade and Commerce that "The provinces play the most important role because it is in their jurisdiction. Our role is to push this idea of more cooperation and more freedom among the provinces" (Senate Standing Committee on Banking, Trade and Commerce 2006: 4). What is startling

about this comment is the way the Minister demoted the federal role on interprovincial trade. He seemed unaware that
interprovincial trade is a matter for the federal jurisdiction.
He stated further that he did not see the need "to impose anything on the provinces, because of the current leadership and
the desire expressed by the provinces to settle this problem"
(Ibid., 8). Despite the AIT's large number of exemptions, omissions and exceptions, despite the widespread agreement that
the AIT has not been effective in significantly reducing internal trade barriers, the Minister nevertheless accepted that the
provinces have 'the desire' to settle the issue. Finally, referring to a federal–provincial meeting on interprovincial trade
barriers, Bernier stated: "[Manitoba] Premier Doer chaired
the meeting. He reports to the confederation. We have leadership from the provincial premiers and provincial governments. The leadership is there" (Ibid., 16). That the leadership
on the issue is supposed to come, and can legitimately come,
from Ottawa seems not to have occurred to Bernier.

By October 2007, the federal position seemed to harden.
In the Speech from the Throne, the federal government
declared:

> Our Government will also pursue the federal govern-
> ment's rightful leadership in strengthening Canada's
> economic union....It is often harder to move goods and
> services across provincial boundaries than across our
> international borders. This hurts our competitive posi-
> tion but, more importantly, it is just not the way a country
> should work. Our Government will consider how to use
> the federal trade and commerce power to make our eco-
> nomic union work better for Canadians (Canada 2007).

This position was confirmed by Bernier's successor, James
Prentice, in comments before the Senate Standing Committee
on Banking, Trade and Commerce. But, like his predecessor,
Prentice was at pains to point out the work being done by
the provinces on internal trade barriers, as if hoping that
Ottawa would not have to act (Senate Standing Committee
on Banking, Trade and Commerce 2008: 11).

Interestingly, it was a senator, not either minister, who
expressed concern during a Senate committee meeting
about a possible consequence of the AIT's weaknesses: the
emergence of trading blocs among the provinces. Senator
Tkachuk stated:

> ...I am not happy that separate agreements are tak-
> ing place among some powerful groups. Ontario and
> Quebec hold most of the consumer market in Canada and
> Alberta and B.C., both wealthy provinces, have signed
> an agreement....[T]his balkanization bothers me and I
> am concerned that Ontario and Quebec might use their
> agreements to keep other provinces out of their markets,
> thereby doing it for selfish motives rather than for national
> motives (Senate Standing Committee on Banking, Trade
> and Commerce 2006: 9).

The fact that two trading blocs are emerging in the country
appears not to be a concern of the federal government.[16]

Conclusion

The overall aim of this chapter has been to demonstrate that
the theoretical framework provides a reasonable explanation for why Ottawa is reluctant to employ its valid constitutional powers. Constructed with two theories, historical
institutionalism and the theory of constitutional abeyances,
the framework holds that the constitutional abeyance pertaining to the founders' views on Canadian sovereignty left
Canada with a foreign judicial institution to adjudicate disputes between the central and sub-national governments.
That institution made a string of judgments that set it and
its successor institution, the Supreme Court of Canada, on a
certain path, making both path dependent and shaping the
political goals and strategies of the executive branch of the
federal government. To extend the metaphor, it was a path
that led away from federal assertiveness. Though Supreme
Court rulings in 1989 and 1990 resuscitated the federal trade

and commerce power, by the time those decisions were made the 'damage' had been done.

In the early 1980s, the Rt. Hon. Pierre Trudeau, rarely shy about using federal power, nevertheless was uncertain about Ottawa's authority to secure the economic union. His uncertainty was justified, given the Supreme Court's rulings in the 1976–80 period. As late as 1987, legal scholar, John Whyte, could remark on the scale of Ottawa's "under-confidence", its "lack of jurisdictional confidence" on trade and commerce matters (Whyte 1987: 267). In the early 1990s, Conservative Prime Minister Mulroney, in the midst of constitutional negotiations with the provinces, more than willing to accommodate provincial power demands, and with recent Supreme Court decisions to support him, had to drop from the bargaining table his very modest proposals for securing the economic union. It is, therefore, simply unrealistic to argue that the federal habit of ignoring interprovincial trade barriers, made possible by successive federal defeats before the JCPC and practiced for many decades, would be overcome in a matter of a few years. The JCPC's decisions cast a very long shadow over the federal political executive. To put it in Pierson's HI language, despite the Supreme Court's 1989–90 decisions, 'norms of appropriateness' had developed which precluded federal use of its interprovincial trade power.

We may also recall Pierson's note regarding the timing of political events. An event that happens "too late," wrote Pierson, may have no effect. The Supreme Court's rulings strengthening the federal trade and commerce power were handed down just at the time when the Mulroney government's constitutional reform efforts had set off a powerful movement toward provincialization, the effects of which were to embolden the provinces and diminish federal jurisdictional self-confidence even further. By the time the Rt. Hon. Jean Chrétien came to power in 1993, Ottawa had neither the will nor the inclination to face down the provinces or use its newly strengthened powers. Rather, the Chrétien government was motivated by a felt need to show that 'federalism works'. And yet, federal action on internal trade barriers probably would have had the approval of the Supreme Court, as well as the support of at least business, parts of the media, the West, probably Ontario, parts of Quebec, the Progressive Conservative party and the Reform party.

If the Supreme Court's rulings had come down a decade earlier, Ottawa's approach to internal trade barriers may have been very different. As it was, by the time the decisions did come down, the federal government was firmly on the path of collaborative federalism.

Endnotes

[1] An earlier version of this paper was presented at a federalism conference held at the University of Ottawa in October 2008. Both papers are based on the first four chapters of my doctoral dissertation in political science.

[2] The Hockin panel on securities regulation, which recommended the creation of a single national securities regulator, made it clear that, if there were jurisdictional problems blocking the creation of "a single comprehensive national securities regime in Canada", the federal government should "consider unilateral action to implement such a regime". The advice provided by the panel's special advisor on constitutional law, Peter W. Hogg, Q.C., "has confirmed that the federal government has the constitutional authority to do so. This opinion is widely held by constitutional lawyers" (Canada 2009b: 62).

[3] Unless otherwise indicated, when I use the word 'nation' or 'national' I am referring to Canada.

[4] Unless otherwise indicated, when I use the word 'Ottawa' I am referring to the Canadian federal government.

[5] A good example of this occurred in the 1990s when the Chrétien government vacated the field of labour force training. In the labour market development agreements that it signed with each province, the federal government acknowledged labour force training to be a provincial responsibility. And yet, in a December 2008 decision on employment insurance, the Supreme Court of Canada ruled that federal training programs were a valid exercise of the federal unemployment insurance power. Clearly the Chrétien government acted too hastily.

[6] A feature of the JCPC that is not well-known is that its president was a senior member of the British Cabinet. Thus, it was inevitable that political factors would enter into the Law Lords' (members of the JCPC

and British House of Lords) deliberations. On the issue of JCPC impartiality, see J. Krikorian, 2000. In this work, Krikorian shows how the judicial committee was significantly influenced by a conflict between the British government and the Irish Free State when it made its decision in the Canadian case, Nadan v The King, in 1926. In its decision, the JCPC determined that Canadian legislation prohibiting criminal appeals to the Committee was invalid.

[7] In a 1998 piece, Janine Brodie and Malinda Smith state that the proposals in this discussion paper would have provided for "a stronger role for the federal government" (Brodie and Smith 1998: 85). It is difficult to understand how they could draw this conclusion. By saying that the economic union was a shared responsibility, and then circumscribing its own 'new' power to manage the economic union, Ottawa was surely diminishing its own capacity to regulate.

[8] Interestingly, the 2007 free trade agreement between Alberta and British Columbia, known as the Trade, Investment and Labour Mobility Agreement (TILMA), eliminates duplicate business registration and reporting requirements so that businesses registered in one province are automatically recognized in the other (Knox and Karabegović 2009: 3).

[9] Many labour law scholars in Europe see the need for labour issues to be regulated by the European-level institutions rather than by the member states. Presently, those institutions are excluded from regulating on labour relations issues, e.g., collective bargaining. The labour issues for which they do have responsibility include worker health and safety, working conditions, and equal treatment. However, according to R. Blanpain et al., the "absurdly complex voting system" makes it extremely difficult to adopt Europe-wide decisions on these issues. As a result, "the ESM [European Social Model] is extremely weak." Because the EU does not have full regulatory authority on labour, and because of the complex voting system at the EU-level "the EU lacks the essential competences, which are needed to organize and establish a full-fledged ESM" (Blanpain et al. 2007: 285–286). Another legal scholar, Philip Syrpis, has written on how the European Court of Justice appears to regard differences in labour laws among the member states of the European Union as problematic and, in its case law, has attempted to minimize those differences (Syrpis 2007). Syrpis himself calls for greater judicial tolerance of regulatory diversity.

[10] While the Quebec Court of Review affirmed the constitutionality of the IDIA, it reversed Justice Lafontaine's decision on a technicality. It found that at the time of the application for a board of conciliation no dispute within the meaning of the Act existed between the workers and the company. It, therefore, ordered the board to stop its proceedings.

¹¹ Advocates of a national labour code argue that provincial control of labour results in a race to the bottom in labour legislation. Legal scholar and former member of the Canada Industrial Relations Board, Véronique Marleau, shares this concern. She has recently written:

> The fully decentralized Canadian labour relations setting is particularly problematic in this respect (Marleau 2006: 119–120).
>
> ...
>
> A fully decentralized framework favours the development of a regulatory race to the bottom because there is no countervailing force capable of offsetting the tendency of jurisdictions to compete for investments and jobs by bringing existing protections to the lowest common denominator. Canadian developments in labour regulation and practice over the last ten years in the various political jurisdictions confirm this prognostic, by showing that the risks of dismantling and regulating downward are real in the absence of a central regulating authority and broad-based bargaining structures (Ibid.).

I might add here that, at a 2008 round-table of senior executives from unions and employers, which I attended, the head of one of Canada's largest unions exclaimed out of exasperation, "Why do we need so many labour codes in this country?" This individual then described the devolution of labour market training as "a catastrophically stupid decision!"

¹² In addition to the Black decision, the Court's rulings in General Motors of Canada v City National Leasing [1989], Morguard Investments Ltd. v De Savoye [1990] and Hunt v T&N PLC [1993] are said to have strengthened the federal trade and commerce power. In Morguard, the Supreme Court determined that recognition of court judgments by all provinces "is inherent in a federation." In Hunt, the Court nullified a Quebec law prohibiting the removal from the province of documents relating to a Quebec business firm.

¹³ It should be stressed that federal-provincial negotiations to remove barriers to interprovincial trade had been going on under the auspices of First Ministers since 1986. There were annual First Ministers meetings at that time and the issue of internal trade was on the table at every meeting.

¹⁴ Marc Lee of the Canadian Centre for Policy Alternatives offered an interesting proposal for the elimination of internal trade barriers. A Senate Committee should be empowered to identify the most egregious trade barriers and then press the country's governments to eliminate those that do not violate any public interest concerns. In these circumstances, the federal government should be prepared to use "federal constitutional powers to resolve the issue if necessary" (Lee 2007: 3).

[15] At the July 2008 meeting of the Council of the Federation, ministers agreed to strengthen the AIT dispute resolution mechanism. Adopting the model used in the Trade, Investment and Labour Mobility Agreement, the ministers approved the use of monetary penalties to a maximum of $5 million. Ontario did not agree to this amendment. On this amendment, Knox and Karabegović write: "It is not clear what impact these changes will have. They appear conditional and equivocal and they do not apply to disputes brought by non-government complainants" (Knox and Karabegović 2009: 16).

[16] It should be noted that the AIT actually allows provinces and territories to enter into separate bilateral or multilateral trade arrangements provided the arrangement further liberalizes trade, there is full disclosure about the arrangement, and the signatories are willing to have other provinces and territories enter the agreement. So, while Senator Tkachuk's concern that Ontario and Quebec will keep other provinces out of their markets does not seem justified, he is right to be bothered by a trade agreement that allows groups of provinces to establish separate agreements among themselves.

References

Adam, Marc-Antoine 2009. "Fiscal Federalism and the Future of Canada: Can Section 94 of the Constitution Act, 1867 be an Alternative to the Spending Power?" In *Canada: The State of the Federation 2006/07, Transitions: Fiscal and Political Federalism in an Era of Change,* eds. J. R. Allan, T. Courchene and C. Leuprecht. Kingston, ON: Queen's University, Institute of Intergovernmental Relations, 295–322.

Baier, Gerald 2002. "Judicial Review and Canadian Federalism." In *Canadian Federalism: Performance, Effectiveness, and Legitimacy,* ed. H. Bakvis and G. Skogstad. Don Mills, ON: Oxford University Press, 24–39.

Black v Law Society of Alberta, 1 S.C.R. 591 (1989).

Blanpain, Roger et al. 2007. *The Global Workplace: International and Comparative Employment Law: Cases and Materials.* Cambridge, UK: Cambridge University Press.

Board of Commerce Act, 1919, and *Combines and Fair Prices Act,* 1919, 1 A.C. 191 (1922).

Brodie, Janine and Malinda Smith 1998. "Regulating the Economic Union." In *How Ottawa Spends 1998–99: Balancing Act: The Post-Deficit Mandate,* ed. L. Pal. Don Mills, ON: Oxford University Press, 81–97.

Brown, Douglas 2002. *Market Rules: Economic Union Reform and Intergovernmental Policy-Making in Australia and Canada.* Montreal and Kingston, ON: McGill-Queen's University Press.

Cameron, David and Richard Simeon 2002. "Intergovernmental Relations in Canada: The Emergence of Collaborative Federalism." *Publius: The Journal of Federalism*, 32: 2: 49–72.

Canada 1865 (February 6). Provincial Parliament of Canada. *Parliamentary Debates on the Subject of the Confederation of the British North American Provinces*. Quebec: Hunter, Rose and Co., Parliamentary Printers.

_____1925. Department of Labour. Judicial Proceedings Respecting Constitutional Validity of the *Industrial Disputes Investigation Act*, 1907 and Amendments of 1910, 1918 and 1920. Ottawa: F. A. Acland, Printer to the King's Most Excellent Majesty.

_____ 1940. Royal Commission on Dominion-Provincial Relations. (Rowell–Sirois Commission 1929–1939) Ottawa.

_____ 1979. Supply and Services Canada. *A Future Together: Observations and Recommendations*. Task Force on Canadian Unity (Rowell-Sirois Commission 1929–1939). Otawa: Supply and Services Canada.

_____1985. Supply and Services Canada. Royal Commission on the Economic Union and Development Prospects for Canada (MacDonald Commission), 2. Ottawa: Minister of Supply and Services.

_____1991. Supply and Services Canada. *Shaping Canada's Future Together: Proposals*. Ottawa: Supply and Services Canada.

_____1995. House of Commons. "Debates." *Hansard*, May 15 and June 19.

_____2007. (October 16). Office of the Prime Minister. *Speech from the Throne*. www.pm.gc.ca. [retrieved April 20, 2008].

_____2009a. Department of Finance Canada. *Canada's Economic Action Plan: Budget 2009*. House of Commons. Ottawa: Department of Finance Canada.

_____2009b. Department of Finance Canada. *Final Report and Recommendations*. Expert Panel on Securities Regulation. Ottawa: Department of Finance Canada.

Citizens Insurance Company of Canada v William Parsons, 1 A.C. 96 (1881).

Chrétien, Rt. Hon. Jean 1980. *Securing the Canadian Economic Union in the Constitution*. Discussion paper. Government of Canada. Hull, QC: Supply and Services Canada.

Cohen, David 1995. "The Internal Trade Agreement: Furthering the Canadian Economic Disunion?" *Canadian Business Law Journal*, 25: 257–279.

de Mestral, Armand 1995. "A Comment." In *Getting There: An Assessment of the Agreement on Internal Trade*, eds. M. Trebilcock and D. Schwanen. Toronto: C.D. Howe Institute, Policy Study 26, 97.

DiGiacomo, Gordon 2009. "Employment Insurance and Parental Benefits." In *Canada: The State of the Federation 2006/07, Transitions: Fiscal* and *Political Federalism in an Era of Change*, eds. J. R. Allan, T. Courchene and C. Leuprecht. Kingston, ON: Queen's University, Institute of Intergovernmental Relations, 323–345.

Doern, G. Bruce and Mark MacDonald 1999. *Free-Trade Federalism: Negotiating the Canadian Agreement on Internal Trade*. Toronto: University of Toronto Press.

Financial Post 1997 (May 22). "Lack of Leadership a Barrier to Freeing Up Internal Trade." Toronto, 68. Canadian Newsstand database. http://proquest.umi.com.proxy.library.carleton.ca/ [retrieved April 19, 2009].

Foley, Michael 1989. *The Silence of Constitutions: Gaps, 'Abeyances' and Political Temperament in the Maintenance of Government*. London, UK: Routledge.

Forbath, William 1991. *Law and the Shaping of the American Labor Movement*. Cambridge, MA: Harvard University Press.

Forsey, Eugene 1974. *Freedom and Order: Collected Essays*. Toronto: McClelland and Stewart Limited.

Gagnon, Lysiane 2007 (Spring). "Quelling Stereotypes." *Tabaret: The Magazine of the University of Ottawa*.

Gaudreault-Desbiens, Jean François 2006. "The Irreducible Federal Necessity of Jurisdictional Autonomy, and the Irreducibility of Federalism to Jurisdictional Autonomy." In *Dilemmas of Solidarity: Rethinking Redistribution in the Canadian Federation*, eds. S. Choudhry, J.-F. Gaudreault-Desbiens and L. Sossin. Toronto: University of Toronto Press, 185–205.

General Motors of Canada v City National Leasing, 1 S.C.R. 641 (1989).

Government of Ontario 1979 (March). Second Report of the Advisory Committee on Confederation: The Federal-Provincial Distribution of Powers. Ontario Advisory Committee on Confederation. Toronto.

Haddow, Rodney 2003. "Canadian Federalism and Active Labour Market Policy." In *New Trends in Canadian Federalism*,. 2nd edition, eds. F. Rocher and M. Smith. Peterborough, ON: Broadview Press, Ltd., chapter 9.

Harrison, Kathryn 2003. "Passing the Environmental Buck." In *New Trends in Canadian Federalism*, 2nd edition, eds. F. Rocher and M. Smith. Peterborough, ON: Broadview Press, Ltd., chapter 12.

Hogan, John 2006. "Remoulding the Critical Junctures Approach." *Canadian Journal of Political Science*, 39: 3: 657–679.

Hogg, Peter W. 1980–81. "Comment on James C. MacPherson's Paper on Economic Regulation and the *British North America Act*." *Canadian Business Law Journal*, 5: 220–224.

Howse, Robert 1992. *Economic Union, Social Justice, and Constitutional Reform: Towards a High but Level Playing Field*. Background Studies of the York University Constitutional Reform Project, Study No. 9. Toronto: York University, Centre for Public Law and Public Policy.

Howse, Robert 1996 (June). *Securing the Canadian Economic Union: Legal and Constitutional Options for the Federal Government.* The Canadian Union Papers. Commentary series. Toronto: C.D. Howe Institute.

Hunt v T&N PLC, 4 S.C.R. 289 (1993).

Jérome-Forget 1995 (March 4). "The Crumbling Walls of Provincial Protectionism: Internal Trade Agreement Shows that Federalism Can be Flexible Enough to Work." Toronto: *Financial Post*, 23. http://proquest.umi.com.proxy.library.carleton.ca/ [retrieved April 19, 2009].

Knox, Robert and Amela Karabegović 2009 (February). *Myths and Realities of TILMA.* Studies in Trade Policy. Vancouver: Fraser Institute.

Krikorian, Jacqueline 2000. "British Imperial Politics and Judicial Independence: The Judicial Committee's Decision in the Canadian Case Nadan v The King." *Canadian Journal of Political Science*, 33: 2: 291–332.

La Selva, Samuel 1996. *The Moral Foundations of Canadian Federalism: Paradoxes, Achievements, and Tragedies of Nationhood.* Montreal and Kingston, ON: McGill-Queen's University Press.

Laskin, Boris 1968. "Reflections on the Canadian Constitution After the First Century." In *Canadian Federalism: Myth or Reality*, ed. J. Peter Meekison. Toronto: Methuen Publications.

Lecours, André 2005. "New Institutionalism: Issues and Questions." In *New Institutionalism: Theory and Analysis*, ed. A. Lecours. Toronto: University of Toronto Press, 3–25.

Lee, Marc 2007 (May 17). *Presentation to the Senate Standing Committee on Banking, Trade and Commerce.* www.progressive-economics.ca/2007/05/17/marcs-testimony-to-the-senate/.

Lemieux, Rodolphe 1907 (June 21). Progressive Policy of the Liberal Administration: Postal Reforms, Labour Legislation. Speech. Aurora, ON.

Liquidators of the Maritime Bank of Canada v The Receiver-General of New Brunswick, A.C. 437 (1892).

MacDonald, Mark 2002. "The Agreement on Internal Trade: Trade-Offs for Economic Union and Federalism." In *Canadian Federalism: Performance, Effectiveness, and Legitimacy*, eds. H. Bakvis and G. Skogstad. Don Mills, ON: Oxford University Press, 138–157.

MacPherson, James C. 1980–81. "Economic Regulation and the *British North America Act.*" *Canadian Business Law Journal*, 5: 172–199.

March, James and Johan Olsen 1984. "The New Institutionalism: Organizational Factors in Political Life." *American Political Science Review*, 78: 3: 734–739.

Marleau, Véronique 2006. "Globalization, Decentralization and the Role of Subsidiarity in the Labour Setting: In Memory of Marco Biagi." In *Globalization and the Future of Labour Law*, eds. J. R. Craig and M. Lynk. Cambridge, UK: Cambridge University Press, 119–120.

Monahan, Patrick 2006. *Constitutional Law*, 3rd edition. Toronto: Irwin Law Inc.

Montreal Street Railway Company v Board of Conciliation and Investigation 44 S. C. (Que.) 350 (1913).

Morguard Investments Ltd. v De Savoye 3 S.C.R. 1077 (1990).

Noël, Alain 2000. *Without Quebec: Collaborative Federalism with a Footnote?* Working paper. Montreal: Institute for Research on Public Policy.

O'Neill, Pierre 1994 (July 20). "Commerce Interprovinciale : La Preuve d'Un Federalisme 'Sclerose'." Montreal: *Le Devoir*, A1. www.library. newscan.com.proxy.library.carleton.ca/ [retrieved April 23, 2009].

Painter, Martin 1991 (June). "Intergovernmental Relations in Canada: An Institutional Analysis." *Canadian Journal of Political Science*, 24: 2: 269–288.

Pearson, Rt. Hon. Lester B. 1968. "Federalism for the Future." In *Canadian Federalism: Myth or Reality*, ed. J. Peter Meekison. Toronto: Methuen Publications, 182–192.

Pelletier, Gerard, ed. 1996. *Against the Current: Selected Writings 1939–1996*. Toronto: McClelland & Stewart Inc.

Pierson, Paul 1993. "When Effect Becomes Cause: Policy Feedback and Political Change." *World Politics*, 45: 4: 595–628.

Pierson, Paul 2004. *Politics in Time: History, Institutions, and Social Analysis*. Princeton, NJ: Princeton University Press.

Poirier, Johanne 2004. "Intergovernmental Agreements in Canada: At the Crossroads Between Law and Politics." In *Canada: The State of the Federation, 2002: Reconsidering the Institutions of Canadian Federalism*, eds. J. Peter Meekison, H. Telford and H. Lazar. Montreal and Kingston, ON: McGill-Queen's University Press, 425–462.

Quebec Liberal Party 1991. *A Québec Free to Choose*. (Allaire Report). Report of the Constitutional Committee of the Québec Liberal Party. For submission to the 25th convention, January 28.

Rocher, François and Miriam Smith 2003a. "The Four Dimensions of Canadian Federalism." In *New Trends in Canadian Federalism*, 2nd edition, eds. F. Rocher and M. Smith. Peterborough, ON: Broadview Press, Ltd., 21–44.

Rocher, François and Miriam Smith 2003b. "Introduction." In *New Trends in Canadian Federalism*, 2nd edition, eds. F. Rocher and M. Smith. Peterborough, ON: Broadview Press, Ltd., 7–17.

Russell, Peter 2004. *Constitutional Odyssey: Can Canadians Become a Sovereign People?* Toronto: University of Toronto Press Inc.

Saywell, John 2002. *The Lawmakers: Judicial Power and the Shaping of Canadian Federalism*. Toronto: University of Toronto Press.

Scott, Frank R. 1977. *Essays on the Constitution: Aspects of Canadian Law and Politics*. Toronto: University of Toronto Press.

Senate Standing Committee on Banking, Trade and Commerce 2006. *Proceedings, Issue 13—Evidence—December 14.* www.parl.gc.ca/39/1 [retrieved April 22, 2008].

Senate Standing Committee on Banking, Trade and Commerce 2008. *Proceedings, Issue 10—Evidence—March 6.* www.parl.gc.ca/39/2 [retrieved April 17, 2008].

Skelton, Oscar 1966. *Life and Times of Sir Alexander Tilloch Galt.* Toronto: McClelland and Stewart Limited.

Smith, Andrew 2008. *British Businessmen and Canadian Confederation.* Montreal and Kingston, ON: McGill-Queen's University Press.

Syrpis, Philip 2007. *EU Intervention in Domestic Labour Law.* Oxford, UK: Oxford University Press. www.oxfordscholarship.com.proxy.bib.uottawa.ca/oso/private/content/law/9780199277209/toc.html. [retrieved April 9, 2009].

Thelen, Kathleen and Sven Steinmo 1992. "Historical Institutionalism in Comparative Politics." In *Structuring Politics: Historical Institutionalism in Comparative Analysis,* eds. S. Steinmo, K. Thelen and F. Longstreth. Cambridge, UK: Cambridge University Press, 1–32.

Thomas, David 1997. *Whistling Past the Graveyard.* Don Mills, ON: Oxford University Press.

Toronto Electric Commissioners v Snider, A.C. 396 (1925).

Tsebelis, George 2002. *Veto Players: How Political Institutions Work.* New York, NY: Russell Sage Foundation.

Vipond, Robert 1991. *Liberty and Community: Canadian Federalism and the Failure of the Constitution.* Albany, NY: State University of New York Press.

Weinstock, Daniel 2001. "Towards a Normative Theory of Federalism." *International Social Science Journal,* 53: 166: 75–83.

Whyte, John 1987. "Federal Powers Over the Economy: Finding New Jurisdictional Room." *Canadian Business Law Journal,* 13: 3: 257–302.

Chapter 2

Asymmetrical Federalism in Canada: Magic Wand or Breaking the Ties that Bind?

Michael D. Behiels

The [British North America] Act places the constitutions of all provinces within the Dominion on the same level; and what is true with respect to the legislature of Ontario has equal application to the legislature of New Brunswick.

—The Liquidators of the Maritime Bank of Canada v The Receiver-General of New Brunswick [1892] A.C., 442.

Introduction

Asymmetrical federalism most certainly is neither a new nor a uniquely Canadian concept. Informal and formal federal asymmetries can be found in virtually every federation worldwide but have only received serious scholarly attention in the past half century (Griffiths 2002; Watts 2005). Indeed, an American political scientist, Charles Tarlton, first used the term in his 1965 analysis of the different relationships among and between American Southern states (Tarlton 1965). "'Asymmetry' may be defined as a feature of complex (multi-level) political systems, in which some units (provinces, member states, etc.) have greater powers and/or undertake broader policy responsibilities than other units" (Leslie 1994: 37–38).

It was only in the late 1980s that asymmetrical federalism became the rage for Quebecois academic, political and media circles. As Canada moved toward its second referendum on secession in 1995, a few English-speaking Canadian academics joined their call for entrenched federal asymmetry for Quebec (Seidle 1994). Federal asymmetry first gained notoriety among the Canadian public when the concept emerged as the central feature of then Prime Minister Brian Mulroney's and Quebec Premier Robert Bourassa's 1987 Meech Lake Constitutional Accord. The highly controversial constitutional accord recognized, in a powerful interpretative clause, Quebec as a 'distinct society' and empowered the Quebec legislature and government to preserve and promote the distinct identity of Quebec (Behiels 1989). Constitutional asymmetry, as embedded in the Meech Lake Accord, was portrayed as a 'magic wand'—an infinitely flexible and powerful concept capable of resolving the constitutional crisis stemming from Quebec political and intellectual classes' rejection of the *Constitution Act, 1982*, particularly its province-based amending formula and its alleged 'centralizing' Canadian Charter of Rights and Freedoms.

A far more comprehensive degree of federal asymmetry, extending well beyond recognition of a distinct Quebec state, was entrenched in the omnibus Consensus Report on the Constitution (Charlottetown Consensus Report) which the Prime Minister and the premiers signed on 28 August 1992 after nearly two years of very difficult and controversial negotiations (Canada 1992). Federal asymmetry was the central doctrine underlying the Aboriginal constitution within the Canadian Constitution. One Canadian political scientist criticized the highly asymmetrical Aboriginal constitutional package for creating parallel Aboriginal self-governing communities which would foster segregation from rather than integration into Canadian society and its institutions of governance (Cairns 2000). Canadians, highly skeptical of these asymmetrical arrangements, resoundingly rejected the complex and incomplete Charlottetown deal in the October 1992 referendum.

Nonetheless, this did not stop the proponents of federal asymmetry from pursuing its extensive application to the functioning of Canadian federalism. Its rejection by Canadians fuelled the re-emergence of the Quebecois secession-ist movement under the leadership of Jacques Parizeau and Lucien Bouchard. Asymmetric federalism achieved its nadir during and following the beleaguered federalists' very nar-row win in the 1995 referendum on Quebec's secession from the federation. Proponents of federal asymmetry and mul-tinational federalism—the former's most recent incarna-tion—contend that these concepts are both necessary and sufficient tools for managing the increasing religious, eth-nic, national and regional conflicts within pluralistic federal states in a globalizing world. Asymmetry, if one is to believe the doctrine's protagonists, is the most recent 'magic wand' capable of curing all the ills of the Canadian federation. On the other hand, critics argue vigorously that excessive asymmetry, especially formalized and entrenched asymme-try, will erode and eventually fracture the fragile ties that bind the already far too decentralist Canadian federation.

The term 'asymmetric' federalism, when used alone, is misleading at best and fundamentally anti-federalist at worst. Like yin and yang, asymmetry can only be under-stood when juxtaposed with symmetry. Why? Because if a federation is to remain a genuine federation, there must be an ongoing dynamic balancing act between symmetrical and asymmetrical forces, powers, and institutions of governance. Indeed, as the Rt. Hon. Pierre Trudeau often reminded us, true federalists are both 'symmetricists' and 'asymmetricists' depending on how and to what end the central and pro-vincial governments exercise their respective jurisdictions. Yet, a great many policy wonks, academics, journalists and politicians have forgotten this basic principle of federalism. They have been developing and promoting the theoretical and ideological foundations for the constitutional entrench-ment of asymmetrical federalism/multinational federalism for the past twenty years. Arguments in favour of the con-stitutional entrenchment of more asymmetrical federalism have been increasingly cloaked in the discourse of liberal communitarian moral and political philosophies and, more recently, in the discourse surrounding the emergence of what is termed multinational federal democracies.

All federal societies and federal democracies face deeply
entrenched and very powerful, historically rooted centrifugal forces that extend from the past into the present (Milne
2005). The Canadian federation, since its inception in the
1860s, is a very prominent example of this reality. Designed
by its framers as a fairly centralist federation, hard-pressed
Canadian governments, with the political, economic and
military assistance of Great Britain, managed to create a
transcontinental state by the time Prime Minister Laurier
took office in 1896. Paralleling this development was the
rise and consolidation, thanks to historic regionalism and
several watershed decisions of the Judicial Committee of
the Privy Council, of the provincial rights movement led
by Ontario's Premier Oliver Mowat and Quebec's Premier
Honoré Mercier. The 'construction' by 1900 of a classical
federation of sovereign—within their 1867 watertight compartments—provincial and central governments was consolidated during the first three decades of the 20th century.
First, this occurred thanks to the remarkable demographic
and socio-economic transformation of Canadian society
during the ebullient Laurier era. Next, it was facilitated by a
second, more dramatic, phase of industrialization throughout central Canada during the Great War and the booming
1920s. When the Great Depression got underway with the
'crash' on Wall Street in 1929, Sir John A. Macdonald's conception of a highly centralized federation was a forlorn and
utterly shattered dream.

The depression of the 1930s, which was followed by a
dramatic expansion of the federal government and state
during and following World War II, allowed Ottawa to
challenge informally the entrenched decentralist vision
of the provinces. The Canadian federation's biggest challenge was to design and implement a range of largely
informal and administrative symmetrical approaches,
institutions and programs in response to regional and provincial needs, while all-the-while ensuring that the centre
holds. This challenge, made painfully evident during the
Great Depression of the 1930s, fuelled the development
of a Keynesian-inspired new federalism during the post

World War II era. Pressured by hard-pressed citizens who demanded and expected improved public services, Ottawa used its taxing and spending powers to propel reluctant provincial governments into the 20th century. That is, Ottawa cajoled highly conservative and recalcitrant provincial governments into providing long overdue social service, health, and education programs to Canadian citizens. Ottawa also provided substantial funding to ensure that all provinces could and would construct the elaborate infrastructure required for the development of financial, commercial and industrial capitalism.

Since the 1950s, the tremendous demographic, social and economic developments, combined with the unmatched prosperity which ensued, propelled, yet again, a remarkably successful era of expansive province-building. This process was led by prosperous and activist Ontario governments under Conservative Premiers Leslie Frost and John Robarts. Spurred on by the ideological 'quiet revolution' of the 1950s, a modern, expansive Quebec state was constructed by an urban, secular, Quebecois middle-class during the 1960s and beyond. It was neo-nationalist Quebecois state builders, led by Liberal Premier Jean Lesage, who articulated an early version of the doctrine of asymmetrical federalism, that is, special constitutional status for an expansive Quebec state. His successor, Union Nationale Premier Daniel Johnson preached the doctrine of *égalité ou indépendance*' (Johnson 1965). The Canadian federation had to be refashioned into an asymmetrical, binational confederation between a highly sovereign Quebec and a reconstituted Canada. René Lévesque's Parti Québécois would portray this ambivalent asymmetrical constitutional arrangement as a sovereignty-association. Meanwhile, Alberta and British Columbia, fuelled by a bonanza of natural resources and expanding urban populations, were quick to build expansive, interventionist governments. Very soon the remaining provinces and territories—thanks largely to resource developments; increased transfer payments; and equalization grants from Ottawa—were able to construct modern bureaucracies to oversee a wide range of public programs in all fields.

As these tremendous centrifugal pressures mounted, Ottawa politicians and senior mandarins were forced to respond to ensure that the centre would hold. This was particularly important once successive Quebec governments, responding to powerful and sustained political pressures from Quebecois neo-nationalist and secessionist movements, demanded additional provincial powers under Section 92 as well as treaty-making powers in every area of provincial jurisdiction. Prime Minister Lester B. Pearson, in power from 1963–68, initially agreed with a degree of symmetrical decentralization, especially in areas of provincial jurisdiction, but rejected in principle, if not always in practice, formal asymmetry. Beginning in 1968, the Canadian government, led by Prime Minister Pierre Elliot Trudeau, set out to counterbalance the growing centrifugal pressures brought on by expansive province-building. First, his government brought an end to Pearson's one-way system of cooperative federalism, which allowed the Quebec state to achieve a degree of *de facto* special status by opting out of shared-cost federal-provincial programs in areas of provincial jurisdiction with full financial compensation. Trudeau became the *bête noire* of Quebecois neo-nationalists and secessionists for shutting down this process of achieving federal asymmetry by stealth (McRoberts 1997).

Ottawa then set in motion what became a protracted process of mega-constitutional negotiations to patriate the *British North America Act, 1867* (BNA) with a region-based amending formula and a Charter of Rights. Eventually, the *Constitution Act, 1982* included a general amending formula and a comprehensive Charter of Rights and Freedoms— one modeled, in part, on the 1948 Universal Declaration of Human Rights as well as the 1966 UN Covenant on Civil and Political Rights and its binding Protocol. Hoping to gain support for an entrenched Canadian Charter, the Trudeau government ratified the UN Covenant and its Protocol in 1977. The Trudeau government's hybrid Charter protected fundamental civil and political rights and the equality rights of every citizen as well as the rights of Canada's official language minority communities, Aboriginal peoples and ethno-cultural communities. Despite the relentless opposition of most premiers, the transformative *Constitution Act, 1982*, with its comprehensive Charter of Rights and Freedoms, altered the paradigm of Canadian constitutionalism. Henceforth, Canada was a constitutional democracy and Canadians were a sovereign people. The Constitution was the supreme law of the land while the executives, the legislators, and the judiciary were the guarantors of the Constitution (Behiels 2003).

This constitutional revolution set in motion a determined provincial government movement, led by Quebec's Premier Robert Bourassa, to challenge the 'Canadianizing' and democratizing forces of the Charter of Rights and Freedoms. Premier Bourassa's plan was to obtain for the Quebec government and legislature a powerful 'distinct society' interpretative clause. This, he believed, would enable them to use the courts to acquire additional jurisdictions and taxing powers for the government and legislature of Quebec to preserve and promote its 'distinct society'—formal federal asymmetry achieved via the courts rather than through a formal constitutional amendment. Canadian citizens from all regions twice rejected—in 1990 by reluctant premiers and in the 1992 referendum—the constitutional recognition of formal federal asymmetry via a Quebec 'distinct society' clause, a third order of Aboriginal self-governments, as well as wholesale decentralization of jurisdictions and spending powers to the provinces (Ibid., 158–173).

In doing so, Canadians help set in motion a political tsunami of retaliation by the Quebecois political and intellectual leaders and classes. Jacques Parizeau's reinvigorated Parti Québécois government, Lucien Bouchard's recently created Bloc Québécois, and Mario Dumont's Action Démocratique du Québec joined forces to fuel, and then adroitly exploit, the backlash among Quebec voters. They held a second referendum on the secession of Quebec in October 1995. The disoriented and disorganized federalists managed to win the referendum by the narrowest of margins, but this win led to the Supreme Court's Reference re Secession of Quebec case in 1998. The Supreme Court's landmark decision stated that

Quebec did not have a right to make a unilateral declaration of independence under either domestic or international law. The federal government of the day, led by Prime Minister Jean Chrétien, followed up the Supreme Court decision with its *Clarity Act, 2000,* which set the parameters for any future referendum on secession. Parliament would have to ensure that the question was a clear one on secession and that there was a clear majority vote in support of secession before undertaking any negotiations (Behiels 1998).

The easy road to Quebec secession was closed. But the narrow defeat of the secessionist forces in the 1995 referendum set in motion a range of attempts by successive Canadian and Quebec governments to implement a certain degree of Quebec/Canada asymmetry through informal administrative arrangements and parliamentary resolutions recognizing Quebec as a 'distinct society'; the *'Québécois et Québécoises'* as a nation; and representation on the Canadian delegation in certain United Nations committees. The current government of Quebec, led by Premier Jean Charest, has achieved some success using this informal approach to asymmetry but still remains unsatisfied and wants to move on to the formal recognition. Consequently, this informal political and administrative approach, and the debate surrounding it, will continue as long as the internal socio-economic, ideological and political conditions fuelling the Quebec government's ongoing demands for greater asymmetry remain strong.

Which kind of asymmetry should federations formally recognize?

All societies, especially federal societies, display a wide range of asymmetries (Brown 2005). Some of these asymmetries are fixed, such as geographic differences and natural resources—both of which tend, most often, to produce lesser or greater economic and social asymmetries for citizens. These kinds of asymmetries, over time, are considered unacceptable. Increasingly, citizens of modern

nation-states demand a wide range of government programs to overcome these regional disparities and thereby
achieve more symmetrical socio-economic conditions and
similar levels of equality of opportunity. Indeed, starting
with Confederation but gaining momentum in the 1920s
and 1930s, Canadians in all provinces and regions have
fought hard to overcome asymmetrical geographic, natural resource and demographic conditions. By the 1950s
Canadians had successfully convinced their national government to use its taxing and spending powers to foster
greater equality of opportunity for all citizens while raising the floor associated with equality of condition for all
public services and programs. Indeed, the *Constitution Act,
1982* entrenched the principle and practice of equalization, which promotes greater symmetry in the delivery of
public services and programs. Entrenchment ensures that
this commitment to symmetry via wealth redistribution
will not be unduly tampered with by the federal executive
and legislative branches of government as the expense of
Canadian citizens in the 'have-not' provinces.

Other asymmetries are the result, so-to-speak, of ongoing human settlement by indigenous peoples, nationalities
and ethno-cultural communities with different cultural,
religious, social and linguistic values—norms and institutions, civic and public. These forms of long-standing human
asymmetry are deemed acceptable, indeed valuable. Nor-
mally, whenever economic, social, military and political
conditions permit, federal societies establish federal systems of governance. Federal systems of governance are one
of the best guarantees for minority communities to preserve
their survival while providing them with opportunities to
promote their development and expansion. Certain crucial
asymmetries deemed central to cultural identity and survival—including language, religion and civil law—are most
often given formal constitutional recognition. In the case of
Canada's highly centralized quasi-federation wherein the
principle of the monarchy trumped that of federalism, the
French-Canadian Catholic nationality obtained majority
control over the government and legislature of Quebec, a

province which exercises full and unfettered sovereignty over a very wide range of local jurisdictions. Further recognition of the French-Canadian nationality involved making the legislature and the courts of Quebec as well as the national Parliament officially bilingual (Vaughan 2003).

A range of well-defined and limited asymmetries have been granted formal recognition within the Canadian Constitution. Other informal arrangements—most involving federal-provincial administrative agreements—have acknowledged Canada's wide range of cultural and linguistic asymmetries. The question that faces us today is whether or not it is both wise and necessary to expand the existing range of well-defined, yet limited asymmetries that are formally recognized within the Canadian Constitution, or whether the Canadian and provincial governments should opt to continue the ebb and flow of informal arrangements in order to manage most of these human asymmetries. Before tackling these questions let us look at the ever-evolving pressures for constitutionally entrenched forms of federal asymmetry.

The compact of provinces and the compact of nations: rationales for asymmetrical federalism

Even before the ink was dry on the *British North American Act, 1867* (BNA Act) two basic ideological rationales, the compact of provinces and the compact of cultures, emerged to challenge the highly centralized, quasi-federal system of governance. Provincial governments, led by Ontario's Oliver Mowat and Quebec's Honoré Mercier, pursued vigorous political campaigns to ensure that the quasi-federal system was turned into a symmetrical form of classical federalism whereby each province was sovereign in areas of provincial jurisdiction (Armstrong 1981). Each province could then use its sovereign powers in the way that it saw fit. If this resulted in the emergence of informal asymmetry, that is, different provincial regimes with unique programs and structures then so be it. The ideological rationale for the compact of provinces theory, drawn from the literature and practice of federalism, was the argument that Confederation was the outcome of a political/constitutional compact of autonomous BNA colonies which then became provinces. In its most radical form, the compact of provinces theory was used by some of its advocates to claim that a province had a right to withdraw unilaterally from Confederation if the central government infringed on its jurisdictions or did not comply fully with the terms of its entry. Political leaders in Nova Scotia, the Northwest Territories, British Columbia and Quebec resorted on occasion to this argument. On most occasions the provincial compact theory was used by advocates and supporters of the provincial rights movement in its protracted campaign to define Confederation as a classical form of federalism, one comprised of equal and sovereign entities. Given that Canada was, by geography and by colonial settlement patterns, a federal society with a federal constitution, the emerging provincial rights movement led by Ontario Premier Oliver Mowat rendered Sir John A. Macdonald's dream of a highly centralist federation obsolete by the 1890s (Cook 1969; Armstrong 1981). This process of province building was aided and abetted by the Judicial Committee of the Privy Council in several important but controversial judicial review decisions involving the Imperial Justices' imaginatively constructed interpretations of Section 91, especially the residual and trade and commerce clauses, and Section 92, especially the property and civil rights clause (Saywell 2002).

The second rationale for the acceptance of formal asymmetry was based on the compact of 'two founding nations' theory. The province of Quebec was the homeland of the French-Canadian and Catholic nationality. Quebec's legislative assembly and legislative council, in partnership with the Catholic Church, were responsible for ensuring the survival and development of the French-Canadian nationality by protecting its language, culture, Catholic religion and the Catholic Church's institutional network, which buttressed much of the French-Canadian society in Quebec. In the decades following Confederation, the concept of 'two founding nations' was extended to embrace all of Canada. How and why? Beginning in the 1870s, several very serious conflicts erupted over the religious, cultural and linguistic rights of the growing Metis, Acadian and French-Canadian minority communities outside Quebec. Thanks in large measure to the role of the Catholic Church missionaries, Quebec's French-Canadian political, clerical and intellectual classes discovered the presence of these beleaguered minority communities. British-Canadian attacks on these minorities were considered to be attacks on the French-Canadian community of Quebec. During several attempts to convince British-Canadians and their provincial governments to respect the religious, cultural and linguistic rights of their compatriots, French-Canadian intellectuals and politicians argued that Confederation entailed a pan-Canadian compact between French Canada and British Canada. Henri Bourassa, the leading French-Canadian nationalist of his time, championed this conception of Canada as a bilingual and bicultural state. Indeed, it took well over half a century for leading Canadian politicians and intellectuals to support Bourassa's conception of a pan-Canadian cultural and linguistic duality (Cook 1969; Silver 1982).

During the 1960s and 1970s, in the wake of Quebec's 'quiet revolution', the Royal Commission on Biculturalism and Bilingualism, and the *Official Languages Act, 1969*, a growing majority of Canadians embraced a far more robust pan-Canadian conception of linguistic duality. The Trudeau government rejected the compact of 'two founding nations' theory for two reasons. The first was sociological and reflected the rapid transformation of a largely bilingual and bicultural Canada into a pluralistic, multicultural and increasingly open society. After WW II, mass immigration, primarily from continental Europe, transformed a declining, increasingly rural and small town Protestant British Canada into several English-speaking, multicultural, rapidly expanding urban/suburban communities (Igartua 2006). Given that Quebec absorbed less than fifteen percent of this mass immigration—nearly all its immigrants settled in the Greater Montreal region—the French-Canadian community of Quebec was slower to feel the cultural and linguistic impacts of these converging phenomena.

Trudeau's second reason for rejecting the constitutional recognition of the concept of 'two founding nations' was political. He did not want Ottawa to give political credibility to the destabilizing constitutional demands emerging from the Quebecois political and intellectual classes. During the 1950s and 1960s, Quebecois nationalists and secessionists radically redefined the concept of pan-Canadian linguistic and cultural duality which flowed from their redefinition of the concept of 'two founding nations.' Quebecois nationalists called for constitutional 'special status'—formal asymmetry through the acquisition of additional jurisdictions, revenues and taxing powers—for Quebec within the existing federation (Behiels 1985; Martel 1997). Trudeau played a leading role in the rejection, by two provincial governments, of the Meech Lake Accord, 1967–1990 on the grounds that it entailed constitutional 'special status' for Quebec and a weakening of the federation via extensive asymmetric decentralization in important jurisdiction and national institutions—Senate and Supreme Court—to all the provinces. Trudeau then played an important role in convincing a majority of Canadians to reject the far more complex and far more asymmetrical Charlottetown Consensus Report in the 1992 referendum for essentially the same reasons (Behiels 1998).

Meanwhile, Quebecois secessionists, who actively supported Quebecois nationalists' campaigns for constitutional 'special status', called for the constitutional recognition of a Quebec/Canada territorial duality via the creation of a highly decentralized, binational confederation. This binational Quebec/Canada would be symmetrical in its recognition of formal equality between the associate states of Quebec and Canada. Yet, in practice this binational confederation would be highly asymmetrical given that the state of Quebec would constitute only one-quarter of the entire population. A majority of Quebecers rejected the concept of a binational confederation of associate states in the 1980 referendum. In the wake of the rejection of constitutional 'special status' for Quebec in the Meech Lake and Charlottetown accords, in October 1995 the Parti Québécois, backed by the Bloc Québécois and the Action Démocratique du Québec, held a second referendum on Quebec's secession from the federation, with or without an association with the 'Rest of Canada'.

The communitarian doctrine: an ideological foundation for asymmetrical federalism

Beginning in 1980s, Quebecois and Canadian academics resorted to new theories and ideologies, primarily the doctrines of 'liberal communitarianism' and multinational federalism, to justify the policy, as well as the implementation, of full-fledged federal asymmetry. Liberal communitarianism and multinational federalism were vaunted as the best policy instruments for Canada's political elites to manage the growing conflicts between competing nationalities, Aboriginal peoples, and ethno-cultural and/or religious communities. Each of these groups competed for formal recognition by, and financial support from, the Canadian state in the hope that they would get the upper hand over their rivals. Nationalist and secessionist Quebecois academics, intellectuals and politicians quickly embraced both liberal communitarianism and multinational federalism to promote their respective campaigns for constitutional 'special status' for Quebec within a restructured, asymmetrical federation or for outright secession.

Several well-known Canadian political philosophers in the 1990s embraced the doctrine of conservative communitarianism, albeit in a highly reworked and reconstructed 'liberal' form. American liberal communitarianism "emerged in the 1980s as a response to the limits of liberal theory and practice. Its dominant themes are that individual rights need to be balanced with social responsibilities and that autonomous selves do not exist in isolation, but are shaped by the values and culture of communities" (Civic Practices Network 2008: 1). The doctrine of communitarianism developed by an expansive school of American academics in the late 1980s and 1990s was based—some argue quite erroneously so (Berkowitz 1995)—on the seminal thinking of John Rawls in his ground breaking work, *A Theory of Justice* (1972).

One of the leading protagonists of communitarianism is the Canadian born and Oxford educated political philosopher Daniel A. Bell. His very popular and quite remarkable *Communitarianism and its Critics* (1993) skillfully used a dialogue style to defend and promote the viability and urgent necessity for a conservative communitarian political philosophy as the foundation for a restructured American society and political system. Most American liberals became fierce critics of Bell and his conservative communitarian prescription for American society and politics (Phillips 1993: 175-196). Bell, not feeling welcomed among liberal American scholars, took a teaching position in the philosophy department at Tsinghua University in Beijing where he applies his conservative communitarian philosophy to Asian societies. Other scholars stepped in quickly to fill the void. They include Amitai Etzioni, a founder of the communitarian movement and author of *The Spirit of Community: The Reinvention of American Society* (1993), and Mary Ann Glendon, whose trenchant critique of the human rights movement, *Rights Talk: The Impoverishment of Political Discourse* (1991), reinforced the growing cleavage between conservative communitarians and liberals.

The communitarian critique of classical liberalism prompted many American liberals—assisted by Joseph Raz's *The Morality of Freedom* (1986) and, yet again, by John Rawls— to rethink their understanding of American liberalism. John Rawls' revisionist study, *Political Liberalism* (1993), advanced a political conception of justice focused not on morality but rather on "an overlapping consensus of reasonable comprehensive doctrines" (Rawls 1993: 134). Rawls' clarification and redefinition of contemporary liberalism prepared the groundwork for the formulation of a liberal communitarian doctrine. American scholars of liberalism rediscovered a liberal communitarian school of thought within American liberal democracy, one that juxtaposed, integrated, and promoted both individual and community interests (R. M. Smith 1993; Mulhall and Swift 1996). One prominent American political philosopher, Michael Walzer, refers to the communitarian critique of liberalism as merely a "communitarian correction" of liberalism (Berkowitz 1995: 64).

The spillover into Canada of this American communitarianism versus liberalism debate came rather quickly. The most prominent and prolific Canadian liberal communitarians include three eminent and erudite political philosophers: Charles Taylor, Will Kymlicka and James Tully. All three political philosophers worked very hard to formulate and disseminate a liberal communitarian doctrine which they believed was more relevant to the pluralistic nature of Canada's federal society with its historic Aboriginal peoples, long established French-Canadian and British-Canadian nationalities, as well as its increasingly numerous and diverse ethno-cultural communities. They applied liberal communitarian doctrine and principles to Canada's political and constitutional conflicts. They argued forcefully that liberal communitarianism, which incorporated the concepts of deep diversity and the politics of constitutional recognition of national, religious and ethno-cultural communities, was the best political philosophy for Canada's political elite to manage conflict in a pluralistic, liberal, federal democracy. Kymlicka, Taylor and Tully sought to entrench formal federal asymmetry thereby making it impossible for future political and intellectual elites to restore important decision-making powers—executive and legislative—back to the central government from formally recognized communities. (Taylor 1993; Kymlicka 1995; Tully 1995)

Liberal communitarian philosophy, deep diversity, and the politics of recognition of collectivities proved to be far too esoteric and idealistic for the vast majority of ordinary Canadians to embrace. On the other hand, educated, liberal, middle-class Canadians paid attention but were difficult to convince. By and large, the majority perceived liberal communitarianism as an oxymoron since, at its core, doctrine is based on conservative values and principles. They correctly saw communitarian doctrine and its adjacent concepts of deep diversity and the politics of recognition as largely advancing the fundamental interests of collectivities, rather than promoting the common good within a liberal democratic society. They believed, like most American critics (Phillips 1993: 10–23), that communitarianism was based on a highly critical assessment of classical liberalism which posits the individual at the core of Western political thought and liberal democratic institutions. A majority of Canadians intuitively understood that all communitarian collectivist ideologies, however formulated, threatened the liberal values and shared citizenship entrenched in the 1982 Canadian Charter of Rights and Freedoms. For these reasons, a majority of Canadians successfully pressured two premiers not to ratify the Meech Lake Constitutional Accord in June 1990. When given the opportunity to have their direct say, a clear majority of Canadians voted against the communitarian Charlottetown Consensus Report in the October 1992 referendum. Both documents were viewed as dangerous constitutional attempts to weaken individual and minority rights so recently enshrined in the Canadian Charter of Rights and Freedoms.

Federal multinational democracies: a proposed European Union prescription for Canadian federal asymmetry

Political scientists specializing in analyzing and promoting the construction of the European Union out of a highly complex set of long-established, competing federal and unitary states—some far more pluralistic and multinational than others—are leading the way in promoting various forms of informal and formal federal asymmetry. Many of these scholars have focused their attention on the restructuring of liberal democratic institutions in the evolving transnational or supra-federation called the European Union. Their goal is to empower regional collectivities, namely the historic minorities and/or nations, most of them stateless, which were subsumed within all the powerful nation-states of Europe during their respective processes of formation. Michael Keating's extensive work focuses on reconciling nation and state in the 21st century. He promotes an informal, pragmatic approach to the recognition of the numerous historic sub-state and stateless nations within the European Union, the United

Kingdom and Canada via a wide range of asymmetrical federal arrangements that promote self-determination but preclude the right of secession (Keating 1988; 2001). The prolific Ferran Requejo combines the ideologies of liberal communitarianism and multinational democracy to make his case for the legitimacy of plural and asymmetrical federalism as it applies to the Spanish case (Requejo 2001).

Michael Burgess is a leading United Kingdom scholar of comparative federalism. As well he is a specialist of the Canadian federation (Burgess 1990), the emerging quasi-federation of the United Kingdom, (Burgess 1995) and the emerging transnational or supra-federation of the European Union, one that comprises both federal and unitary nation states. Burgess maintains that decentralized, asymmetrical federalism is the only form of democratic governance that will enable the multinational European nation-states to function effectively and efficiently as a supra-federation know as the European Union (Burgess 1989). Burgess analyses the British intellectual tradition of federalism with its deep roots in the halcyon days of the British Empire and the imperial federation movement. He argues that the United Kingdom should draw upon this intellectual tradition to recognize the multinational nature of the United Kingdom by supporting a significant devolution of Westminster's powers to national parliaments in Scotland, Northern Ireland and Wales. The United Kingdom should also support the construction of the European Union, an asymmetric transnational federation in the making (Burgess 1995).

Burgess' analysis and prescriptions for asymmetric multinational federations are reinforced by many scholars of the European Union. Belgium's troubled and highly decentralized territorial, binational federation has been the focus of considerable analysis given that a successful resolution of its constitutional crisis remains elusive (Lijphart 1981; Jaumain 1997). Post-Franco Spain, with its constitutionally recognized Catalonian, Basque and Andalucian autonomous communities, has attracted immense scholarly attention (Keating 1988; Moreno 2001; Requejo 2001). Robert Agranoff, an American federalism scholar, analyses the various factors driving the ongoing demands within the emerging Spanish federation for the recognition of a wide range of formal and informal federal asymmetries. He also analyses the central government's concerted attempts to counter these asymmetries with institutionalized mechanisms of symmetry. Drawing on the work of Luis Moreno, Agranoff demonstrates how the central government uses its constitutional status and the constitutional court, as well as a complex process of multilateral intergovernmental negotiations and agreements to construct a symmetrical/asymmetrical Spanish federation of provinces and autonomous national communities comprising one or several provinces (Agranoff 1994; 1999). "Today Spain," writes Agranoff, "is both symmetrical and asymmetrical in governance, reflecting the forces of unity and diversity in one of the world's oldest nation states. This has occurred by what one could call 'management' of asymmetrical forces through intergovernmental relations (IGR)" (Agranoff 2005: 1–2).

All of these scholars have focused their attention on the restructuring of liberal democratic institutions in an evolving European Union so as to empower collectivities, namely the historic minorities or nationalities which had been subsumed within the all powerful nation-states of Europe.

In the wake of Canada's political and constitutional crises brought on by the failed Meech Lake Constitutional Accord and the Charlottetown Consensus Report, several political scientists specializing on Quebec readily embraced formal and informal federal asymmetries as applied within the European Union's and the United Kingdom's multinational democracies. Few of these Canadian scholars take heed of Peter Leslie's well-substantiated argument that there is a very significant difference in both the theory and practice of asymmetry within federations and confederations. In his view, the European Union is not an emerging federation but rather a centralized/decentralized confederation of nation-states (Leslie 1994). In the European Union, asymmetry is rejected, conceded and/or imposed depending on which policy areas are involved. The main objective of the European Union's flexible and pragmatic approach to policy

implementation is to achieve increasing integration of the
nation-states within a stronger confederation of Europe.
Advocates of asymmetry in Canada, Leslie warns, should
always differentiate between asymmetry within the existing Canadian federation or asymmetry as it would apply
to a Canada/Quebec binational Confederation following a
negotiated secession of Quebec (Ibid.).

This important distinction between federal and confederal systems is seldom made. McGill political scientist,
Alain-G. Gagnon, a strong advocate of liberal communitarian doctrine as well as the concept of multinational
democracies as per the European Union, applies both concepts to argue for the recognition of formal asymmetry
for the Quebecois nation, either within the existing Canadian federation or between a constructed Canada/Quebec
asymmetrical binational confederation. He advances a
comprehensive critique of liberal theory as being exces-
sively individualist, egalitarian and universalist. In his
view, classic liberal theory places far too high a premium
on democratic stability at the cost of cultural diversity
and justice. He maintains that a collectivist liberal communitarian concept of the good and a genuine deliberative
democracy of small republics require the acceptance and
implementation of formal federal asymmetry for the Quebecois nation. In practice, Gagnon argues, formal asymmetry requires the entrenchment of special constitutional
status for the 'nation' of Quebec as well as the wholesale
rejection of the homogenizing, centralizing and demo-
cratically illegitimate 1982 Canadian Charter of Rights
and Freedoms. The implementation of federal asymmetry
would trump the classical liberal principle of the equality of individuals and of provinces. This would empower
formally recognized nations such as Quebec by enabling
them to pursue collective affirmative action with the goal
of attaining equality of outcome rather than equality of
treatment. He argues that Canada's acceptance of federal
asymmetry for the Quebec nation, contrary to classical liberal theory, will restore political stability while enhancing
deliberative democracy within the Canadian federation. If

this approach is not acceptable, the Quebecois nation has no choice but to opt for a Quebec/Canada binational confederation (Gagnon 2001).

During the Charlottetown Consensus Report's round of mega-constitutional negotiations, Canada was redefined by several scholars as a multinational federation comprising three, not two, founding nations. These included the Quebecois nation of Quebec, the English-speaking nation of the 'Rest of Canada', and the Aboriginal First Nations comprising Indian, Metis and Inuit peoples. These scholars rejected three models: the wholesale decentralization of the Canadian federation based on the concept of the equality of the provinces; a binational Canada/Quebec confederation; and a decentralized confederation of three distinct nations. Instead, these scholars advocated the restructuring of the Canadian federation to recognize its three nations within an asymmetrical framework. A new constitutional arrangement should recognize the province of Quebec as a 'distinct' society empowered to preserve and promote the Quebecois nation. Some scholars argued that this should not mean 'special' constitutional status for Quebec and emphasized that Quebec's MPs would lose certain executive and legislative powers. Others, less concerned with the West Lothian issue, promoted the recognition of 'special' constitutional status for Quebec.

Finally, an asymmetrical arrangement should recognize and create a 'Third Order of Government' empowering the Aboriginal nations to proceed with full-fledged Aboriginal self-government. The English-speaking Canadian nation in the remaining provinces and territories would then be able to choose between greater centralization in Ottawa or a policy of asymmetric decentralization whereby provincial government could opt-out of any and all national programs and obtain full financial compensation (Resnick 1994; Webber 1994). Finally, three Quebecois political scientists questioned the validity of the European Union's multinational democracies, especially Belgium and Spain, as adequate models for the resolution of crisis confronting Canada's multinational federation. "In other words, a *sui generis* case like

Canada could only be solved by a *sui generis* solution, one
that avoids Belgian particularism, while at the same time
going beyond Spain's hierarchical institutionalization of collective identities" (François Rocher, Christian Rouillard and
André Lecours 2001: 200). Canada, they concluded, would
only resolve the question of the Quebec nation's role within
the federation if there was a prolonged period of crisis that
rendered the Canadian federation completely unstable.

Managing conflict and accommodating diversity: alternative approaches

Strong advocacy by many academics, politicians and journalists of multinational, liberal communitarian, asymmetric
federalism is by no means universal. Indeed, a majority of
English-speaking Canadian academics, journalists and politicians remain very skeptical of all forms of formal asymmetry, federal and confederal. A strong majority—over eighty
percent—of Canadians intuitively understand that federal asymmetry, if pushed too far, will "break the ties that
bind". They are not fooled by the 'magic wand' metaphor
preached by the artists of asymmetry (Newman 1994: 60).
Once entrenched in the political culture and formalized in
the Constitution, radical asymmetric federal and confederal
systems of governance—as is the case with Belgium and
increasingly with Spain—generate ongoing political instability. In the lead up to the referendum of 1995, political instability was fueled by the failure of mega-constitutional negotiations that pushed hard for federal asymmetry as well as
by Ottawa's ballooning deficit and debt. Canadians quickly
realized that this rising tide of political instability threatened
to end in the disintegration of the federation. "In this polar-
ized public climate," David Milne reminded Canadians,
"all of the inventiveness and ingenuity of Canada's asymmetrical artists may be of little help" (Milne 1994: 107). For
Milne, reaching a consensus on formal asymmetries, and
how they should be implemented, requires a very special
set of conditions. First, there must be a return to the pre-

confederation 'spirit of consociationalism' which was re-placed by the federal constitutional arrangement. Politicians of the Colony of the Canadas needed to move beyond the consociational, binational form of governance that had cul-minated in political deadlock. Second, Canadians would have to embrace, once again, elite accommodation, that is, a highly discredited process of executive federalism by eleven men in suits. Since neither of these developments was likely to occur in an increasingly democratic and far less defer-ential Canadian society, Canadians had only two realistic options: strengthen national unity or accept the secession of Quebec (Milne 1994).

Richard Simeon and Daniel-Patrick Conway remind us that federalism is Janus-faced. Federal governance can be, and often is, used to "perpetuate and intensify the very con-flicts it is designed to manage" (Simeon and Conway 2001: 34). Federalism provides, as some have observed, minority elites with powerful institutional tools and fiscal resources associated with sub-states to pursue nation-building via extensive federal asymmetry. When pushed to the extreme, sub-state elites use these powers and institutions to pursue outright secession. This minority–majority power struggle produces an undesirable political culture of federal brib-ery and provincial blackmail (Dion 1994). During the 1992 referendum on the Charlottetown Consensus Report, then Prime Minister Trudeau warned Canadians not succumb to Quebec's blackmail for extreme federal asymmetry. "Each new ransom paid to stave off the threat of schism will sim-ply encourage the master blackmailers to renew the threat and double the ransom" (Trudeau 1996: 274). Limited and quite specific forms of federal asymmetry were possible and some were already present within the Canadian fed-eration. What was neither probable nor desirable, according to Dion, was the acceptance of an extreme form of federal asymmetry, namely a Quebec/Canada binational confedera-tion. Why? Because Quebec's MPs would exercise very little authority in the federal Cabinet, the House of Commons and the Senate. They would not be able to vote on jurisdictional matters delegated to the exclusive authority of Quebec's

National Assembly. This dynamic would enable MPs from the other provinces and territories to govern Canada in their best interests thereby widening the institutionalized chasm between Canada and Quebec. A Quebec/Canada binational confederation would be a recipe for incessant political conflict, deadlock and ultimately secession (Dion 1994).

Federalism is a dynamic process of 'bringing together' and 'holding together' diverse cultural and linguistic communities. Canada's federal structure was the necessary but not the sufficient condition for 'bringing together' and the 'holding together' of the majority British-Canadian community and the minority French-Canadian community for over a century following Confederation. Federalism, nonetheless, is neither the unique nor the primary cause of ongoing political conflict between the Canadian and Quebec governments and political classes since the 1960s. There are often much deeper factors at play. The socio-economic transformation of Quebec's French-Canadian majority community generated a Quebecois neo-nationalism centered on Quebec state building by an expansive Quebecois secular, urban, educated middle class. These profound developments were bound to generate a power struggle between the new Quebec state and the increasingly interventionist Canadian state (Behiels 1985; Simeon and Conway 2001). Similarly, the demographic, socio-economic, cultural transformation of British Canada into an English-speaking multicultural Canada, with Ontario taking the lead, fuelled several parallel developments. New cleavages based on social class, ethnicity, gender and Aboriginality emerged to challenge the historic fault-lines. This growing pluralism accelerated the process of rapid state building by more diverse provincial political, bureaucratic and economic elites. Over time, some of these new provincial elites broke ranks with the established British-Canadian elites whose members had governed Canada, both provincially and federally, since Confederation (Igartua 2006). The longstanding dynamic of Anglophone–Francophone elite accommodation was challenged by the 1960s. Once this process of province building was well underway, Western premiers, led by Peter Lougheed,

promoted the concept of the equality of the provinces so as
to justify a sharp curtailment of Ottawa's taxing and spending powers and to exert greater provincial control over
national institutions, namely the Senate and the Supreme
Court (Behiels 2005; Simeon and Conway 2001). The second trend was the strengthening and coming together of
the national civil, political and equality rights movement.
By the late 1970s the Canadian human rights movement
was powerful enough to assist the Trudeau government in
entrenching a comprehensive Canadian Charter of Rights
and Freedoms in the *Constitution Act, 1982* (Behiels 2003;
Igartua 2006). These parallel transformations were driven
by robust, competing neo-nationalisms: a Quebecois ethic
nationalism—often masquerading as a civic nationalism—
centered on the Quebec state, and a pan-Canadian pluralistic, civic neo-nationalism centered on the Canadian state.
By the late 1970s these competing Quebecois and Canadian nationalisms were challenged by a nascent Aboriginal
nationalism which fuelled the Aboriginal peoples drive for
self-government outside or within a restructured multinational federation (Cairns 2000).

Is formal federal asymmetry the necessary and sufficient
condition to prevent the Canadian federation from coming
apart in the early 21st century? The vast majority of Canadians do not think so, given that federalism is Janus-faced;
its competitive institutions, watertight compartments and
players can, and do manage conflict, but they are more likely
to perpetuate and intensify conflict. Several scholars, politicians and journalists argue that there are more effective,
less risky approaches to managing conflict and accommodating diversity in a pluralistic federation than institution-
alizing federal asymmetry. "Thus it may be that the arenas
for reform of Canadian federalism lie less in the institutions of federalism themselves than in the broader framework in which federalism is embedded" (Simeon 2000: 16).
The emerging consensus among scholars is that the best
approach is through reinvigorated mechanisms and institutions of intrastate federalism. Revitalized intrastate federalism, they maintain, will foster greater and more effective

representation of the full range of provincial and national interests at the centre. Canada's central institutions—Cabinet, Parliament and the courts, as well as political parties and the electoral system—need to be reformed to ensure the full participation of a wide range of minorities in national and regional politics. Our omnipotent executive branch and the continued dominance of the executive federalism are throw backs to the 19th century that do not reflect the reality of Canadian democracy in the 21st century. Canadians are no longer deferential to their politicians and bureaucrats. All forms of elite accommodation—backroom deals among premiers, ministers, and their senior mandarins and advisors—are now perceived as a usurpation of citizens' democratic rights. Canadian and provincial Cabinets must learn to operate in more open, accountable and cooperative ways (Simeon and Conway 2001; Savoie 2006).

This is a difficult goal to achieve. Why? Canada's highly compartmentalized federation of watertight jurisdictions is inherently competitive and combative. Former Prime Minister Paul Martin, succumbing to pressures from all the premiers gathered in their newly-assembled Council of the Federation, offered them a new health accord based on the principle of asymmetry for every province. This proved to be merely a political cover for enabling the Quebec government to exercise *de facto* exclusive control over health care with unconditional financial compensation (Gregg 2005). The current government led by Prime Minister Harper, using the rhetoric of 'open federalism', is determined to return Canada to this outmoded, rigid conception federalism (Dunn 2008). Instead, Canadians and their leaders need to rethink the allocation of jurisdictional and taxing powers assigned under Sections 91 and 92 because they constitute an impediment to flexible, informal and dynamic governance that best serves the needs of citizens. A more cooperative and bargaining dynamic can be created between the central and provincial governments by establishing more concurrent jurisdictions, perhaps with 'paramountcy' assigned very judiciously to one level or the other in order to break deadlocks.

The House of Commons and the Senate and their permanent committees must take on an expanded and more active role in the formulation of policy as well as carrying out a far greater scrutiny of legislation. This enhanced, more activist role is particularly important. Why? Because as guarantors, along with the executive and judicial branches, of Canada's constitutional democracy, the House of Commons and the Senate have the responsibility to ensure that all legislation is 'Charter proofed'. MPs and Senators should not defer to the executive and senior mandarins in the Justice Department to carry out this task. MPs and Senators cannot shirk their respective responsibilities and then complain bitterly and dishonestly that the Charter has turned Canada into a 'jurocracy' because Supreme Court justices, by default, have become lawmakers. The Supreme Court was also created to defend and promote the rights of the linguistic and religious minorities. This role was expanded quite dramatically by the Charter of Rights and Freedoms in 1982 (Kelly 2005).

More importantly, the Senate's role as Canada's central institution of intrastate federalism is to defend and promote the federal nature and structure of Canada's constitution. In theory, the appointed Senate is duty bound to defend and promote—with all the powers assigned to it that are equivalent with those assigned to the House of Commons, except for money bills—the interests of the regions and provinces. In practice this intrastate function was thwarted when successive prime ministers, beginning with Sir John A. Macdonald, allowed party politics and patronage to take precedence over the Senate's primary function (D. E. Smith 2003). Would an elected Senate restore the intended role of this crucial institution, one that is central to every modern federation? There is no doubt that elected senators, regardless of their political persuasion, would feel compelled by their constituents to put their loyalty to their regions and provinces before their loyalty to their party. Senators would have to hash out, at the very centre of the federation, the difficult political compromises so necessary to its stability and development. The power of the premiers, represented by the Council of the Federation, and the role of federal-provincial conferences would be diminished. Cabinet and the MPs in the House of Commons would have to learn to share power in all matters pertaining to the provinces with elected senators. One result may be the emergence of negotiated legislative and administrative asymmetrical deals—ones required to satisfy the differing and ever evolving needs of the regions and provinces (J. Smith 2009). Given the evolving nature of the conditions underlying any and all asymmetrical arrangements, it would not be wise or necessary to entrench them in the Constitution.

Some have argued that there is a strong urgency for Senate reform to enhance the intrastate federalist dimension given that Canada's main political parties, and the all-powerful Cabinets and excessive deferential caucuses they produce, have not been able to fulfill this intrastate function for quite some time. Beginning in the late 1950s, Prime Minister John Diefenbaker's Progressive Conservative Cabinet and party lacked any meaningful and effective representation from the province of Quebec. Things did not improve under the Rt. Hon. Robert Stanfield and the Rt. Hon. Joe Clark. By the 1960s, Canada's longstanding 'governing party', the Liberal party, while overly dominant in Quebec, ceased to have any meaningful representation from the Prairie provinces. The Liberal cabinets and caucuses of the Rt. Hon. Lester B. Pearson and the Rt. Hon. Pierre Trudeau had a difficult time to respond to the changing needs of the three Prairie provinces. When then Prime Minister Brian Mulroney's Conservative party began the process of undermining the Liberal bastion in Quebec, his failed attempts at mega-constitutional politics quickly transformed Ontario into the bastion of the Liberal party. Currently Prime Minister Harper's Conservative government is weak in every region and province except in Alberta and British Columbia. Canada's regional-based federal parties no longer have the ability and/or the desire to defend and promote a strong central government, one which can counterbalance effectively both the natural and very powerful political centrifugal forces within the federation.

Conclusion

A close analysis of the Canadian federation, as well as many other federations, reveals the existence of limited formal asymmetries entrenched in the Constitution. The same scrutiny reveals the presence of ever-evolving and ever-changing legislative and administrative asymmetrical arrangements which are required for the central government to exercise stable and effective governance given the inherently asymmetrical nature of federal societies and the politics which flow from this reality. What this analysis also demonstrates is that these natural and political asymmetries require constant and effective rebalancing by various formal and informal symmetries if federal systems of governance are to remain dynamic and stable federations.

A limited number of informal asymmetrical legislative and administrative arrangements, if well designed and properly managed, do not threaten the stability of federations. Why? Because a reasonable degree of informal asymmetry can be counterbalanced with informal symmetrical arrangements. Major conflicts invariably emerge in federations when specific political elites, backed by sizeable constituencies, demand constitutional recognition of asymmetry, entailing additional powers for well-defined national communities with sub-states of their own. Such formal asymmetry can and usually does threaten the long-term viability of the federation. There is no magic wand for managing conflict and accommodating diversity in federations. The best that citizens and their political classes can do is to counterbalance any and all forms of informal and formal asymmetry with well-designed forms of judicious informal and formal symmetry. Since the socio-economic and political disaster of the Great Depression, Canada's pragmatic federal system of governance has met various challenges quite successfully. Let's hope Canadians continue to do so in the 21st century, especially now that we are confronted once again with a major recession bordering on a depression.

References

Agranoff, Robert 1994. "Asymmetrical and Symmetrical Federalism in Spain: An Examination of Intergovernmental Policy." In *Evaluating Federal Systems*, ed. Bertus De Villiers. Dordrecht: Martinus Nijhoff, 61–90.

Agranoff, Robert 1999. "Intergovernmental Relations and the Management of Asymmetry in Federal Spain." In *Accommodating Diversity: Asymmetry in Federal States*, ed. Robert Agranoff. Baden-Baden: Nomos.

Agranoff, Robert 2005. *Federal Asymmetry and Intergovernmental Relations.* Kingston, ON: School of Policy Studies, Queen's University, Asymmetry Series (17).

Armstrong, Christopher 1981. *The Politics of Federalism. Ontario's Relations with the Federal Government.* Toronto: University of Toronto Press.

Balthazar, Louis 1995 (March). "Quebec and the Ideal of Federalism." In *Annals of the Academy of Social and Political Science (ANNAL-AAPSS)* 538: 1: 40–53.

Behiels, Michael D. 1985. *Prelude to Quebec's Quiet Revolution. Liberalism versus Neo-nationalism, 1945-1960.* Montreal and Kingston, ON: McGill-Queen's University Press.

Behiels, Michael D. 1989. *The Meech Lake Primer. Conflicting Views on the 1987 Constitutional Accord.* Ottawa: University of Ottawa Press.

Behiels, Michael D. 1998. "Who Speaks for Canada? Trudeau and the Constitutional Crisis." In *Trudeau's Shadow: The Life and Legacy of Pierre Trudeau*, eds. J. L. Granatstein and Andrew Cohen. Toronto: Random House, 309–331.

Behiels, Michael D. 2003. "Pierre Elliott Trudeau's Legacy: The Canadian Charter of Rights and Freedoms." In *The Canadian Charter of Rights and Freedoms: Reflections on the Charter After Twenty Years*, eds. Joseph Magnet et al. Toronto: Butterworths, 148–173.

Behiels, Michael D. 2005. "Premier Peter Lougheed, Alberta and the Transformation of Constitutionalism in Canada, 1971-1985." In *Forging Alberta's Constitutional Framework*, eds. Richard Connors and John M. Law. Edmonton, AB: University of Alberta Press, 411–458.

Bell, Daniel A. 1993. *Communitarianism and its Critics.* Oxford, UK: Clarendon Press.

Berkowitz, Peter 1995 (Fall). "Communitarian Criticisms and Liberal Lessons." *The Responsive Community*, 54–64.

Brown, Douglas 2005. *Who's Afraid of Asymmetrical Federalism? A Summary Discussion.* Kingston, ON: School of Policy Studies, Queen's University, Asymmetry Series (16).

Burgess, Michael 1989. *Federalism and European Union: Political Ideas, Influences and Strategies in the European Community, 1972-87.* London, UK: Routledge.

Burgess, Michael, ed. 1990. *Canadian Federalism: Past, Present and Future.* Leicester, UK: Leicester University Press.

Burgess, Michael 1995. *The British Tradition of Federalism.* Leicester, UK: Leicester University Press.

Burgess, Michael 2001. "Competing National Visions: Canada–Quebec Relations in a Comparative Perspective." In *Multinational Democracies,* eds. Alain-G. Gagnon and James Tully. Cambridge, UK: Cambridge University Press, 257–274.

Cairns, Alan C. 2000. *Citizens Plus: Aboriginal Peoples and the Canadian State.* Vancouver: University of British Columbia Press.

Canada 1992. *Consensus Report on the Constitution* 1992. (Charlottetown Consensus Report) Charlottetown, August 28. 1992. Final Text, and Draft Legal Text, October 9, 1992.

Civic Practices Network 2008. *Civic Dictionary: Communitarianism.* Prepared by Carmen Sirianni and Lewis Friedland. www.cpn.org/tools/dictionary/comunitarion.html [consulted March 24, 2010].

Cook, Ramsay 1969. *Provincial Autonomy, Minority Rights and the Compact Theory, 1867-1921.* Ottawa: Queen's Printer.

Coulombe, Pierre 2001. "Federalist Language Policies: the Cases of Canada and Spain." In *Multinational Democracies,* eds. Alain-G. Gagnon and James Tully. Cambridge, UK: Cambridge University Press, 242–256.

Courchene, Thomas J. 2006. "Variations on the Federalism Theme." *Policy Options,* 27: 7: 46–54.

Courchene, Thomas J. 2007. "Alberta: The New Dominant Player in Confederation." *Policy Options,* 28: 6: 66–71.

Dion, Stéphane 1994. "Le fédéralisme fortement asymétrique: improbable et indésirable." In *Seeking a New Canadian Partnership: Asymmetrical and Federal Option,* ed. Leslie F. Seidle. Montreal: Institute for Research on Public Policy, 133–152.

Dunn, Christopher. 2008. "Explaining Canada's Open Federalism/Federalism of Openness." In *The Federal Nation,* eds. Phil Davies and Iwan Morgan. London, UK: Palgrave, Part I.

Etzioni, Amitai 1993. *The Spirit of Community: The Reinvention of American Society.* New York: Crown Publishers.

Gagnon, Alain-G. 2001. "The Moral Foundations of Asymmetrical Federalism: a Normative Exploration of the Case of Quebec and Canada." In *Multinational Democracies,* eds. Alain-G. Gagnon and James Tully. Cambridge, UK: Cambridge University Press, 319–337.

Gagnon, Alain-G. and Raffaele Iacovino 2007. *Federalism, Citizenship, and Quebec*. Toronto: University of Toronto Press.

Gibbins, Roger 2005. *Western Asymmetry*. Kingston, ON: School of Policy Studies, Queen's University, Asymmetry Series (12).

Glendon, Mary Ann 1991. *Rights Talk: The Impoverishment of Political Discourse*. New York: The Free Press.

Graefe, Peter 2005. *The Scope and Limits of Asymmetry in Recent Social Policy Agreements*. Kingston, ON: School of Policy Studies, Queen's University, Asymmetry Series 2005 (10).

Gregg, Allan 2005 (February). "Quebec's Final Victory." *The Walrus*, 2: 1: 50–61.

Griffiths, Ann L., ed. 2002. *Handbook of Federal Countries, 2002*. Montreal and Kingston, ON: McGill-Queen's University Press.

Igartua, José E. 2006. *The Other Quiet Revolution: National Identities in English Canada, 1945-71*. Vancouver: University of British Columbia.

Jaumain, Serge, ed. 1997. *La réforme de l'État... et après? L'impaxt des débats institutionnels en Belgique et au Canadaé*. Brussels: Éditions de l'Université de Bruxelles.

Jérome-Forget, Monique 1994. "Brinkmanship and Renewal of Canadian Federalism: A High Stakes Game." In *Seeking a New Canadian Partnership: Asymmetrical and Federal Option*, ed. Leslie F. Seidle. Montreal: Institute for Research on Public Policy, 19–25.

Johnson, Daniel 1965. *Égalité ou indépendance*. Montreal: Edition de l'homme.

Jung, Saskia 2005. *German Federalism—Still a Model of Symmetry?* Kingston, ON: School of Policy Studies, Queen's University, Asymmetry Series (11).

Keating, Michael 1988. *State and Regional Nationalism. Territorial Politics and the European State*. London: Harvester-Wheatsheaf.

Keating, Michael 2001. "So Many Nations, So Few States: Territory and Nationalism in the Global Era." In *Multinational Democracies*, eds. Alain-G. Gagnon and James Tully. Cambridge, UK: Cambridge University Press, 39–64.

Kelly, James B. 2005. *Governing with the Charter: Legislative and Judicial Activism and Framers' Intent*. Vancouver: University of British Columbia Press.

Kymlicka, Will 1995. *Multicultural Citizenship: a Liberal Theory of Minority Rights*. Oxford, UK: Clarendon Press.

Laforest, Guy 2005. *The Historical and Legal Origins of Asymmetrical Federalism in Canada's Founding Debates: A Brief Interpretative Note*. Kingston, ON: School of Policy Studies, Queen's University, Asymmetry Series (8).

Lecours, André 2005. *Speaking of Asymmetry. Canada and the Belgian Model.* Kingston, ON: School of Policy Studies, Queen's University, Asymmetry Series (7).

Lenihan, Donald G. et al. 2007. "Canadian Federalism: Adapting Constitutional Roles and Responsibilities in the 21st Century." *Policy Options,* 28: 4: 89–95.

Leslie, Peter M. 1994. "Asymmetry: Rejected, Conceded, Impose." In *Seeking a New Canadian Partnership: Asymmetrical and Federal Option,* ed. Leslie F. Seidle. Montreal: Institute for Research on Public Policy, 37–69.

Lijphart, Arend, ed. 1981. *Conflicts and Coexistence in Belgium: the Dynamics of a Culturally Divided Society.* Berkeley: Institute of International Studies, University of California.

Maclure, Jocelyn 2005. *Beyond Recognition and Asymmetry.* Kingston, ON: School of Policy Studies, Queen's University, Asymmetry Series (9).

Manfredi, Christopher 1997 (September). "The Charter and Federalism: A Response to Professor Balthazar." Occasional paper. Montreal: McGill Institute for the Study of Canada.

Martel, Marcel 1997. *Le deuil d'un pays imagine: Rêves, lutes et déroute du Canada français. Les rapports entre le Québec et la francophonie canadienne (1867-1975).* Ottawa: University of Ottawa Press.

McRoberts, Kenneth 1997. *Misconceiving Canada: The Struggle for National Unity.* Toronto: Oxford University Press.

Milne, David 1994. "Exposed to the Glare: Constitutional Camouflage and the Fate of the Federation." In *Seeking a New Canadian Partnership: Asymmetrical and Federal Option,* ed. Leslie F. Seidle. Montreal: Institute for Research on Public Policy, 107–131.

Milne, David 2005. *Asymmetry in Canada, Past and Present.* Kingston, ON: School of Policy Studies, Queen's University, Asymmetry Series (1).

Moreno, Luis 2001. *The Federalization of Spain.* London, UK: Frank Cass.

Morton F. L. (Ted) 2005. *Equality or Asymmetry? Alberta at the Crossroads.* Kingston, ON: School of Policy Studies, Queen's University, Asymmetry Series (5).

Mulhall, Stephen and Adam Swift 1996. *Liberals and Communitarians.* Oxford, UK and Cambridge, MA: Blackwell.

Newman, Peter C. 1994 (July 1). "Canada is the Solution Looking for a Problem." *Maclean's,* 107: 60.

Pelletier, Benoît 2005. *Asymmetrical Federalism: A Win-Win Formula.* Kingston, ON: School of Policy Studies, Queen's University, Asymmetry Series (15a).

Phillips, Derek L. 1993. *Looking Backward: A Critical Appraisal of Communitarian Thought.* Princeton, NJ: Princeton University Press.

Rawls, John 1972. *A Theory of Justice*. Oxford, UK: Oxford University Press.

Rawls, John 1993. *Political Liberalism*. New York: Columbia University Press.

Raz, Joseph 1986. *The Morality of Freedom*. Oxford, UK: Oxford University Press.

Resnick, Philip 1994. "Toward a Multinational Federalism: Asymmetrical and Confederal Alternatives." In *Seeking a New Canadian Partnership: Asymmetrical and Federal Option*, ed. Leslie F. Seidle. Montreal: Institute for Research on Public Policy, 71–89.

Requejo, Ferran 2001. "Political Liberalism in Multinational States: the legitimacy of plural and asymmetrical federalism." In *Multinational Democracies*, eds. Alain-G. Gagnon and James Tully. Cambridge, UK: Cambridge University Press, 110–132.

Roberts, John 2005. *Asymmetrical Federalism: Magic Wand or 'Bait and Switch'*. Kingston, ON: School of Policy Studies, Queen's University, Asymmetry Series (14).

Rocher, François, Christian Rouillard and André Lecours 2001. "Recognition Claims, Partisan Politics and Institutional Constraints: Belgium, Spain and Canada in a Comparative Perspective." In *Multinational Democracies*, eds. Alain-G. Gagnon and James Tully. Cambridge, UK: Cambridge University Press, 176–200.

Savoie, Donald J. 2006. "Intrastate Federalism and the Civil Service." In *Continuity and Change in Canadian Politics: Essays in Honour of David E. Smith*. Toronto: University of Toronto Press, 64–88.

Saywell, John T. 2002. *The Lawmakers. Judicial Power and the Shaping of Canadian Federalism*. Toronto: University of Toronto Press.

Seidle, Leslie F. 1994. "Constitutive Principles and the Elusive Canadian Vision." In *Seeking a New Canadian Partnership: Asymmetrical and Federal Option*, ed. Leslie F. Seidle. Montreal: Institute for Research on Public Policy, 7–17, 221–225.

Seidle, Leslie F. 2005. *Public Opinion on Asymmetrical Federalism: Growing Openness or Continuing Ambiguity?* Kingston, ON: School of Policy Studies, Queen's University, Asymmetry Series (2).

Silver, A. I. 1982. *The French-Canadian Idea of Confederation, 1864-1900*. Toronto: University of Toronto Press.

Simeon, Richard 2000 (January–February). "Let's Get at the Basic Question Indirectly." *Policy Options*, 21: 1: 11–16.

Simeon, Richard and Daniel-Patrick Conway 2001. "Federalism and the Management of Conflict in Multinational Societies." In *Multinational Democracies*, eds. Alain-G. Gagnon and James Tully. Cambridge, UK: Cambridge University Press, 338–365.

Smith, David E. 2003. *The Canadian Senate in Bicameral Perspective*. Toronto: University of Toronto Press.

Smith, Jennifer 2005. *The Case for Asymmetry in Canadian Federalism*. Kingston, ON: School of Policy Studies, Queen's University, Asymmetry Series (6).

Smith, Jennifer, ed. 2009. *Senate Reform: Once More into the Breech*. Kingston, ON: School of Policy Studies, Queen's University.

Smith, Rogers M. 1993 (September). "Beyond Tocqueville, Myrdal, and Hartz: The Multiple Traditions in America." *American Political Science Review*, 87: 3: 549–566.

Tarlton, Charles D. 1965 (September). "Symmetry and Asymmetry as Elements of Federalism." *Journal of Politics*, 27: 861–874.

Taylor, Charles 1993. *Reconciling the Solitudes: Essays on Canadian Federalism and Nationalism*, ed. Guy Laforest. Montreal and Kingston, ON: McGill-Queen's University Press.

Telford, Hamish 2005. *Survivance Versus Ambivalence: The Federal Dilemma in Canada*. Kingston, ON: School of Policy Studies, Queen's University, Asymmetry Series (13).

Trudeau, Rt. Hon. Pierre Elliott 1996. "Quebec's Blackmail." In *Against the Current. Selected Writings 1939-1996*, ed. Gérard Pelletier. Toronto: McClelland & Stewart, 262–274.

Tully, James 1995. *Strange Multiplicity: Constitutionalism in an Age of Diversity*. Cambridge, UK: Cambridge University Press.

Tully, James 2001. "Introduction." In *Multinational Democracies*, eds. Alain-G. Gagnon and James Tully. Cambridge, UK: Cambridge University Press, 1–33.

Vaughan, Frederick 2003. *The Canadian Federalist Experiment: From Defiant Monarchy to Reluctant Republic*. Montreal and Kingston, ON: McGill-Queen's University Press.

Watts, Ronald L. 2005. *A Comparative Perspective on Asymmetry in Federations*. Kingston, ON: School of Policy Studies, Queen's University, Asymmetry Series (4).

Webber, Jeremy 1994. *Reimagining Canada: Language, Culture, Community, and the Canadian Constitution*. Montreal and Kingston, ON: McGill-Queen's University Press.

Chapter 3

Prime Minister Harper's Open Federalism: Promoting a Neo-liberal Agenda?

Brooke Jeffrey

> *Canada is a Northern European welfare state in the worst sense of the term, and very proud of it.*
> —Stephen Harper (1997)

Introduction

Like the Rt. Hon. Pierre Elliott Trudeau, Prime Minister Stephen Harper spelled out his views on Canadian federalism in considerable detail before becoming prime minister. But Trudeau had nearly sixteen years to implement his vision, most of the time with the benefit of a strong majority; at the time of writing, Harper has had only three years of minority government. Despite these limitations, the outline of Harper's 'new' approach to Canadian federalism is beginning to take shape, and his vision of 'open federalism' is clearly antithetical to Trudeau's pan-Canadian approach.

Although this would be significant in itself, the real extent of the change envisaged by 'open federalism' is demonstrated by the yawning gulf that exists between the Reform/Alliance-based Harper and his former opponents in the Progressive Conservative party. Progressive Conservatives historically espoused a more decentralized view of the federation than Liberals, especially in the post-war era. But the open federalism of Harper's new Conservative party is far more decentralist in some respects and far more radical in others. One striking indicator of this divergence is the fact that Harper appears ready to give the provinces a say in areas of federal responsibility, in addition to withdrawing the federal government entirely from areas of provincial or shared jurisdiction. The 2006 Conservative platform, Stand Up for Canada, made this abundantly clear when it declared "A Conservative government will support the creation of practical intergovernmental mechanisms to facilitate provincial involvement in areas of federal jurisdiction where provincial jurisdiction is affected...." It even suggested the provinces' Council of the Federation could take the lead on a number of issues formerly managed by the federal government. (Conservative Party of Canada 2006)

The Hon. Sinclair Stevens, a former Progressive Conservative Cabinet minister and fierce critic of the new Conservative party and Harper's open federalism, has written "this is the first time in Canadian history that a national political party has embraced a provincial rights agenda" (Stevens 2006). His views were shared by former Progressive Conservative Prime Minister Joe Clark, who shocked many of his colleagues when he declared he would rather support Paul Martin—"the devil we know"—than Stephen Harper, because he was "extremely worried" about Harper's ideological approach, his views on the federation, and his leadership style (Clark 2004).

Some scholars have suggested Harper's concerns about the current state of Canadian federalism are primarily procedural in nature, reflecting his desire to see a more consultative, collaborative, open and transparent federal-provincial relationship. Although never a populist, Harper's statements about the so-called 'democratic deficit' lend some credence to this argument. Harper's letter to the Council of the Federation on January 13, 2006 specifically underlined his commitment "to initiate a new style of open federalism which would involve working more closely and collaboratively with the provinces...." This commitment was reinforced in his speech to the Montreal Board of Trade in April of the same year, when he declared "the time has come to establish a new relationship with the provinces, a relationship that is open, honest and respectful" (Harper 2006).

Other commentators, such as Michael Behiels, have highlighted the constitutional basis for Harper's vision, noting he has often advocated a 'return' to a classic form of federalism with watertight compartments where there is little or no need for intergovernmental relations of any kind (Behiels 2008). Harper's stated preference for 'disentanglement' and his oft-repeated comment that Ottawa "should do what the federal government is supposed to do", instead of persistently "sticking its nose into provincial and local matters, while at the same time neglecting what it had to do", provide ample support for this argument (Harper 2006). The constitutional rationale for Harper's vision was underlined in his open letter to the *National Post*, where he called for "renewed respect for the division of powers between the federal and provincial governments..." and stressed the need to "re-establish a strong central government that focuses on genuine national priorities like national defence and the economic union, while fully respecting the exclusive jurisdiction of the provinces" (Harper 2004).

Still other observers, notably Keith Banting, have pointed to the partisan political and electoral considerations which appear to underpin Harper's approach to federalism (Banting 2006). His emphasis on Quebec and the fiscal imbalance are frequently cited in support of this argument, as is the remarkably candid analysis of Harper's long-term political strategy that was provided by his former senior adviser and mentor, Tom Flanagan.

All of these elements must be considered when examining Prime Minister Harper's highly decentralist vision. However, they are largely concerned with process and strategy, or what Peter Leslie has referred to as the "narrow, precise face" of open federalism (Leslie 2006). By contrast, this chapter is intended to focus on the broader but much less precise 'face' of open federalism, namely its underlying policy objectives and likely consequences. Specifically, the chapter examines the potential role and impact of open

federalism on the welfare state in Canada. As such it is necessarily speculative, exploring the philosophical underpin-
nings of Harper's federal vision by drawing on his earlier,
less guarded comments before taking over the leadership
of the Conservative party, as well as his statements once in
office and the subsequent actions of his government. Since
Harper himself said in 2005, "I don't think my fundamental beliefs have changed in a decade", the use of the earlier material does not seem too great a leap of faith, and the
accumulated empirical evidence is certainly suggestive.

As Leslie has noted, Harper's stated objectives for
open federalism—of 'developing' the social and economic
union—are not only closely interrelated but motivated by
a consistent worldview of the role of the state, one which
is both minimalist and assertive. More importantly, "such
objectives not only call for a review of the conduct of intergovernmental relations, but open up questions of broad
scale political design…At stake is the kind of country that
Canada is and should become" (Ibid., 45).

This analysis concludes that an important but unstated
objective of open federalism is to further the neo-liberal
agenda which prompted Harper to enter politics in the first
place, and which underpins his ideological approach to
government as a whole. As a result, it suggests much of the
existing architecture of the welfare state would be at risk if
he were able to obtain a majority and implement his new
federal vision.

Prime Minister Harper's early political views

Stephen Harper was one of the earliest converts to Preston
Manning's Reform party, and Harper's speech at the party's
founding convention in Winnipeg in 1987 was described by
Manning as brilliant. In it, Harper embraced the idea of a
truly free market economy and dismissed Canadians' reliance on state-run social welfare. His comments on federalism, however, were limited to the standard complaints
about western alienation and central Canadian dominance.

Like other Reform hopefuls, Harper ran unsuccessfully for federal office in the 1988 federal election. Unlike most of his cohorts, though, he continued his direct involvement with the party afterwards, becoming the party's national policy director and one of Manning's principal advisers. Harper eventually left his formal paid party post, but he continued to play a major role in the development of the 1993 Reform platform (the Green Sheet) through his position on the party's national executive. Various accounts of that platform process have outlined the calculated efforts of Harper and the national executive to tone down some of the more radical and extreme views of Reform party members, as expressed through party resolutions at conventions. In fact, Harper was credited with having actually changed the direction of some resolutions between Winnipeg and the subsequent policy convention in Saskatoon which immediately preceded the drafting of the platform (Dabbs 1997).

Nevertheless the party's Green Sheet was widely criticized, even in western Canada, for its extremist views. One need look no further than some of its twenty 'guiding principles' to determine why the *Edmonton Journal* saw the platform as "shrill and intolerant" while the *Calgary Herald* described it as "strident and repugnant", allowing the *Globe and Mail*'s evaluation of the party as "narrow-minded and disturbing" to appear moderate by comparison (Jeffrey 1999: 343).

Reform's use of code words to convey different impressions to different audiences was first evident in the Green Sheet—again something generally credited to Harper and the national executive. The party's promotion of a 'balanced' immigration system, for example, was interpreted favourably by moderates and racists alike, each of whom read what they wanted into the deliberately ambiguous language (Dobbin 1991: 20). But even this ambiguity was not sufficient to conceal the size of the gap between the values of the Reform party and mainstream Canadian political culture. Few observers could miss the fact that Reform opposed official bilingualism and multiculturalism when the party's platform declared it supported "the principle that individuals or groups are free to preserve their cultural heritage using their own resources." The values gap was even more obvious when the platform addressed the issue of the welfare state. Here again, the role of government was nowhere to be found. Instead, the Green Sheet declared "We believe Canadians have a personal and collective responsibility to care and provide for the basic needs of people who are unable to care and provide for themselves." For greater certainty, the text went on to state "We would actively encourage families, communities, non-governmental organizations and the private sector to reassume their duties in social service areas" (Reform Party of Canada 1993).

Reform won only nineteen percent of the popular vote in the 1993 election. Nevertheless it finished a close third to the Bloc Québécois, the Official Opposition, by virtue of its concentration of support in western Canada. This support, in turn, was the direct result of the collapse of the Progressive Conservative party and the coalition of alienated westerners and 'soft' Quebec nationalists put together by former Prime Minister Brian Mulroney to achieve two majority governments. Among the most important factors in the party's defeat were Mulroney's two failed attempts to provide constitutional recognition for Quebec as a 'distinct society'. It was the Reform party's opposition to the Meech Lake and Charlottetown accords—a position adopted reluctantly by Preston Manning at the express urging of Stephen Harper— that cemented the party's support in western Canada.

As a result of Reform's unexpected success, Stephen Harper was finally a Reform MP in Ottawa. There he watched in frustration as the party failed to make any headway. Reform was often treated with scorn and derision by the governing Liberals, to say nothing of the central Canadian media. This was especially painful when some of his more extreme colleagues spoke their mind. Comments such as Deborah Gray's "We believe Medicare is for the sick and not the poor" and Paul Forseth's criticism of Old Age Security as "welfare for the aged" did little to advance Reform's cause as far as Harper was concerned, since his aim was to form a government, not serve as a thorn in the side of

Prime Minister Jean Chrétien's Liberals. Worse still, it was clear that Manning had no intention of compromising on basic principles. He continued to believe Canadians would eventually come around to his way of thinking if only it was properly explained. But Harper was increasingly convinced that Canadians were simply too liberal to accept a frontal assault on the welfare state, and opinion polls confirmed his view (Jeffrey 1999).

During the 1995 Quebec referendum, Manning held discussions with the US ambassador about Canada's future in the event of a 'yes' vote. Meanwhile Harper—who by then was the party's unity critic responsible for intergovernmental affairs—was preparing a twenty-point plan to achieve something he referred to as 'new federalism.' The plan provided an early glimpse into Harper's vision of Canadian federalism, one in which the role of the federal government would be greatly reduced and power further decentralized to the provinces. Asked how this plan would impact national unity, given that Canada was already among the most decentralized federations in the world, Harper insisted national unity would be strengthened by creating stronger provinces. His proposed changes, Harper declared, "will assert the autonomy of the provinces and the power of the people well into the future" (Stevens 2006: 2).

Open federalism in theory: a return to past constitutional practice?

It is instructive to note that after this watershed declaration the issues of constitutional jurisdiction and provincial rights became key rallying points for Harper's approach to federalism. Coincidentally his direct criticism of the welfare state soon faded from public view. In addition, although the majority of his twenty points involved the effective transfer of significant powers and fiscal resources to the provinces, this was to be achieved by administrative means rather than constitutional reform. As Harper said at the time, he did not want to "re-open old constitutional wounds." He also made it clear that he felt constitutional reform was unnecessary, since the changes he had in mind "simply require a (federal) government that is willing to act" (Harper 1995).

Yet Harper's stated rationale for open federalism was the need "to return to the original principles of the constitution" and "revert" to the practice of federalism "at the time of Confederation" (*Canadian Press* 2008). The problem with this argument, as Behiels and others have noted, is that it is not factually accurate. In Canada's case, the classic federalist idyll of watertight compartments and two separate but equal levels of government is a myth, and always has been. British political scientist K. C. Wheare actually described Canada as a "quasi-federal" system in the early years under Sir John A. Macdonald, precisely because of the number of areas of shared constitutional jurisdiction and the predominance of the federal government's powers, including reservation and disallowance (Wheare 1967). Although the Laurier era saw a considerable degree of decentralization take place by virtue of decisions rendered by the British Judicial Committee of the Privy Council, the provinces once again took a back seat to the federal government during two World Wars and a Great Depression, notably through the introduction of federal income tax and unemployment insurance.

Harper's commitment to a further decentralization of the federation also flies in the face of the intent of the original framers of the Canadian constitution, who were well-known for their determination to ensure a strong central government and their fears of an American-style federation in which the states were perceived—especially during the throes of a disastrous Civil War—as having far too much power. Similarly, Harper's vitriolic opposition to the use of the federal spending power since World War II—"this outrageous spending power gave rise to a domineering and paternalistic federalism..." (Harper 2005)—ignores the fact that this power is not only constitutionally legitimate and unrestrained, but was deliberately envisaged by the Fathers of Confederation.

Nor, as Harper has repeatedly asserted, was the federal government aggressively asserting its spending power when these programs were developed. On the contrary, as Tom Kent has pointed out "it is difficult to believe that the clever Stephen Harper is a true believer in so myth-based a misreading of federal-provincial bargaining. The myth is about how Ottawa began to subsidize major provincial programs. It did not barge in. Initially, it was dragged in..." (Kent 2008).

The principal use of the federal spending power since World War II has been to create the modern welfare state. The so-called 'golden age' of cooperative federalism was the very antithesis of Wheare's classic watertight compartment version. Lacking an amending formula or other constitutional means to resolve the vertical imbalance between jurisdiction and revenues, the Canadian social safety net was built through intergovernmental administrative cooperation. The major initiatives were structured as federal-provincial cost-sharing programs that depended for their very existence on the federal spending power. And, with the federal government's introduction of minimum national standards as the *quid pro quo* for its participation, they were a quintessential expression of the pan-Canadian vision of federalism.

In short, a return to the past is not something that open federalism could realistically accomplish, and Harper can hardly be unaware of this. However, his discourse does allow him to link his new Reform/Alliance based-Conservative party with the old Progressive Conservative party, a tactic that achieves the political objective of making open federalism appear more legitimate and less threatening. Hence his frequent references to the party's "roots that stretch back to Confederation" and his assertion that "It was Conservatives...led by John A. Macdonald and Georges-Etienne Cartier and their allies in other provinces, who laid the foundations of Confederation..." (Harper 2004). This tactic, as noted above, has infuriated dyed-in-the-wool Progressive Conservatives such as the Rt. Hon. Joe Clark and the Hon. Sinclair Stevens—and even prompted lawsuits—but it has not deterred Harper from pressing the point.

Open federalism in theory: defending provincial rights?

This apparently deliberate obfuscation raises some important questions. Why is it necessary and what is the real purpose behind the constitutional and procedural justifications? One possible answer lies in early comments made by Harper himself about the welfare state. For example, in 1997 when he had left politics and was serving as vice-president of the National Citizens' Coalition—a Canadian organization whose official slogan is "more freedom through less government"—Harper delivered a startlingly blunt and critical assessment of Canada's political situation to a meeting of the Council for National Policy, a right-wing American think tank. The very first 'fact' he offered his audience about Canada was that "it is a Northern European welfare state in the worst sense of the term, and very proud of it" (Harper 1997). Four years later, Harper was president of the National Citizens' Coalition and, as such, was one of six signatories to an open letter to Alberta premier Ralph Klein in the aftermath of the 2000 federal election (Alberta Agenda 2001). In it, the authors decried the Liberal government's criticism of Klein's controversial approach to health care, including his creation of 'truth squads' to promote the benefits of privatization, and his repeated demands that no conditions of any kind be attached to federal funding for health care.

The 'Firewall Letter' took the provincial rights approach to a new extreme. It urged Klein to adopt an Alberta Agenda that would cut the province off from the influence of the federal government as much as possible. The recommendations included: withdrawing from the Canada Pension Plan; creating a provincial police force to replace the RCMP; and "resuming provincial responsibility for health-care policy." The authors argued "each province should raise its own revenue for health care", with poorer provinces relying on equalization. Anticipating that the federal government would challenge this plan in the courts, they declared "If we lose, we can afford the financial penalties that Ottawa may try to impose under the *Canada Health Act*" (Ibid.).

Although the constitutional defence of provincial jurisdiction was raised by the authors as the primary motivation
for their letter, this soon gave way to a long list of economic
considerations. In fact, the letter concluded with a revealing
warning. "An economic slowdown, perhaps even a recession, threatens North America, and a hostile government in
Ottawa will be tempted to take advantage of Alberta's prosperity, to redistribute income from Alberta to residents of
other provinces..." (Ibid.).

Soon after, Harper dismissed the efforts of the newly-
created Commission on the Future of Health Care in
Canada (Romanow Commission) as "not only useless but
dangerous."

Nevertheless, he was also acutely aware of the political
resistance that Preston Manning and his successor, Stockwell
Day, had continued to encounter by speaking too candidly
about their views on social programs. Day's desperate effort
to moderate the extremist image of the Canadian Alliance
party with his hand-written "No two-tier medicine" sign
during the 2000 Leaders Debates was a classic case of failed
damage control. In numerous public opinion polls, Canadians agreed the Alliance party was still far too extreme and
did not share their views on a number of important issues,
most noticeably social policy.

As a result, by the time Harper became the leader of the
new Conservative party in March 2004, he was far more
circumspect about his own views on health care and social
welfare in general. His speeches now focused almost exclusively on the need to restrain the federal spending power as
a means to protect provincial jurisdiction, and on decentralization as the best way to preserve national unity, especially
with respect to Quebec.

After the June 2004 election, when unguarded comments
by backbenchers such as Randy White and Cheryl Gallant
undermined Harper's attempts to distance himself from the
extremist label, he took firm measures to prevent any recur-
rence of such remarks. He also redoubled his own efforts to
stress the provincial rights argument. Hence the 2005 Conservative party platform, which allocated three full sections

to "federalism", "reform of the federation", and "the fiscal imbalance". It stated the party "is committed to the federal principle and to the notion of strong provinces within Canada." The platform also promised the party would "ensure that the use of the federal spending power in provincial jurisdictions is limited", and "authorize the provinces to use the opting out formula with full compensation if they want to opt out of any new or modified federal program in areas of shared or exclusive jurisdiction" (Conservative Party of Canada 2005).

In a speech in Quebec City on December 19, 2005, during the election campaign, Harper went further. He declared that his approach to federalism would involve "expanding" or "developing" the social union by allowing the Council of the Federation to play the lead role. The federal government's actions, he said, would be limited to "complementing and supporting" those of the provinces (Leslie 2006).

By 2008, hoping for a majority government after having secured a minority in 2006, the Harper Conservatives' platform reiterated these commitments with some important additions. One section on open federalism was entitled "respecting the provinces and territories" and promised, somewhat paradoxically, that a re-elected Harper government would recognize provincial jurisdiction "as spelled out in the *Constitution Act, 1867*" by "enshrining our principles of federalism in a new Charter of Open Federalism." Further voluntary limitations on the federal spending power were also promised. Now, any new shared-cost program would not even proceed without the consent of the majority of provinces, and provinces could still choose to opt out with compensation "so long as the province offers a similar program with similar accountability structures" (Conservative Party of Canada 2008).

This terminology, as students of Canadian constitutional reform will immediately recognize, is strikingly reminiscent of the discourse used in the Meech Lake and Charlottetown accords. Opponents of those deals—who supported Trudeau's pan-Canadian vision of federalism—decried the elimination of the concept of 'minimum national standards'

in favour of much more ambiguous language. They argued
the changes would diminish rather than enhance accountability, and lead to a race to the bottom in terms of standards. Some, including Trudeau himself, also argued the
changes would inevitably lead to a 'checkerboard Canada'
in which access to social programs and services would differ dramatically from one province to another. In short, the
Harper Conservatives were proposing to achieve by administrative means what Meech and Charlottetown had been
unable to accomplish through constitutional reform.

In an interview with L. Ian Macdonald published in *Policy
Options* shortly after he became prime minister, Harper indicated that, if he were to be successful, the role of the federal
government would be limited to little more than defence, foreign policy and the economic union (Macdonald 2007).

Open federalism in theory: promoting a neo-liberal agenda?

Many of his statements suggest that Stephen Harper's
objectives are not only more ambitious but far more coherent than former Prime Minister Brian Mulroney's. Where
Mulroney's arguments were almost entirely political,
Harper's have been consistently supported by two prominent neo-liberal themes.

The first, as demonstrated earlier, is a Canadian variation on the states' rights argument favoured by right-wing
politicians in the United States. The most successful proponent of states' rights was undoubtedly former President Ronald Reagan, who appointed the ultraconservative
William Rehnquist as Chief Justice of the Supreme Court.
Reagan was one of a number of prominent American politicians who argued in favour of restraining the 'federal
power'. From Barry Goldwater's rejection of the New Deal
and George Wallace's opposition to desegregation, to the
Rehnquist court's decisions on abortion, the equal rights
amendment, gay rights and affirmative action, the modern
use of the 'states' rights' argument has served as a code

for right-wing politicians who want to dismantle various aspects of the liberal agenda.

Proponents of states' rights were conspicuously successful in achieving their objectives under Reagan. In addition to securing appointments of like-minded activists to the Supreme Court—a move designed to ensure their influence long after Reagan's departure—they came together to form the Federalist Society, an organization of high-powered right-wing Republican lawyers and academics. The society was led in the early days by Robert Bork at Yale. Although Bork failed in his attempt to join the Court, other Federalists such as Antonin Scalia, Samuel Alito and Sandra Day O'Connor succeeded. Other members of the Federalist Society went on to take key posts in Republican administrations, including Edwin Meese as Reagan's Attorney General, C. Boyden Gray in the White House under George Bush, and no fewer than five assistant attorneys-general and senior counsel to the Senate Judiciary Committee.

The Federalists are widely seen as the driving force behind President George W. Bush's unprecedented decision to eliminate the American Bar Association's role in evaluating candidates for the Supreme Court. Similarly, Stephen Harper has been a consistent opponent of the Canadian Supreme Court, and has introduced a variety of measures since taking office to limit its powers and circumvent the established appointments process.

The constitutional arguments of the Federalists also bear a striking resemblance to those used by Prime Minister Harper. The Federalists "are 'originalist' in their approach to the Constitution, meaning they favour strict textual readings designed to shear back constitutional principles developed during the more liberal Warren court era...in order to leach power away from 'big government' in Washington" (Landay 2000). Their stated objectives are to promote dramatic reductions in federal powers, primarily through court challenges, by ensuring greater respect for states rights as outlined, in their view, in the constitutional division of powers. Among their most striking victories are the 1999 American Trucking v EPA decision, which rolled back various federal environmental standards as being *ultra vires*, and their successful defence of California's right to introduce anti-affirmative action measures—Proposition 209.

Some scholars have also argued that the states' rights argument can be seen as a precursor or complement to the business community's drive for deregulation and the privatization of government services. For example, a commentator for the Federalist Society proudly claimed the American Trucking decision "will save industry in the neighborhood of US$ 45 billion per year."

Harper has also advanced a second neo-liberal theme, put forward by conservative American economists who believe federal systems are ideal for achieving their free market objectives. As Canadian political economist Adam Harmes has demonstrated, prominent American economists of the Friedrich Hayek school of thought, from Milton Freidman to James Buchanan, have promoted the merits of federalism as a means of restraining what they see as the 'market-inhibiting tendencies of governments' (Harmes 2006). Specifically, Harmes notes there is a widely held view that decentralization of a federation will provide for more competition among sub-national units, and that tax measures (rather than regulation and legislation) are the best way for both levels of government to achieve an optimal competitive economy.

Perhaps the best-known proponent of this argument in recent years has been Grover Norquist, an economist who founded Americans for Tax Reform in 1985 at the request of President Reagan. Norquist subsequently participated in the drafting of the Republican's 1994 Contract with America and became a close confidant of Newt Gingrich. Norquist argues the power of the federal government can be constrained by non-constitutional means through a reduction in revenue. It was Norquist who introduced the now-famous conservative mantra that the solution is "to starve the beast". An early supporter of the candidacy of George W. Bush, Norquist has been widely credited with engineering many of the tax cuts and deregulation measures introduced by the Bush administration (Friedman 2005).

Given the significant influence of American neo-liberal thinkers in shaping Stephen Harper's political outlook (Flanagan 2007), his adaptation of these two arguments to the Canadian situation, and specifically to the welfare state, does not seem farfetched. Indeed, Harper's Masters' thesis not only rejected Keynesian economics as wrong-headed and ineffective, but praised the free-market arguments of Hayek and Friedman.

Both the provincial rights theme and the "starve the beast" idea have been articulated in Canada by right-wing economists and think tanks such as the Fraser Institute for some time. In their 1978 report, *Canadian Confederation at the Crossroads: The Search for a Federal-Provincial Balance*, the authors not only recommended that provinces be required to finance education at all levels, but that the federal government should give up tax room, rather than providing transfer payments, to fund this arrangement (Walker 1978).

More recently, the Canadian Council of Chief Executives (CCCE) produced a discussion paper which included a more broadly-based proposal along the same lines. It suggested the federal government transfer the GST to the provinces and eliminate all of its transfer payments. Among the stated advantages of this approach was the fact "it would encourage the federal government to focus on its core responsibilities instead of continuously looking for ways to intrude in provincial jurisdiction." Among the disadvantages, the report acknowledged "a shift in tax room would…reduce the federal ability to ensure national standards in areas of provincial jurisdiction." The report also acknowledged that, "absent offsetting changes in the equalization program", the impact of "transferring tax room would widen the gap between have and have-not provinces" (Canadian Council of Chief Executives 2006).

The CCCE report is virtually a mirror image of the positions put forward by the new Conservative party in its platform and convention resolutions, and repeated in statements by Stephen Harper. In his discussion of open federalism over time, Harper—trained as an economist and heavily influenced by the right-wing tendencies of the so-called 'Calgary School'—has made frequent reference to the use of various tax measures as a means of achieving the 'disentanglement' of jurisdictions that he envisages.

Nowhere was this more clearly expressed than in the new Prime Minister's speech to the Montreal Board of Trade in April of 2006. Referring to his government's intention to deal with the fiscal imbalance, he stressed, "Let me be clear, we will develop specific proposals...And let me tell you what they will not include: they will not include increasing federal spending in areas of exclusive provincial jurisdiction." A subheading in the official text of that speech specifically highlighted "Tax reduction: the ultimate decentralization", and promised significant tax reductions, including the possibility of transferring tax room to the provinces, rather than increased transfer payments (Harper 2006).

At first glance Harper's Montreal declaration seems to contradict his party's election platform only a few months earlier. On closer examination, however, it becomes apparent that the wording for the relevant passage in Stand Up for Canada has been carefully drafted to suggest a range of possibilities, while committing to none. "A Conservative government", it reads, "will fix, in collaboration with the provinces, the problem of the fiscal imbalance by increasing the amounts allocated to provincial governments, by reducing taxes, *or* by transferring tax points to the provinces", a pledge which may have reassured many voters but actually left them in the dark about the party's likely choice (Conservative Party of Canada 2006, italics added for emphasis).

By contrast, there was little doubt about the intent of Harper's later commitment to transfer tax points to the provinces. An article in the *Globe and Mail* by columnist John Ibbitson declared, "Mr. Harper's most important liberal initiative...is his plan to download taxing powers to the provinces, accompanied by a pledge to keep Ottawa out of provincial areas of jurisdiction." In fact, Ibbitson foresaw this move would eventually "return the federal government to something closer to the role of the night watchman state..." (Ibbitson 2006: A7). In short, this exploration of possible underlying motives for Stephen Harper's vision of open federalism suggests the provinces will assume a pivotal role in preserving or dismantling the welfare state.

Open federalism and the Harper government's record

Beginning with the Mulroney government's unprecedented move to unilaterally redraw the formula for federal transfer payments, the Chrétien government's subsequent implementation of the Canada Health and Social Transfer (CHST) to achieve deficit reduction, and the adoption of the Social Union Framework Agreement (SUFA) in response to the fallout from the Quebec referendum of 1995, several recent federal measures have already allowed the provinces more scope than ever before. Taken together, these measures have produced a number of unintended consequences and significantly weakened the welfare state. Even more significant, however, is the provincial response to these measures. It provides ample evidence of the likely negative trends that would emerge if a further dramatic decentralization of social programs resulted—as Harper has suggested—in unfettered provincial ability to design as well as administer those programs. Harper is surely only too well aware of this recent trend. In fact, he appears to be counting on the provinces to accomplish what he cannot, due to political constraints.

Certainly the precedents set by earlier Progressive Conservative and Liberal measures, virtually all of which were introduced as a result of immediate political pressures rather than any commitment to an alternative agenda, have so far allowed Harper to move towards his vision of open federalism with little serious opposition, if not impunity. This is largely because he appears—at least superficially— to be moving in the same direction as his immediate predecessors, and the real extent of his divergence from the pan-Canadian norm has been minimized.

Taken together, the problems posed by the CHST, the SUFA and former Prime Minister Paul Martin's enthusiastic defence of an increasingly asymmetrical model of federalism—especially with respect to Quebec—have inevitably provided Stephen Harper with an ideal opportunity to combine his partisan criticism of the Liberals' 'paternalistic' and 'invasive' approach to provincial jurisdiction with a valid policy concern about 'one-off deals' that belied principles of fairness and equity. It was this devastating political combination that allowed him to begin to advance his own vision of open federalism, secure in the knowledge that Canadians were already concerned about the direction the country was taking.

Nevertheless, the Harper government's actions during its first three years in power were not entirely consistent with his stated vision, nor did they advance that vision as far and as fast as Harper's original rhetoric might have suggested. Indeed, several observers have argued that Harper's open federalism was always a partisan tool that quickly became the victim of political opportunism.

Since taking office in January 2006, the Harper government has proceeded to implement some of its commitments regarding open federalism quite aggressively. In other policy fields it has taken strong federal initiatives that appear to fly in the face of its decentralist vision. This apparent mixed message has led some observers, including a former Clerk of the Privy Council, to conclude that Harper may be more opportunistic and less ideologically driven than previously thought (Spector 2009).

While there is clearly some truth to this argument—epitomized by Harper's opportunistic introduction of the Quebec nation resolution in the House of Commons during the last Liberal leadership race—an analysis of his government's record to date suggests the Prime Minister has not succumbed to this phenomenon to the extent Norman Spector has argued. This analysis suggests a more nuanced situation in which a genuine commitment to the neo-liberal agenda has had to be tempered with political realism, particularly in a minority situation. Indeed, the fact that Harper has already managed to have an impact on the operation of Canadian federalism suggests a level of commitment unlikely to disappear in the long run, and certainly not in the event of a majority government.

This has not always been apparent. For one thing, Harper has been the beneficiary of a happy convergence of political pressures and ideological positioning on certain issues. As a result no right-wing justification was necessary for some of his government's decisions, which could be easily defended on other grounds. Moreover several of the apparent inconsistencies between Harper's decentralist rhetoric and his centralizing actions are misleading and do not necessarily reflect ideological inconsistency. It is important to note that the classic neo-liberal discourse of the Hayek school not only favours considerable decentralization of power in a federation, but also supports the aggressive use of the central power for specific economic aims (Harmes 2007). Hence Prime Minister Harper's consistent references over time to the economic union, along with defence and foreign policy, as legitimate responsibilities of the federal level of government, and his lack of interest in provincial economic input.

In power, Harper's emphasis on the economic union has translated quite quickly into a concern with the removal of internal trade barriers and the push for a national securities regulator. A former Mulroney cabinet minister, the Hon. Tom Hockin, was the man appointed by Finance Minister Jim Flaherty to chair an expert panel that examined the latter issue and the panel's final report defended the creation of such a national regulator on constitutional grounds. "The federal government has a 'constitutional' right to impose a regulator that would have authority to pre-empt existing provincial agencies" the report said. In his foreword to the report, Hockin himself stressed "Canadians are ill-served by such a Balkanized system…and we are assured by our constitutional advisor that the federal Parliament has the constitutional authority to enact legislation that would provide for comprehensive capital markets regulations in Canada" (Canada 2009). Harper's determination to pursue this issue in the face of staunch opposition from Quebec suggests his commitment to this belief is far stronger than his concern about political gain in the province.

Following in the footsteps of the Chrétien government's unilateral tax measures, and his own predilection for tax measures over regulation, Harper has also introduced more direct social policy initiatives than many Canadians recognize. This is largely because several of them reflect Harper's neo-liberal bias and some run directly counter to the aims of the major cost-shared social programs, creating a situation in which the federal level is now undermining some of the federal-provincial programs it funds.

At the same time, following Grover Norquist's dictum to "starve the beast" by cutting revenues, Harper's early fiscal measures included a significant reduction in the GST and a variety of tax cuts for individuals and businesses, all of which has left the government more vulnerable with the advent of the economic crisis. The Harper government has also reduced funding for a variety of federally-funded social programs, such as youth employment and workplace skills training, adult literacy programs and social development partnership programs (most notably federal support for the internationally acclaimed drug injection site in Vancouver). Agencies such as the National Crime Prevention Centre and the Canada Food Inspection Agency have also seen dramatic reductions in federal funding, even as funding for the military has skyrocketed.

Then, too, there have been several attempts by Harper to rein in the federal government and achieve more *de facto* devolution of power to the provinces through structural change, for example, with electoral legislation; Senate reform; and various measures in the *Federal Accountability Act*. Even more revealing of Prime Minister Stephen Harper's determination to implement his vision of open federalism was his handling of the Conservatives' 'tough on crime' agenda during the 2008 election. When Harper's proposal to introduce a life sentence for 'criminals' as young as fourteen was widely panned in Quebec, he merely added a proviso that the minimum age could remain at sixteen in that province, despite the fact the criminal code is an exclusive area of federal jurisdiction.

This move, widely seen as driven by political expedi-
ence, was nevertheless entirely consistent with his commitment to allow provinces a say in areas of federal
responsibility, and his willingness to tolerate asymmetrical arrangements. It was also unprecedented and provoked considerable controversy. A *Globe and Mail* editorial
lamented that the inevitable result would be a "patchwork
nation"—an astonishing critique of Harper's position
from a paper which had supported both the Meech Lake
and Charlottetown accords. Arguing, "there should be
one criminal law for Canada", it concluded that although
some of the Conservatives' other justice measures might
have had merit, "by breaking with a principle of federalism as old as Canada, Mr. Harper is diverting the debate"
(*Globe and Mail* 2008).

Nevertheless political considerations undoubtedly played
a part in some budget decisions. As Banting has noted, the
2006 Budget blatantly recognized this fact when it committed the Harper government to extend funding for existing
shared cost programs in health and post-secondary education because "there is a clear consensus among Canadians
on the importance of support for health care, postsecondary
education and training, and infrastructure...". On the other
hand, it appears the decentralist thrust of open federalism
will not prevent the Harper government from taking the
lead when it wants to, for example by introducing federal-
provincial measures that actually support the neo-liberal
agenda, such as their 2006 platform commitment to create
a new cost-shared program with provinces and municipalities "to put at least 2,500 more police on the beat in our cities
and communities" (Banting 2006).

Political necessity has also forced the Harper government
to take some actions it would never have contemplated
under normal circumstances. After more than two years
in power, Harper still demonstrated little interest in meeting with the premiers on any issues, since they were not
necessary to implement his plans. Only the recent global
economic meltdown and the political fallout from the 2008

federal election—which saw Harper fall short of his coveted majority, in large part, due to his lack of sensitivity to public opinion on the economic crisis—caused him to spend more time on intergovernmental relations. Harper's fear of being held responsible for the economic downturn apparently forced him not only to consult the premiers, but to table a budget that repudiates most Conservative financial principles (Behiels 2008).

Despite this, however, it should be noted that calls for federal investment in social infrastructure (such as a national child care plan), environmental technology or even employment insurance (EI) reform, as part of a federal stimulus package, have all fallen on deaf ears. Meanwhile the Prime Minister has virtually removed environmental and Aboriginal issues from the national agenda by refusing to deal with them in the intergovernmental forum, arbitrarily relegating them to the provincial arena. He has even reduced the growth in federal equalization payments, despite loud protests from Quebec Premier Jean Charest.

Portents of things to come can also be found in the October 2008 Speech from the Throne, where the dual concepts of aggressive federal intervention on the economic union, coupled with an abdication of the federal role in the social union, were strongly reinforced. The Harper government's commitment to legislate limits to the federal spending power, and to allow provinces to opt out of existing national schemes with full compensation if they set up their own, served notice that the underlying rationale for open federalism is alive and well.

In short, there would seem to be every reason to believe Prime Minister Harper would aggressively implement more of his neo-liberal agenda in the event of a majority government. This point was made emphatically by Tom Kent, who unwittingly may have provoked the December 2008 coalition crisis by urging all parties to oppose Harper's plan to further limit the federal spending power (Kent 2008).

Conclusion: open federalism versus the welfare state

On the surface, at least, there would seem to be little advantage in the government bringing about such a dramatic confrontation at the best of times, let alone during a minority, unless a compelling ideological rationale exists.

In addition, the Harper government's apparent determination to decentralize power within the Canadian federation is at odds with the direction taken by virtually every other western democracy in light of current (and common) social issues and concerns. As numerous observers have pointed out, social policy issues everywhere have become increasingly horizontal in nature—a scenario for which the traditional 'silo' structure of government administration is already a problem. Federalism adds another layer of complexity to the policy development mix but other federal jurisdictions are moving towards integrated solutions, not separate and isolated approaches to these new and emerging social issues. In Europe the concept of social cohesion is promoted as an economic as well as a social good—an approach supported by conservative and socialist parties alike. Similarly, in the new America of President Barack Obama, an unprecedented level of popular support for a strong federal role in the development of social policies—and in ensuring the integration of such policies—is emerging as well.

In Canada's case, not only federal and provincial governments but municipalities and Aboriginal nations are directly involved in delivering social services. From social housing and municipal infrastructure to public transit, child care and environmental protection, the costs and administrative interdependence are too great to enable one level of government to design or administer effective programs alone, as Prime Minister Harper would prefer.

Then too, recent experience has shown that the absence of a strong federal presence means the likelihood of developing new social architecture, or of even maintaining current programs, is slim. This suggests that open federalism would inevitably lead to a patchwork set of programs providing wildly unequal services. Since such programs have historically comprised an important element of national identity, this scenario could also lead to what journalist Andrew Coyne has called "destructive sectionalism", rather than the greater national unity Harper has predicted. Indeed, Coyne argues that Harper's vision, if implemented, would lead to "the ebbing attachment of its citizens to the 'idea' of Canada, which is now becoming an association of princely states, duchies and caliphates run by regional pashas" (Coyne 2008).

Seen in this light, the perils of further decentralizing the Canadian federation—already the most decentralized in the world—and, in particular, of decentralizing the operation of the social programs comprising the welfare state, are significant for many reasons. Not only have these programs served as an important part of the glue that binds Canadians in all regions of the country, but they have been recognized by Quebecers as a crucial aspect of the confederation bargain. As Lucien Bouchard repeatedly argued during the 1995 referendum, Quebecers could choose the separation option with little cost if the federal government was perceived to have diminished the benefits of the social safety net.

In practical terms the ability of a country with so much geography and so few people to provide the social services that citizens expect—regardless of where they live—is clearly dependent on a coordinated approach led by the federal government, providing the certainty of minimum standards and the resources to fund comparable programs in all regions. Yet Prime Minster Stephen Harper's decision to cut taxes and eliminate the federal surplus effectively reduced the role of the federal government by default, even before the current economic crisis emerged. Still, the vast majority of Canadians, as Harper himself has recognized, are committed to the welfare state. They expect such programs to be delivered regardless of jurisdictional responsibilities. In the end, his government's ability to implement significant changes by stealth, through the back door of open federalism, may well be limited by this important aspect of the dominant political culture.

Nowhere is this more apparent than in Quebec. As Harper learned to his dismay, when attempting to resolve the so-called fiscal imbalance, and then again during the 2008 election, Quebecers' attitudes towards the welfare state are diametrically opposed to the neo-liberal agenda. It seems apparent that no attempt by Prime Minister Harper to placate Premier Jean Charest will likely prove sufficient (Yakabuski 2008). Moreover Harper's ability to position the new Conservative party as the real federalist alternative in Quebec has been derailed, partly by his minimalist approach to the role of the federal government in social and cultural areas, and partly by his determination to proceed with a more centralized federal management role in others, such as the economic union.

It will therefore be interesting to see whether Harper's second term in office, although constrained to some extent once more by a minority situation, will result in further measures to implement his vision of open federalism, regardless of political fallout. Alternatively, will he be captured by the pursuit of power, if not the Canadian tradition of compromise? Having demonstrated such determination to achieve his earlier objectives of merging the Right and forming a government, it is difficult to believe that Prime Minister Harper will be willing to risk those accomplishments by pursuing his neo-liberal agenda too aggressively or overtly. On the other hand, his blatantly partisan approach to the budget, which led to the coalition debacle of December 2008, demonstrated that he may be less politically adept than expected but more ideologically driven than any previous prime minister. If so, either his hold on power will be brief, or the negative consequences for the welfare state, and for national unity, could be substantial.

References

Alberta Agenda 2001 (January 27). "Open Letter to Premier Ralph Klein." Signed by Stephen Harper, Tom Flanagan, Ted Morton, Rainer Knopff, Andrew Crooks and Ken Boessenkool.

Aucoin, Peter 1986. "Politicized Incompetence: Mulroney's Brokerage Politics." *Canadian Journal of Political Science, 29:* 17.

American Trucking Associations, Inc., et al. v United States Environmental Protection Agency, DCC, No. 97–1440 (1999).

Banting, Keith G. 2006. "Open Federalism and Canada's Economic and Social Union." In *Open Federalism: Interpretations, Significance.* Kingston, ON: Institute of Intergovernmental Relations, Queen's University, 77–86.

Behiels, Michael, ed. 1989. *The Meech Lake Primer.* Ottawa: University of Ottawa Press.

Behiels, Michael 2008 (November 17). "Harper Finds a Use for the Premiers." *Ottawa Citizen,* A-11.

Boismenu, Gérard and Jane Jenson 1999. "A Social Union or a Federal State?" In *How Ottawa Spends 1998-99,* ed. Leslie A. Pal. Toronto: James Lorimer.

Canada 2009. Expert Panel on Securities Regulation (Hockin Report). "Creating an Advantage in Global Capital Markets." Final report. Ottawa: Department of Finance.

Canadian Council of Chief Executives 2006 (February). *From Bronze to Gold: A Blueprint for Canadian Leadership in a Transforming World.* Ottawa: Canadian Council of Chief Executives.

Canadian Press 2008 (June 24). "Tories True Quebec Nationalists, Harper Says." Stephen Harper campaign speech. Montreal.

Clark, Rt. Hon. Joe 2004 (April 26). Question Period. CTV.ca. www.ctv.ca/servlet/ArticleNews/story/CTVNews/1082910779022_14/?hub=TopStories [consulted March 25, 2010].

Conservative Party of Canada 2005. Policy Declaration, adopted at the National Policy Convention, Montreal, March 19, 2005.

_____2005. *Stand Up for Canada,* Federal election platform.

_____2008. *True North Strong and Free,* Federal election platform.

Courchene, Thomas J. 2000 (July/August). "A Mission Statement for Canada." *Policy Options.* Montreal: Institute for Research in Public Policy, 21: 6–14.

Coyne, Andrew 2008 (August 5). "The Quiet Devolution." *Ottawa Citizen,* A-12.

Dobbin, Murray 1991. *Preston Manning and the Reform Party.* Toronto: James Lorimer.

Dabbs, Frank 1997. *Preston Manning: The Roots of Reform.* Vancouver: Greystone Press.

Flanagan, Tom 2007. *Harper's Team.* Montreal and Kingston, ON: McGill-Queen's University Press.

Friedman, Thomas 2005 (September 7). "Osama and Katrina." *New York Times,* OpEd.

Globe and Mail 2008 (September 23). Editorial, A-2.

Harmes, Adam 2006. "Neo-liberalism and Multilevel Governance." *Review of International Political Economy*, 13: 5: 725–749.

Harmes, Adam 2007. "The Political Economy of Open Federalism". *Canadian Journal of Political Science*, 40: 2: 417–437.

Harper, Stephen 1995. "The New Canada Plan." Reform Party of Canada.

Harper, Stephen 1997. Council for National Policy (USA). Speech.

Harper, Stephen 2004 (October 27). "My Plan for 'Open Federalism'." *National Post*, A19.

Harper, Stephen 2005. "Harper Announces Conservative Platform for Quebec." Address to the Quebec City Chamber of Commerce. December 19.

Harper, Rt. Hon. Stephen 2006. "Prime Minister Harper Outlines his Government's Priorities and His Open Federalism Approach." Speech to the Montreal Board of Trade. Montreal, April 20.

Hobson, Paul and François St. Hilaire 2000. "The Evolution of Federal-Provincial Fiscal Relations." In *The State of the Federation 1999-2000*, ed. Harvey Lazar. Kingston, ON: Queen's University, Institute of Intergovernmental Relations, 159–188.

Holden, Michael 2006 (January 4). "Equalization: Implications of Recent Changes." Ottawa: Parliamentary Research Branch, PRB 05-91E.

Ibbitson, John 2006 (February 21). "Judicial Reform: It's the Newest 'liberal' Initiative." *Globe and Mail*, A7.

Jeffrey, Brooke 1999. *Hard Right Turn: The New Face of Neoconservatism in Canada*. Toronto: Harper Collins.

Jeffrey, Brooke 2006. "From Collaborative Federalism to the New Unilateralism: Implications for the Welfare State." In *Continuity and Change in Canadian Politics*, eds. Hans Michelman and Cristine de Clercy. Toronto: University of Toronto Press.

Kent, Tom 2008 (February). "The Harper Peril for Canadian Federalism." *Policy Options*, 29: 2: 12–16.

Landay, Jerry 2000 (March). "The Conservative Cabal That is Transforming American Law." *Washington Monthly*. www.washingtonmonthly.com/features/2000/0003.landay.html [accessed April 29, 2010].

Leslie, Peter 2006. "The Two Faces of Open Federalism." *Open Federalism: Interpretations, Significance*. Kingston, ON: Institute of Intergovernmental Relations, Queen's University, 39–66.

Macdonald, L. Ian 2007 (February). "A Conversation with the Prime Minister." *Policy Options*. Montreal: Institute for Research on Public Policy, 5–11. www.irpp.org/po/archive/mar06/interview.pdf [accessed April 29, 2010].

Osborne, Lars 2000."Poverty Trends and the Canadian Social Union."
In *Canada: The State of the Federation: 1999-2000*, ed. Harvey Lazar.
Kingston, ON: Institute for Intergovernmental Relations, Queen's
University, 213–238.

Reform Party of Canada 1993. "Green Sheet." Party platform. Available at
www.www.zoklet.net/totse/en/politics/political_documents/reformpt/
html [accessed April 9, 2010].

Stevens, Hon. Sinclair 2006 (May). "One Canada or Ten?" www.BLOC-
HARPER.com [retrieved August 10, 2008].

Spector, Norman 2009 (March 17). "Harper the Pragmatist." *Ottawa
Citizen*, A13.

Walker, Michael ed. 1978. *Canadian Confederation at the Crossroads: Search
for a Federal-Provincial Balance*. Vancouver, BC: The Fraser Institute.

Wheare, K. C. 1967. *Federal Government*, 4th edition. New York: Oxford
University Press (OUP).

Yakabuski, Konrad 2008 (October 2). "Harper's Open Federalism Not
Rich Enough for Charest." *Globe and Mail*, B2.

Chapter 4

Is Canada Ready for a New Universal Social Program? Comparing the Cases of Universal Medicare in the 1960s and 'Universal' Child Care in the New Millennium[1]

Cheryl N. Collier

On April 29, 2005 Prime Minister Paul Martin and Manitoba Premier Gary Doer, along with their respective federal and provincial social services ministers, announced an 'agreement in principle' on early learning and child care (ELCC). The agreement set out a "long-term vision, principles, and goals to guide the development of regulated early learning and child care for children under six," which would expand on a five-year plan the Manitoba government previously had in place (Government of Manitoba 2005).[2] Although the terms and conditions of the agreement were specific to Manitoba, the agreement was not entirely unique. It was one of ten bilateral agreements reached between the federal government and each of the provinces following two years of broader federal, provincial and territorial negotiations, between 2003 and 2005, on a national ELCC vision. At the conclusion of these broader negotiations, the federal government committed CA\$ 5 billion in the February budget for new ELCC spending over five years in collaboration with provincial and territorial levels of government (Canadian Intergovernmental Conference Secretariat 2005). During the Manitoba announcement, Prime Minister Martin suggested that this was perhaps the first step toward a long-promised Canadian universal child care program:

> The Agreement in Principle between Canada and Manitoba marks a major milestone that will move us toward a shared vision for early learning and child care. More agreements will follow. Decades ago, it was a series of such agreements that led to the creation of Medicare in Canada—a program that now helps to define us as Canadians (Government of Manitoba 2005: 1).

Even though there are some similarities between the policy framework that eventually produced universal Medicare and the 2005 federal/provincial/territorial consensus agreement, resulting in ELCC bilateral deals, Canada was still without a universal child care program in 2009.

This chapter attempts to gain a greater understanding of why universal child care did not materialize following the 2005 announcements. Drawing on neo-institutional theories of public policy it will examine how relevant institutional frameworks, ideas and interests guided federal-provincial hospital and medical insurance negotiations, particularly between 1957 and 1961, culminating in the *Medical Care Act, 1966*.[3] It will then compare this broader universal policy framework to the more recent ELCC negotiations, focussing mainly on the 2000–2005 federal/provincial/territorial multilateral framework and consensus negotiations and concluding with a look at the current ELCC policy context in 2009. Despite similarities in the bilateral cost-sharing nature of both social programs, their lengthy paths to consensus agreements and some similar national guiding principles, important differences in institutional and ideational frameworks help us understand divergent policy outcomes in terms of universality. In both cases, even though interests had some impact on outcomes, our illustrations show that these were less significant than the impact of institutions and ideas.

Universal social programs and the Canadian welfare state

According to Keith Banting, "universality lies at the very heart of the development of the welfare state in Canada and indeed in most industrial nations" (Banting 1985: 7). This is especially the case since the establishment of universal programs for specific groups (the elderly, unemployed) or for specific purposes—for example, health care—have historically been such dominant Canadian welfare state themes (Ibid., 8). Universal welfare state programs are desirable to federal states because they can connect individuals more directly to the federal government essentially erasing "difference in social policy attitudes across regions" (Ibid., 13). Universal social programs can also provide a modest level of security to individuals over time. Titmuss argues that they also reaffirm citizenship rights (1968). While selected or targeted welfare state programs usually involve some level of means testing and foster "both the sense of personal failure and the stigma of a public burden", universal social programs do not involve any "humiliating loss of status, dignity or self respect" (Burke and Silver 2006: 377).

Banting defines universal programs as those that "cover the entire [relevant] population...and provide gross benefits, which are not reduced with income or wealth" (Banting 1985: 7).[4] The concept of universality is central to Canadian health care policy and has been since before the advent of universal Medicare. Former Saskatchewan Premier Tommy Douglas, one of the key architects of universal health care first provincially and then federally, insisted that health care must be available to every resident not just in theory, but in practice (Armstrong, Armstrong and Fegan 1998). Ever since, "equity based on need alone" and not one's ability to pay, has been the central distributive principle of Canadian health care (Burke and Silver 2006: 375).

Universality has also been one of the main pillars of a desired national child care program amongst Canadian child care advocates. The 1970 report by the Status of

Women Commission included a call for a federal universal child care program as one of its four central recommendations (Canada 1970). Canadian feminist movements, as well as provincial and federal child care advocacy organizations, further argue that child care needs to be universally accessible, available, affordable and of high quality to, among other things, assist women in their goals toward societal equality (Collier 2006).[5] Thus the aim of universality as a desired policy outcome is one of a number of important similarities between Canadian health care and child care policies.

Comparing health care and child care policy development in Canada

Before highlighting other important similarities between health care and child care policy development in Canada it is important to make a clarification regarding the main question posed in the title of this chapter, "Is Canada Ready for a New Universal Social Program?" The obvious answer to this question in a broad social policy context is 'yes', evidenced by the federal Conservative government's 2006 implementation of the universal child care benefit (UCCB) shortly after being elected. The universal child care benefit, which transfers CA$ 100 per month, per child to parents of children under the age of six, clearly fits Banting's definition (stated above) of a program available to the entire relevant population that provides gross benefits[6] unlimited by income or wealth. However, while the UCCB is similar to other Canadian universal social programs—particularly the 1944 family allowance to which it is often compared (Collier and Mahon 2008)—it falls solely under federal jurisdiction as a direct cash transfer to individuals. Health care and child care programs, on the other hand, fall under provincial jurisdiction.[7] Any federal involvement in health care policy is through the use of the federal spending power which transfers program funding to the provinces. This shared-cost nature of health care policy necessarily results in heightened negotiation between two levels of government as opposed to opportunities for unilateral state action. This has also introduced obstacles particular to any long-term goal toward universality in program delivery (Aucoin 1974). Armstrong and others argue that the task of providing universal health care in Canada in reality is "never completed, but rather must be seen as a process evolving in response to new needs and possibilities" (Armstrong, Armstrong and Fegan 1998: 32). Many of these new challenges arguably continue to place pressure on the sustainability of universal standards in the health care policy arena in the present day (Maioni 2008).

Like health care, child care has been a shared-cost, welfare-state program between the federal and provincial (and sometimes municipal) levels of government, particularly since the advent of federal Canada Assistance Plan (CAP) block funding transfers to the provinces beginning in 1966 (Collier 2006).[8] Therefore, child care policy advocates, like those in the health care field, must navigate a difficult area between federal and provincial jurisdiction which can at times hinder efforts to achieve universality in program delivery. Thus the question of whether Canada is ready for a new universal social policy is much more complicated to answer in areas of provincial jurisdiction where program delivery is often contingent on funding from both the federal and provincial levels on a shared-cost basis. This theme will be revisited later in the comparative analysis.

There are other similarities between Canadian health care and child care policy that help justify their comparative worth for this analysis. Both of these social programs have had lengthy and tumultuous histories leading up to bilateral shared-cost consensus agreements and more definitive action at the federal level under the umbrella of national standards. Along the way, each policy has seen the provinces step in with important policy innovations that have helped raise the profile of the issue nationally. By the time the federal *Hospital Insurance and Diagnostic Services Act* was passed on May 1, 1957, it had been thirty-eight years since health insurance first appeared as a Liberal party election issue. It would take another ten years until national medical insurance was introduced (1966–67) and four years after that until the bilateral Medicare details with the ten provinces were ironed out (Taylor 1987). In the meantime, Saskatchewan went ahead and pioneered a provincial hospital insurance program in 1947 and later a province-wide medical insurance program in 1959 (Ibid.). These initiatives led the way for some of the other provinces to establish health insurance programs to help convince the federal government to take the lead and use its spending power to establish national legislation in both areas.[9]

National-level child care policy has a similar long, slow history in Canada. As mentioned, advocacy demands for a national universal child care program have been around since at least 1970 when they were first articulated federally in the report of the Royal Commission on the Status of Women. While the 2005 bilateral deals were not the first federal attempt toward a 'national' child care program[10], they were arguably the closest the federal government has come to establishing a federally-funded national-level program since 1970. Similar to health care, two provinces made moves toward province-wide comprehensive publicly-funded child care programs in the void left by the lack of concrete federal action over thirty-five years. The first and most significant provincial child-care program was established in Quebec in 1997 when it introduced the only publicly-funded child care program in North America (Jenson 2002).[11] This was followed by the short-lived introduction of a similar program in British Columbia in 2000.[12] While the British Columbia program was not in place long enough to impact federal level activity, the publicly-funded Quebec child care program is often cited by child care researchers as a flawed, but important, example of how child care can become "a publicly provided citizenship right" (Jenson, Mahon and Phillips 2003: 149).[13]

A third important similarity between Canadian health care and child care programs at the point in which they reached federal-provincial (and in the case of child care, territorial) consensus, is how they both were guided by overarching national guidelines. Although the federal approach to the 1957 hospital insurance act closely followed the model established first in Saskatchewan, the federal government agreed to provide the provinces with a level of flexibility in how they operationalized a national hospital insurance scheme. However, in order to qualify for federal financial support, the provinces needed to meet certain national standards within this flexible framework. In particular, hospital care needed to be universal, accessible, comprehensive and readily available to all (Armstrong, Armstrong and Fegan 1998).

Some of these same principles were repeated during the 1965 federal-provincial conference to discuss national Medicare proposals. Federal and provincial representatives generated four guiding principles for a national Medicare program including that it must cover a "comprehensive range of medical services", be "universal", be "portable between provinces" and "administered by a public agency" (Gray 1991: 43). Both sets of these guiding principles were defined more precisely and brought under one piece of legislation in the *Canada Health Act* (CHA) of 1984. The CHA clearly articulated a national commitment to five principles of health care: "public administration, comprehensiveness, universality, portability and accessibility", and identified specific penalties to any of the provinces that failed to live up to those principles, particularly regarding 'extra billing' of patients for medical service delivery (Armstrong, Armstrong and Fegan 1998: 30).

The 2005 ELCC bilateral agreements reached between the provinces and the federal government stated that provincial ELCC programs needed to follow what were known as the 'QUAD principles'. QUAD stood for quality, universality, accessibility and developmental. Quality was defined as 'evidence-based practices' in support of early childhood education. Universality meant 'universally inclusive' in support of all children of diverse needs including Aboriginal children; children with disabilities; and children of different cultural and linguistic origins. In order for programs to be 'accessible' they needed to be broadly "available and affordable to all", including flexibility in the range of options provided. Finally, developmental meant that the care should "strengthen the learning and developmental component... to meet the cognitive, physical, emotional and social development needs of children" through evidence-based practices.[14]

Both sets of guiding principles are similar by including key concepts of accessibility and universality in program delivery. Yet there are important differences between these sets of principles as well. The Canadian health care principles included specific calls for public administration of health care delivery and portability between jurisdictions, whereas neither of these was included in the QUAD child care principles. Conversely, the latter principles include a developmental element particular to child care service delivery that was not necessary for the *Canada Health Act*. Another important distinction is that the health care principles were enshrined into legislation in the 1984 CHA, whereas the child care principles remained outside the legislative framework and without enforceable penalties for non-compliance. In order to better understand the similarities and differences between these two policy cases, the chapter now turns to a discussion of the comparative framework.

A neo-institutional comparative public policy framework

Although neo-institutionalism naturally emphasizes the role of institutions in its conceptualization of the formation of public policy alternatives, newer versions of institutional and historical institutional theory also include the impact of ideas and interests on policy decision making. According to John L. Campbell, institutions or "the formal rules and procedures governing policy making" serve as filters to "which ideas penetrate the policy-making process and are adopted and implemented as policy" (Campbell 2002: 30).[15] Daniel Béland adds that historical institutionalism, based on the "assumption that a historically constructed set of institutional constraints and policy feedbacks", also structures the behaviour and influence of political actors and interest groups (Béland 2005: 1).[16] Despite variations in approaches as to the relative explanatory weight which should be assigned to each, it is clear within this newer institutional literature that in order to gain a better understanding of public policy decisions, it is important to identify and consider the impact of relevant institutions, interests and ideas.[17] Campbell argues that we should not consider these factors on their own, but should aim to "better understand the connections between ideas, institutions, and interests" (Campbell 2002: 33).

Since an important aspect of both health care and child care policy in Canada involves the ways in which policy actors can navigate the challenges posed within the institution of federalism, the neo-institutional approach seems particularly useful for this comparative analysis.

Even though the policy road leading to universal Medicare in 1966 and the *Canada Health Act, 1984* had been very long, it is the bilateral health care negotiations which took place between 1957 and 1961 (leading up to the 1966 *Medical Care Act* (Medicare)) as well as further bilateral deals with the provinces ending in 1971 that operationalized this legislation that will be compared to the federal/provincial/territorial early learning and child care negotiations which took place between 2000 and 2005.

Canadian universal hospital insurance and Medicare in the 1960s

Federal-provincial negotiations surrounding, first, universal hospital insurance in the late 1950s, and then later, universal Medicare in the mid-to-late 1960s–early 1970s, largely fell within an era of executive 'cooperative' federalism characterized by cooperation between federal and provincial governments. While, for the most part, both levels of government were jurisdictionally autonomous, the federal government was often the dominant actor in federal-provincial relations through the use of its formidable spending powers. This era of cooperation helped establish the welfare state in the decades following the end of World War II with the federal government taking the lead in welfare state expansion (Cameron and Simeon 2002). The social mood of frustration after years of deprivation following the Depression and the war served as a backdrop to Medicare policy. During these years, ideas of social liberalism were dominant and state expansion of social policy helped define what would be known as the "golden age" of the Canadian welfare state (Mahon 2006). At the same time, the political landscape was experiencing a new surge of left-wing influence from the social-democratic Cooperative Commonwealth Federation, both federally and in many provinces. The governing federal Liberals were struggling to respond to all of these pressures without alienating many of its core, more conservative, members. The Canadian Medical Association (CMA), representing professional doctors in the country, along with commercial insurance providers were sceptical of the introduction of hospital insurance. Interest-based opposition grew stronger particularly when discussions turned to expanding insurance to cover all medical services. Yet even though these interests exerted some influence, they were no match for the institutional and ideational forces that drove policy change in this era.

Institutional framework

It took a while to gain federal and provincial consensus on the issue of hospital insurance in the years leading up to the 1957 federal act. These early years included a failed 1945 federal-provincial conference where disagreement over the scope of the problem and the wording of national initiatives remained quite strong (Taylor 1987). The federal framework of cooperative federalism that characterized the Canadian policy landscape from the end of World War II until the beginning of the 1960s, however, helped facilitate national legislation in the long run (Cameron and

Simeon 2002). During this era of federalism, the federal spending power was a key policy instrument used to facilitate federal state involvement in areas of provincial jurisdiction. Increased cooperation was enhanced and "close professional relationships developed among provincial and federal officials and ministers within specific policy areas" (Ibid., 50).

Many of the policies generated during this cooperative period resulted from joint decision-making between relatively separate jurisdictions operating within "close and frequent consultation" (Gray 1991: 17). Both the national hospital insurance and national Medicare bilateral deals emulated this cooperative shared-cost model. Four years after the federal government passed the *Hospital Insurance and Diagnostic Services Act* in 1957 all of the provinces had negotiated hospital insurance plans—some of which preceded the 1957, federal act but were later reaffirmed under principles of universality. Even though the plans themselves were varied because the provincial governments remained the "chief decision-makers in health care," the federal government was able to use its spending power to ensure compliance with national standards (Armstrong et al. 1998: 15).

Despite the fact that the 1966 national Medicare act and subsequent provincial agreement reached in 1971 arguably fell outside of the cooperative federalism framework period as typified by Cameron and Simeon,[18] there were still elements of cooperative federalism evident in the outcome of this policy. The lure of federal cost-sharing incentives proved too persuasive for the provinces, some of which had already begun expanding insurance into the wider medical arena. By the end of 1971, all ten provinces had signed deals which, added together, constituted a national plan. This plan quintessentially fit the cooperative federalism framework because it was achieved through "interlocking ten provincial plans, all of which shared certain common features" (Burke and Silver 2006: 378).

The impact of ideas

Overarching ideational frameworks

World War II brought with it an acute demand for hospital care, not only from the returning wounded, but also from those already in the country who wanted a certain level of quality health care but could not afford it. This mood of "rebellion against the universal risks of unemployment and sickness, disability and old age, widowhood and poverty" was prevalent in the years following the end of the war and the earlier Depression (Armstrong, Armstrong and Fegan 1998: 8). This broader social landscape shaped efforts to develop the Canadian welfare state between the 1940s and into the 1970s. This policy context also fit well under a "moderate Keynesian social liberalism" label (Mahon 2006: 1).

Rianne Mahon argues that Canada and other Anglo-American countries fall within an overarching liberal regime framework. Thus Canada embraces key roles for markets and families and occasional supplements from "modest state supports."[19] However, Canadian liberalism has not remained static over time, but has gone through a number of important changes. Mahon places these within a "varieties of liberalism" framework (Ibid.). She argues that this 'varieties of liberalism' framework can aid our understanding of welfare state policy development over time and for the purposes of this study can shed light on some of the constraints placed on government policy making at different points in time.

Thus negotiations toward hospital and medical care insurance in Canada in the late 1950s and into the 1960s, according to Mahon, would fall under a social liberalism rubric, which emphasized the "positive freedoms of opportunity and person development" (Ibid., 3). Social citizenship grew in importance during this era and the role of the state expanded to create "the conditions for all to develop their full potential, even if this involved measures to counteract the impact of market forces" (Ibid.). This ideational social liberal framework helps us understand how the provinces could be convinced to embrace national health care principles and standards, particularly those that spoke of universality and accessibility. Clearly these health care principles enhance individual social citizenship and issues of personal security which are central within a social liberalism framework.

Partisan ideology and the influence of key political actors
Gwendolyn Gray and Malcolm Taylor both argue that competition between political parties at the federal and provincial levels, along with the rise of the social democratic Cooperative Commonwealth Federation (CCF, later NDP) are important factors to consider in understanding why universal hospital and medical insurance policies were politically successful (Gray 1991; Taylor 1987). Although the CCF did not form a national government, it was elected to the official opposition in Ontario in 1943 and, more importantly, won the Saskatchewan provincial election in 1944. Not only was the party as a whole committed to "freely available" health care services (i.e., Regina Manifesto 1933), but CCF Saskatchewan Premier Tommy Douglas was a tireless advocate for Medicare. Douglas not only ensured that both hospital and medical insurance were established provincially, he then eventually became a federal member of Parliament to push for Medicare's adoption on the national stage as well (Armstrong, Armstrong and Fegan 1998).[20] The strength of the Left had an important impact on minority Conservative and Liberal governments, especially between 1962 and 1968. The persuasive power of the Left continued to influence federal health care policy even during the implementation of the 1984 *Canada Health Act*, when the Liberals presided over a majority government. According to Gray, the Left helped keep the health care issue on the agenda both federally and provincially and "inside and outside the House of Commons" (Gray 1991: 185).

Taylor also argues that the federal Liberal party, despite struggles within its own caucus, extra-parliamentary membership and at times its leadership, was instrumental in securing universal Medicare in Canada. He suggests that even though the twenty-year period between 1945 and 1965 saw a complete full circle change in Liberal attitudes toward Medicare "from initiation to reluctant acquiescence to initiation," a major factor in the eventual adoption of national Medicare was "the long-term commitment of the Liberal party to health insurance" (Taylor 1987: 332, 352). This long-term commitment inside the party was strong even during years of Liberal minority status in the mid-1960s. Taylor not only points to the party itself, but also singles out specific Liberal health ministers who doggedly pursued the issue throughout their tenures, including the Hon. Ian Mackenzie who held the portfolio between the mid 1930s until June 1944 (Ibid.); the Hon. Paul Martin [Sr.] who served as health minister during the early to mid-1950s, working under constant opposition from the more conservative-minded Prime Minister Louis St. Laurent (Ibid.); and the Hon. Alan MacEachen who served as health minister during the minority years when national Medicare became law (Ibid.).[21]

The role of interests
The two most influential organized interest groups[22] involved in the Canadian health care debates leading up to and throughout the 1960s both provincially and federally, were the Canadian Medical Association, representing Canadian doctors, and the commercial insurance companies.[23] Yet despite the fact that both were mainly opposed to government provision of national hospital and medical insurance, their opposition tactics were largely unsuccessful compared to the forces of powerful state and political actors.

Although the CMA did not strongly oppose national hospital insurance when it was first being negotiated in the early 1940s, it eventually moved against the proposal later in the decade (Taylor 1987; Armstrong, Armstrong and Fegan 1998). According to Armstrong and others, even though the doctors "were happy to have the government pick up the tab for those who could not pay for insurance, they did not want the government to control all hospital insurance" (Armstrong, Armstrong and Fegan 1998: 14). However, this position eventually softened when the doctors realized they could use the new universal system to their own advantage, including ordering hospital care without worrying about a patient's ability to pay and generally being responsible for less paperwork than in the past (Ibid.).

Commercial insurance companies were less easily swayed and remained opposed to hospital insurance, promoting the private US insurance system as a preferred model for Canada (Ibid.). Their arguments in support of this system largely fell on deaf ears as the federal government's own research showed weaknesses in this approach. Thus it was decided that private insurance companies could not compete with the public scheme, but they could cover 'extras' including dental work, prescription drugs, etc. (Ibid.).

Both the CMA and commercial insurance providers were more strongly opposed to provincial and national Medicare insurance. Doctors in Saskatchewan went so far as to protest the move by going on strike in 1962 after the legislation came into effect. Although the battle was "bitter and long", the provincial government prevailed, ultimately offering only minor concessions to appease striking doctors (Ibid.). When the fight for universal Medicare moved to the national stage, both the CMA and the commercial insurance providers pushed the federal Conservative government of Prime Minister John Diefenbaker to launch a Royal Commission on Health Services to perhaps derail or at least postpone the process (Ibid.). But the resulting Hall Report released in 1964 concluded, much to the disappointment of the doctors and private insurance providers, that "the best solution for Canada is the establishment of a comprehensive, universal Health Services Programme" (Gray 1991: 43).

On the other side of the health care debate, and one of the major interest groups in support of public hospital and medical insurance, was the Canadian labour movement. It essentially agreed with the Hall Report and the conclusion that health care was a public service rather than a market one (Armstrong, Armstrong and Fegan 1998). In the end, however, neither the support of organized labour, nor the opposition of the doctors or commercial insurance providers were cited as having much influence on the federal-provincial negotiations, despite their varied efforts.

The policy context of national hospital insurance and Medicare in the 1960s

In summary, the neo-institutional analysis above helps explain the federal-provincial consensus agreements leading to the *Hospital Insurance and Diagnostic Services Act* of 1957 and subsequent bilateral deals, along with the 1966 Medicare act and related bilateral deals finalized in 1971. The fact that both of these universal programs were achieved within a complex shared-cost framework can be attributed to the intergovernmental openness typified by cooperative federalism and the invitation to broaden the welfare state in a post-war and post-depression environment characterized by moderate Keynesian social liberalism. Political action was hastened by the strength of social democratic political forces on the Left as well as through the long-term commitments of individuals in the CCF and the federal Liberal party who facilitated positive outcomes. Both parties also wholly embraced the legitimacy of the federal spending power and its ability to facilitate a leadership role for the federal government—a key component of policy success. While major organized interests both for and against universal hospital and medical insurance were active within the health care policy community during this time frame, neither side was particularly influential in determining policy outcomes.

Canadian universal child care? The 2000 multilateral framework on early learning and child care and the 2005 federal-provincial bilateral agreements

The federal/provincial/territorial multilateral framework on early learning and child care began in 2000, reached an agreement on initial early learning and child care (ELCC) funding in 2003 (Canada 2004) and then after two more years of negotiations, finalized the QUAD principles and set the groundwork for the separately negotiated bilateral deals that were concluded later in 2005. These series of multilateral ELCC negotiations took place within an era of 'collaborative' federalism where national goals are achieved by some or all of the eleven governments and three territories acting collectively. What distinguishes collaborative federalism from the era of cooperative federalism, which informed the universal health care negotiations analyzed above, is that the former does not necessarily offer opportunities for or see the federal government acting within a leadership or equal role to the provinces, whereas the latter sees a much more equal distribution of power leaving more room for federal leadership through the constitutional use of the federal spending power (Cameron and Simeon 2002). Along with this, the multilateral child care negotiations were impacted by more 'inclusive liberalism'. Inclusive liberalism falls somewhere between social liberalism and neo-liberalism, by embracing a commitment to the market alongside social investments to better an individual's place within it (Mahon 2006). Federally, the political landscape was entering an era of some instability with minority governments elected in 2004 and 2006. While this left room for the Left to have some minor impact, the Left was not as influential as it was during universal health care debates. Pro-child care advocacy interests, including the leading national voice—the Child Care Advocacy Association of Canada—had always been quite weak at the national level and this did not change much during this period, especially since the multilateral framework did not open many doors to interest involvement.

Institutional framework

To understand the dynamics of the multilateral negotiations between 2000 and 2005, it is important to step back a bit further in time to 1996–97 when the federal government introduced the Canada Health and Social Transfer (CHST). The CHST replaced Canada Assistance Plan (CAP) funding arrangements that the provinces had been using to fund child care programs across the country since the late 1960s. CAP funding was a fifty-fifty cost-sharing program for social services, including child care, between the federal government and the provinces. Limits on CAP funding began in 1990 when a cap was put on CAP dollars to the three richer 'have' provinces at the time (British Columbia, Alberta and Ontario), but the significant reductions came in 1996–97 with the introduction of the CHST, which replaced CAP. The CHST combined CAP funding with separate transfers for health care and reduced the entire amount. Essentially, all social-program funding suddenly had to compete with health care funding within provincial budgets and, as health care costs rose, social services lost the fight for limited federal dollars. The fact that all of this funding represented a significant reduction in federal shared-cost transfers exacerbated the problem even further (Collier 2006).

In the aftermath of the 1996–97 CHST, the provinces got together on their own, much in line with the era of collaborative federalism described by Cameron and Simeon,[24] to initiate the national children's agenda (NCA) which the federal government later joined in 1999 (Mahon 2006). This is significant because the power relationship between the federal and provincial governments clearly had shifted within the lead-up to the multilateral framework in what could be seen as an era of distrust. Following the introduction of the CHST, the provinces knew that they could no longer rely on the federal government to come through with important social service cost-sharing transfers even though those transfers were crucial to the delivery of those social services, and this is especially so for child care. Therefore, whereas the federal government always needed to 'buy into' federal/provincial/territorial arrangements in the past, the significance of federal funding guarantees over the long term is arguably greater in this era of mistrust under collaborative federalism.

The other institutional body that guided the multilateral ELCC framework negotiations, at least in the beginning, was the Social Union Framework Agreement (SUFA) of 1999. Like the NCA, SUFA was initiated "to come to terms with the somewhat dysfunctional state of federal-provincial relations on social policy and fiscal issues" (Noël, St-Hilaire and Fortin 2003: 3). SUFA's stated objectives were, among others, to better manage the interaction between the two levels of government and to ensure sustainability in social program funding in a non-constitutional setting (Ibid.). Although Noël and others suggest that the NCA and the multilateral framework agreement were somewhat successful extensions of SUFA principles, most researchers have been critical of the potential of SUFA to solve intergovernmental wrangling over social program delivery (Ibid.; Cameron and Simeon 2002).

Regardless, the impetus behind the multilateral framework negotiations, which followed directly from the NCA and use of the SUFA principles to guide intergovernmental negotiations, in general fit well under the collaborative federalism model. This institutional framework also explains potential shifts in power between the two levels (three, including the territories[25]) that likely occurred during the negotiations themselves, making it more difficult for the federal government to take a leadership role, particularly in establishing national principles or standards to guide a 'national' or 'universal' child care program, or to ensure compliance thereof. Indeed the lack of inclusion of a portability requirement or a public administration delivery requirement within the QUAD principles, such as those that were included in the *Canada Health Act*, indicates that the federal government was likely weaker inside of these negotiations than was the case during those for universal health care four decades ago. Rianne Mahon and Susan Phillips argue that this lack of a leadership role means that participants in these multilateral negotiations (including the NCA and the SUFA) likely are more concerned with the relationships between the actors and their respective "political image[s]" than the actual policy outcomes (Mahon and Phillips 2002).

Another two features of collaborative federalism that were evident in the multilateral framework negotiations were that first, any agreements reached would likely have to be followed up with separately negotiated bilateral deals and second, that this allows for considerable asymmetry, resulting in a form of "checkerboard federalism" (Cameron and Simeon 2002). While bilateral deals were present with both of the policy areas being compared in this chapter, some of the earlier universal health care bilateral deals informed or preceded the actual setting of the national principles themselves and this arguably created more opportunity beforehand to secure compliance on a broader range of common principles. It is possible that the cooperative federalism era of universal health care allowed provincial policy innovations to impact the resulting federal model of universality. With child care and the multilateral framework bilateral negotiations, this was not the case.[26] In fact, even though the 2005 separately negotiated bilateral deals follow the broad QUAD principles, they are very diverse in focus, ranging from spending on ECE training in Manitoba to the expansion of child-care spaces at the junior and senior kindergarten level in Ontario to a CA$ 100 per month stay-at-home-parent benefit for licensed nursery or other approved early childhood development programs in Alberta.[27] Clearly the separate deals were comparatively asymmetrical and because the multilateral negotiations failed to ensure a baseline level or type of child-care delivery across the country, there was no mechanism in place to correct that asymmetry in the future.[28] The portability and public administration requirements established for universal health care arguably helped keep any asymmetry between the provinces at a much lower level than was and is the case with child care services.[29]

The impact of ideas

Overarching ideational frameworks
Much has been written about the shift to neo-liberalism that has been embraced by Western governments, including Canada, beginning in the late 1970s and lasting well into the 1990s in an era of globalization.[30] During these years, states looked to the ideals of competitiveness, efficiency and an embrace of classical liberal principles that privileged a freer

hand for the market in order to thrive in a global world. However, many researchers have noted a softening to this approach even while governments continue to embrace neo-liberal principles in order to remain competitive. This newer era of 'inclusive liberalism', beginning in Canada in the later 1990s, can be seen to sit somewhere between neo-liberalism and the social liberalism of the past that saw the expansion of the welfare state and the introduction of universal health care programs. Inclusive liberalism seeks to meet the challenges of economic globalization by empowering individuals through modest social supports or 'carrots'—which were also championed under social liberalism—to encourage them to be full worker–citizens and contribute to global competitiveness, which is also embraced under neo-liberalism (Mahon 2006).

According to Mahon, inclusive liberalism was evident with the 'activation' programs that the Liberal government introduced in the late 1990s and early 2000s. These programs put the emphasis on the individual and aimed to 'enable' that individual within society using incentives such as "foundations for lifelong learning, early childhood development and education" (Ibid., 18). Mahon also sees the national children's agenda (and resulting multilateral framework negotiations and agreements) as being synonymous with inclusive liberalism "at least in rhetoric".

Of particular importance is the fact that it seemed to reopen the way for universality, reasserting the goal of ensuring provision of an equivalent level of children's services across the provinces. Thus, the NCA committed the federal and provincial governments to work together to develop a comprehensive, cross-sectoral and long term strategy to ensure that *all* Canada's children receive the best possible opportunity to develop to their full potential (Ibid.).

Thus, the move away from neo-liberalism toward a more inclusive liberalism framework appears, at least on the surface, to open the door toward universality in federal/provincial/territorial negotiations. The fact that a national set of guiding QUAD principles were agreed upon in 2005 and that these would be subject to reporting within the provinces[31] does indicate an openness to a level of universality that would not have been possible within a strictly neo-liberal framework (Government of Manitoba 2005; Canada 2004). The question remained, however, whether this potential for universality was merely rhetorical in nature or whether it would be operationalized.

Partisan ideology and influence of key political actors

The partisan federal landscape began from a position of relative government stability with the Liberal party of the Rt. Hon. Jean Chrétien holding majority party status in the House of Commons between 1993 and 2003. At the same time, the opposition went through various periods of disarray. The Progressive Conservative party—the major party of opposition in the past when the Liberals were in power—suffered a humiliating defeat in 1993 and left with only two seats. Afterward, the party essentially split into three factions. One stayed true to the Progressive Conservative label and centre-right principles; the second, the Reform/Alliance party, was more decidedly right-wing with a political base in the West; and the third was basically a federal representative for Quebec's drive towards secession under the label of the Bloc Québécois.[32] The NDP on the left was not the same federal force that it was when it was operating as the CCF during the 1960s health-care negotiations. The immediate beneficiary of opposition disarray was the Liberal party, which was rewarded with successive majorities until 2004.

However, by the time of the 2004 election, politicians on the Right were able to regroup under the Conservative party label and gained strength; the Bloc Québécois remained strong in Quebec; and the NDP was able to recover some of its former strength representing the voice of the centre-left but not as strong as it had been during the fight for universal Medicare. This new reconfiguration of the federal parties resulted in two successive minority governments in 2004 and 2006, the first Liberal and the next Conservative. Though the Liberals remained in power in 2004 under a new leader, Prime Minister Paul

Martin, the minority position of the federal government likely impacted the on-going multilateral framework negotiations by weakening federal opportunities for leadership along the lines already discussed under collaborative federalism. Even though universal Medicare came to fruition under a Liberal minority government, things were different in 2004. Ideological energy was arguably on the Right instead of the Left and the collaborative federal model facilitated provincial tendencies toward decentralization, much more in line with neo-liberal, right-wing ideals. This again would hamper efforts to reach true universality in child-care policy and helps explain the somewhat more limited nature of the national QUAD principles negotiated for child care when compared with those included in the *Canada Health Act*.

At times, support for the minority Liberal government on important pieces of legislation came from the NDP giving some room for further influence from the Left.[33] The most obvious example of this influence came in April 2005 when the NDP negotiated inclusions in the Liberal budget in order to secure NDP support and ensure its passage (CBC News April 2005). None of these particular inclusions involved child care and there was no evidence the Left had any impact on the multilateral ELCC framework negotiations or the agreement reached that same year. Clearly, the Left was not in the same position of influence that it once held during the golden years of social liberalism and welfare state expansion.

The role of interests

Child care advocacy at the national level has traditionally been weaker than at the provincial level where program delivery actually occurred (Collier 2006). Even though feminist groups were the first to articulate a need for a national child care program in the early 1970s as an emancipatory right for women, this message did not influence the debate during the multilateral framework negotiations. One reason for this lack of influence has been the tendency for child care to be defined as a gender-neutral

family issue more in line with neo-liberalism and inclusive liberalism where the focus has shifted wholly to the
child (Mahon 2006). Thus women's movement actors are
seen by government and other social policy advocates as
"radical, adversarial, and irrelevant" (McKeen and Porter
2003: 128).

At the same time, the nature of intergovernmental
negotiations under collaborative federalism and more specifically the SUFA, NCA and the multilateral framework
negotiations focused more on intergovernmental actors
and "marginalize[d] an already weakened advocacy community" (Mahon and Phillips 2002: 206). Despite this,
the national child-care advocacy community continued
to work to influence the child-care debate, most notably
under the leadership of the Child Care Advocacy Association of Canada (CCAAC). The CCAAC has tried to widen
its influence and appeal within the child-care policy community by joining forces with other like-minded advocacy
groups. Coalitions, such as Campaign 2000, were active on
the child-care file during the multilateral framework negotiations. However according to Mahon and Phillips, these
coalitions focussed more on a wider "children's agenda"
which can speak well for a collective but ends up watering
down child-care interests inside of it (Ibid.). Thus child-
care advocacy interests have had little impact on the multilateral framework negotiations, despite remaining active
throughout this period.

The policy context of "universal" child-care agreements, 2000–2005

This neo-institutional analysis helps us understand the
federal/provincial/territorial child-care multilateral framework agreement and subsequent bilateral deals negotiated
under the QUAD principles between 2000 and 2005. The
reduced leadership role of the federal government, along
with greater potential for asymmetry in policy results,
worked against any potential for universality found under

an inclusive liberalism framework. The fact that inclusive liberalism was not as strong a vehicle for discussions of universality as social liberalism had been, also helps explain why the QUAD principles were not as comprehensive and strong as the national principles later enshrined under the *Canada Health Act*. Instability in government after 2004 also helped weaken federal actors, while at the same time opening the door for some very limited and weak influence from the Left—although no evidence of this influence was found on child care *per se*. Likewise, child-care advocacy interests were also weakened by the intergovernmental process and by being forced to work within broader child-focussed interest coalitions.

In the end, the overall policy context for child care negotiations included potential avenues for universality alongside potential roadblocks and detours embedded in the system itself.

Federal child-care policy, 2006–2008

The minority Conservative party elected first in early 2006 and again in the fall of 2008, initially campaigned on child care as one of its five main priorities. Once elected, the Conservatives made good on this promise by putting its own stamp on child care—without negotiating with the provinces beforehand—much different than both 2000– 2005 and from the 1960s with health care. Prime Minister Stephen Harper also indicated that he would be approaching federalism from a new standpoint—'open federalism'— which seemed to place even greater power in the hands of the provinces than in the past. Actions by the Conservatives made some question whether the Canadian state was turning back to neo-liberalism (Mahon 2006; Collier and Mahon 2008). Even though this was another minority government, it did not court support from other political parties, but instead remained committed to its own campaign agenda. Child-care interests that were already weak remained so during these years.

Institutional framework

While it is too early to tell whether or not Canada has experienced a significant change in federalism since the election of the Conservatives in 2006, it is a matter of record that Prime Minister Harper is at least rhetorically committed to approaching federalism from a different perspective. Harper campaigned in 2005 using the phrase 'open federalism', stating that it was a different approach from previous iterations because it would 'respect' the constitutional division of powers between different levels of government and would recognize "a commitment to redress the fiscal imbalance in the Canadian federation" (Courchene 2007: 16). According to Thomas Courchene, this 'new' federal approach was evident in the 2007 federal budget, although it is unclear how different this is from collaborative federalism. Courchene argues that the 2007 bugdet "resurrects aspects of the Meech Lake Accord and even SUFA in terms of how Ottawa will henceforth approach the exercise of the federal spending power" (Ibid., 16). In other words, the federal government would not act unilaterally with regard to new shared-cost social programs that fall under provincial jurisdiction but would ask for majority provincial consent ahead of time and allow the provinces to opt out and receive compensation if they provide "similar programs with comparable accountability structures" (Ibid., 17).

If this can be construed as being different from collaborative federalism, it would be that it further decentralizes social policy making and weakens the federal government even more in its ability to utilize the federal spending power in new policy areas. Even though the Conservative's introduction of its first child-care policy initiative in 2006—the Universal Child Care Benefit (UCCB)—was done without provincial consultation, this was not in a cost-shared area of responsibility. Beyond that, the Conservatives have chosen to reduce child-care transfer amounts to the provinces negotiated by the previous government through the bilateral deals. This reduction of transfers was also made without any significant input from the provinces, but *was* in an area of shared responsibility. Thus the Conservative government could be seen to be following an open federalism model in that it was only proactive in areas of federal responsibility and negatively pulled away from earlier federal financial commitments in areas of shared-cost but jurisdictional provincial responsibility.

The impact of ideas

Overarching ideational framework

Again, it is likely too early to conclude that Canada has moved away from an inclusive liberal framework to something entirely different, however, Mahon does argue that recent decisions by the Conservative government appear to fall outside of an inclusive liberal rubric. She argues that the so-called UCCB is much more neo- than social-liberal because it rewards high income single breadwinner families more than working parents (Mahon 2006). Further, she sees the Conservative government's approach to past social policy initiatives in areas such as elder care and poverty as a move back to neo-liberalism by shifting responsibility for social well-being back to the family, market and community instead of an inclusive approach that would allow for state supports to improve labour market functionality (Ibid.).

Partisan ideology and influence of key political actors

While the Conservative government is more likely than the Liberals to approach social policy from a small 'c' conservative or neo-liberal position, its minority status likely softens this to a certain extent as successful federal governing parties in Canada historically stay closer to the centre of the political spectrum ideationally (Clarke et al. 1996). This means, however, that the Conservatives are likely less open to any influence from the Left in the area of social policy than would be the case under a minority Liberal government. Despite the fact that a severe economic downturn in late 2008 opened up the need for the federal Conservatives to work with opposition parties in the House of Commons to stay in office, to date there is no evidence of outside partisan influence in the child-care arena. In fact, the economic downturn has recently forced the child-care issue to the margins of federal public policy debates.

The role of interests

Generally the same interest groups and coalitions remain in place from the previous child-care period, although the Conservative's move away from the bilateral deals of 2005 and willingness to spend money on the UCCB instead of on the actual creation of child-care spaces did prompt the formation of a new coalition in 2006 called Code Blue for Child Care (Integration Network Project 2007). Despite new activity, advocacy influence is likely lessened further by the presence of a more right-wing Conservative governing party that has traditionally been less open to child care advocacy both provincially and federally over the years.[34] The fact that the intergovernmental process has remained the same or is even further decentralized, would help to solidify this situation. Thus, the present political landscape suggests that national child care interests will continue to be shut out of the child care policy community.

The policy context of 'universal' child care, post 2005

Present indicators from a neo-institutional perspective seem to suggest that any prospects for universality in the child-care field are weaker in the current political context than in previous years when the bilateral deals were first negotiated. Both child-care policy directions introduced by the Conservative government—the UCCB and the Child Care Spaces Initiative (CCSI)—are examples of a move away from traditional intergovernmental discussion on the child-care file in favour of lone federal government action in areas of sole federal jurisdiction. The UCCB in fact is not a 'child-care' policy except in name alone as the taxable transfer of CA$ 100 per month/per child for children under six years of age can conceivably be spent on anything parents desire. What is clear is that the cost of monthly child care far exceeds the yearly CA$ 1,200 before tax benefit[35] and it does not help create child-care spaces or help parents find those spaces in their respective communities.

The Conservatives other child-care policy, the Child Care Spaces Initiative, failed to ever get off the ground. When it was first announced in the 2006 budget, the initiative offered businesses up to CA$ 250 million in tax breaks to create child-care spaces and facilities on their own, thereby bypassing the provinces altogether. To pay for this and the UCCB, the Conservatives also announced the cancellation of the bilateral agreements in 2006. However, since the child-care spaces initiative program failed to entice businesses to actually create child-care spaces, the Conservatives were forced to temporarily restore some of the child-care transfer spending to the provinces in the 2007 budget to show they were addressing the spaces issue.[36] Unfortunately, these transfers were greatly reduced from the original bilateral deals negotiated in 2005.[37] Despite the fact that the provincial transfers have not been completely halted, their decreased value has left the provinces scrambling to keep long-term child-care commitments made since 2005, thus increasing the likelihood that some of these bilateral initiatives will be cancelled altogether.[38]

Conclusion

It appears that even though some progress was made toward the goal of a universal child care program in 2005, the current policy context does not seem conducive to ensuring that potential becomes reality in 2009 or beyond. Much has changed since the introduction of universal hospital and medical care during the 1960s and these changes in federal structure and in ideational landscape have created what appear to be insurmountable obstacles for a new universal cost-shared program in Canada as opposed to greater opportunities. Even the movement made in 2005 on the child-care file was tenuous due to the state of intergovernmental relations and the instability in the overarching ideational culture and within the government itself. Those factors have yet to see improvement to the present day and, in the case of the ideational framework, the present situation is particularly hostile to social policy expansion. It is clear, too, that the factors in place that produced the 'golden age' of the welfare state in Canada are very much in the past. Decentralizing movement away from cooperative federalism to collaborative and perhaps open federalism is particularly distressing in that the federal government appears to have all but abandoned its ability to use the federal spending power to take a leadership role in policy areas of provincial responsibility. Recent cuts to the federal GST also indicate a willingness to abandon federal tax room that facilitates the use of the federal spending power. The recession in 2009 also promises to have longstanding detrimental impacts on federal fiscal health, further complicating any future federal government initiatives to revive the spending power if and when a regime change in Ottawa occurs.

The fact that inclusive liberalism does not appear to have fully taken hold of the Canadian political culture, which remains open to neo-liberal ideology and practice, also works against the prospects for a universal child-care program in the new millennium. Despite the fact that advocates are still committed to this goal, the policy framework does not give them a strong voice within the larger policy community. It appears that significant institutional and ideational change would be necessary to bring universal child care to Canada. This type of change appears next to impossible in the short term and still unlikely in the long term.

Endnotes

[1] An earlier version of this chapter was presented at the 2007 meeting of the Canadian Political Science Association. My thanks to Michael Orsini, who served as discussant and provided useful feedback on that paper

and to Gord DiGiacomo who provided very helpful comments on sub-sequent versions. Any errors of fact or interpretation remain my own.

2   Details of specific bilateral early learning and child care agreements between the provinces and the federal government were obtained from Rianne Mahon through personal communication, June 2006. The Manitoba bilateral agreement included federal transfers totalling CA$ 176 million scheduled for the years 2005 to 2010 for wage and benefit increases to provincial child care workers, training and recruit-ment, replacement staff during training and tuition support in early childhood education (ECE) programs.

3   The analysis also includes the subsequent bilateral deals that followed the *Medical Care Act* of 1966 (Medicare Act) and ended in 1971.

4 Banting uses "gross benefits" as most Canadian universal programs and benefits are taxed and if these were excluded, "there really are no uni-versal programs in Canada" (Banting 1985: 7).

5   Child care and early learning advocates argue that there is an impor-tant educative benefit for children with this type of care as well (Collier 2006).

6   The universal child care benefit is a taxable benefit (Mahon 2006).

7   Health care constitutionally falls under provincial jurisdiction under Section 92 (7) of the *Constitution Act*. Child care is not specifically men-tioned in the Constitution but falls under provincial jurisdiction in Section 92 (13) along with other social programs.

8   It is important to note that education constitutionally falls under pro-vincial jurisdiction and this can help justify provincial action in the child care arena particularly since the 'early learning' aspect of child care programs is often emphasized in ELCC program delivery.

9   According to Malcom G. Taylor, "no provincial government failed to send its official to Regina to learn at firsthand how the program oper-ated and what policies and procedures could be adapted to their home provinces" (Taylor 1987: 104). British Columbia, Alberta, Ontario and Newfoundland all had hospital insurance plans in place prior to fed-eral legislation in 1957 (Ibid.).

10 In 1988, the federal Conservative government introduced Bill C-144, a National Strategy on Child Care, which died on the order paper in the Senate before it could become law (Phillips 1989).

11 This program addressed a number of areas within family policy reform but is best known for its introduction of a five-dollar-a-day provin-cially funded child care program where parents regardless of income would pay five dollars each day for child care services that cost much more than that to provide. The province provided direct grants to child care centres to fill the gap between the fees and actual operating costs

(Jenson 2002). The cost of child care was later raised to seven dollars a day but the concept of universality remained intact.

[12] This child care plan was set to provide after-school care for children under the age of 12 years of age for a cost of seven dollars a day and would have been only the second publicly-funded child care program in North American after Quebec. Even though it was not immediately as comprehensive as the Quebec plan, the British Columbia announcement marked the first phase in a longer-term program to extend child care to cover a broader age-range of children and to expand the length of care. However, the program was terminated after a 2001 provincial election brought in a change in governing party (Collier 2006).

[13] Friendly and White argue that Quebec's unique status in Canada likely renders its child care program more of an exception inside the country rather than a model that could or should be followed in other jurisdictions (Friendly and White 2008).

[14] Personal communication from Rianne Mahon, June 2006.

[15] He cites authors in this tradition including Hall 1989, Weir and Skocpol 1985, Jasper 1990, and Risse-Kappan 1994 (Campbell 2002: 30).

[16] Béland cites Pierson 1994 and Skocpol 1992.

[17] This approach is also supported in the policy community/network literature. For a comprehensive review of that literature, see Skogstad 2005.

[18] They argue that a shift from cooperative to a more competitive federalism occurred between the early 1960s and the mid-1970s, when the 'quiet revolution' in Quebec helped heighten competitive tensions within Canada, particularly between the provinces, which put pressure on larger goals of cooperation (Cameron and Simeon 2002).

[19] Mahon (2006) references the well-known welfare state classification scheme by Esping-Andersen (1990; 1999).

[20] Douglas's commitment to health care was also deeply personal. For more information, see Armstrong, Armstrong and Fegan 1998.

[21] According to Senator J. S. Grafstein, MacEachen was instrumental in guiding Medicare "through the tremulous debates in the House where Medicare was almost derailed" (Grafstein 1997).

[22] This chapter does not include all of the interests involved in the health care policy community. Assessments of which interests were most influential were made after consulting the secondary empirical evidence on the formative years of Canadian health care.

[23] Other medical service interests (including the Canadian Hospital Council and the Canadian Dental Association) were also on-side with the CMA during this period, but the CMA remained the largest and most influential (Taylor 1987).

[24] Collaborative federalism allows for provincial agreements that do not necessarily (at least initially) involve the federal government (Cameron and Simeon 2002).

[25] Information regarding negotiations with the territories is not included in this analysis as specific data was not immediately available to the author.

[26] It is important to note that Quebec, the only province with anything close to a model 'universal' child care program in place that could inform the multilateral discussions, chose not to sign onto SUFA. It also chose not to participate fully in the multilateral framework negotiations, although it did negotiate separate funding for its own child care program following the consensus agreement of 2005. This, of course, also limited the ability of the final agreement to be informed by the Quebec child care program.

[27] Personal communication from Rianne Mahon, June 2006.

[28] This was aided by the fact that the QUAD principles were not legislated whereas the *Canada Health Act* principles were.

[29] For more on the current variation in child care services delivery countrywide, see Child Care Canada at http://www.childcarecanada.org/ECEC2004/.

[30] See, for example, Brodie 1996; Bashevkin 2000, 2002.

[31] The provinces were not required to report to the federal government, only to their respective electorates, on how federal money was spent. Thus an important measurement of accountability was never established, arguably making it much more difficult to establish and sustain universal/national standards in program delivery.

[32] This is a truncated summary of the changes in 1993. For more see, for example, MacIvor 2006, pages 108–111.

[33] This level of influence was not static due to slight shifts in party membership in the House of Commons, which changed the dynamic of partisan influence by benefiting different parties at different time points.

[34] See Collier 2006.

[35] After tax the UCCB could amount to as little as CA\$ 600 per year per child. Child care costs range from a high of CA\$ 8,000 per year for a child under three years of age to approximately CA\$ 3,000 per year for before and after school care (Kershaw 2007: 35).

[36] The decision to temporarily abandon the CCSI and to restore some provincial funding came after wide consultation with businesses, private stakeholders, alongside the provinces and municipalities. This was the first time the provinces were actually consulted on the overarching federal child-care policy framework and it was done out of necessity since the original plan to bypass the provinces was unsuccessful. For more, see Collier and Mahon 2008.

[37] According to the CCAAC, the Conservatives pledged CA$ 250 million
per year (essentially the amount of the original CCSI) to the provinces
whereas the bilateral deals promised CA$ 1.2 billion, for a net loss of
CA$ 950 million (CCAAC 2007).

[38] This has so far varied cross-provincially. Manitoba has pledged to
make up for the federal short-fall on its own, while British Columbia
has pledged child care cuts in the wake of lost funding (Government of
Manitoba 2007; Government of British Columbia 2007).

References

Armstrong, Pat, Hugh Armstrong with Claudia Fegan M.D. 1998.
*Universal Health Care: What the United States Can Learn from the Canadian
Experience.* New York: The New Press.

Aucoin, Peter 1974. "Federal Health Care Policy." In *Issues in Canadian
Public Policy,* eds. G. Bruce Doern and V. Seymour Wilson. Toronto:
Macmillan, 55–84.

Banting, Keith 1985 (May). "The Role of Universality in the Canadian
Welfare State." In *Report of the Policy Forum on Universality and Social
Policies in the 1980s - Policy Forum Series 8,* eds. Alan Green and Nancy
Olewiler. Kingston, ON: John Deutsch Institute for the Study of
Economic Policy, Queen's University, 7–16.

Bashevkin, Sylvia 2000. "Rethinking Retrenchment: North American
Social Policy during the Early Clinton and Chrétien Years." *Canadian
Journal of Political Science,* 33: 1: 3–36.

Bashevkin, Sylvia 2002. *Welfare Hot Buttons: Women, Work, and Social Policy
Reform.* Toronto: University of Toronto Press.

Béland, Daniel 2005 (February). "Ideas and Social Policy: An Institutionalist
Perspective." *Social Policy & Administration,* 39: 1: 1–18.

Brodie, Janine 1996. "Canadian Women, Changing State Forms, and
Public Policy." In *Women and Canadian Public Policy,* ed. J. Brodie.
Toronto: Harcourt Brace, 1–28.

Burke, Mike and Susan Silver 2006. "Universal Health Care: Normative
Legacies Adrift." In *Canadian Social Policy: Issues and Perspectives,* 4th
edition, ed. Anne Westhues. Waterloo: Wilfred Laurier University
Press, 375–396.

Cameron, David and Richard Simeon 2002 (Spring). "Intergovernmental
Relations in Canada: The Emergence of Collaborative Federalism."
Publius: The Journal of Federalism 32: 2: 49–71.

Campbell, John L. 2002. "Ideas, Politics, and Public Policy." *Annual Review
of Sociology,* 28: 21–38.

Canada 1964. Royal Commission on Health Services (Hall Report). Volumes I and II. Ottawa.

_____1970. Royal Commission on the Status of Women in Canada. Report. Ottawa: Information Canada.

_____2004. Multilateral Framework on Early Learning and Child Care. www.socialunion.gc.ca/ecd/2004/english/page00.html [accessed April 8, 2010].

_____2007. "1944 - Family Allowance Program: Supporting Canadian Children." http://canadianeconomy.gc.ca/english/economy/1944family. html [consulted May 15, 2007].

Canadian Intergovernmental Conference Secretariat 2005 (February 11). "Federal-Provincial-Territorial Social Services Ministers Reach Consensus on Early Learning and Child Care." News release. www. socialunion.ca/news/feb11.html [consulted October 2, 2006].

CBC News 2005 (April 27). "PM shells out $4.6B for NDP's support." www.cbc.ca/canada/story/2005/04/26/martin-layton050426.html [consulted May 15, 2007].

CCAAC (Child Care Advocacy Association of Canada) 2007. "The Financial Reality behind the Federal Child Care Spaces Initiative: A Mismatch of Mythic Proportions." www.childcareadvocacy.ca/resources/pdf/Financialreality_behind_spaces_initiative_Oct06.pdf [consulted May 16, 2007].

Child Care Canada. www.childcarecanada.org/ECEC2004 [consulted March 26, 2010].

Christian, William and Colin Campbell 1990. *Political Parties and Ideologies in Canada*, 3rd edition. Toronto: McGraw-Hill Ryerson.

Clarke, Harold et al. 1996. *Absent Mandate: Canadian Electoral Politics in an Era of Restructuring*, 3rd edition. Toronto: Gage.

Collier, Cheryl N. 2006. "Governments and Women's Movements: Explaining Child Care and Anti-Violence Policy in Ontario and British Columbia, 1970-2000." Ph. D. dissertation. Toronto: University of Toronto.

Collier, Cheryl and Rianne Mahon 2008. "One Step Forward, Two Steps Back: Child Care Policy from Martin to Harper." In *How Ottawa Spends 2008-2009: A More Orderly Federalism?* ed. Alan Maslove. Montreal and Kingston, ON: McGill-Queen's University Press, 110–133.

Cooperative Commonwealth Federation 1933. "Regina Manifesto."

Courchene, Thomas 2007 (April). "A Blueprint for Fiscal Federalism." *Policy Options*. Montreal: Institute for Public Policy Research, 16–24. www.irpp.org/po/archive/apr07/courchene.pdf [accessed April 29. 2010].

Friendly, Martha and Linda A. White 2008. "From Multilateralism to Bilateralism to Unilateralism in Three Short Years: Child Care in

Canadian Federalism, 2003-2006." In *Canadian Federalism: Performance, Effectiveness, and Legitimacy*, 2nd edition, eds. Herman Bakvis and Grace Skogstad. Don Mills, ON: Oxford, 182–204.

Government of British Columbia 2007 (February 28). Ministry of Children and Family Development. "For the Record: Child Care in B.C." www. mcf.gov.bc.ca/childcare/ [consulted May 15, 2007].

_____2007 (March 16). Ministry of Children and Family Development. "Letter to Child Care Providers." www.mcf.gov.bc.ca/childcare/ [consulted May 15, 2007].

Government of Manitoba 2005 (April 29). "Moving Forward: Governments of Canada and Manitoba Sign an Agreement on Early Learning and Child Care" *Legislative Electronic Publications*. www.gov.mb.ca/chc/press/top/2005/04/2005-04-29-07.html [consulted May 10, 2007].

_____2007. "Province Invests in 500 More Child-Care Spaces, Centre Construction, Early Childhood Educators' Wages and Lower Fees," News release. http://news.gov.mb.ca/news/index,print. html?archive+2007-04-01&item+1438 [consulted May 5, 2007].

Grafstein, Sen. J. L. 1997 (April 17). "The Alan J. MacEachen Lecture in Politics." www.stfx.ca/academic/political-science/Allan%20J.%20Ma cEachen%20Lecture%20Series/Intro_AJ_JG.html [consulted March 6, 2009].

Gray, Gwendolyn 1991. *Federalism and Health Policy: The Development of Health Systems in Canada and Australia*. Toronto: University of Toronto Press.

Integration Network Project 2007. "The Integration Network Project: Bridging caring and learning for young children." www.inproject.ca/News_and_Views/index .php [consulted on May 16, 2007].

Jenson, Jane 2002. "Against the Current: Child Care and Family Policy in Quebec." In *Child Care Policy at the Crossroads: Gender and Welfare State Restructuring*, eds. Sonya Michel and Rianne Mahon. New York: Routledge, 309–332.

Jenson, Jane, Rianne Mahon and Susan D. Phillips 2003. "No Minor Matter: The Political Economy of Childcare in Canada" In *Changing Canada: Political Economy As Transformation*, eds. Wallace Clement and Leah Vosko. Montreal and Kingston, ON: McGill-Queen's University Press, 135–160.

Kershaw, Paul 2007. "Measuring Up: Family Benefits in British Columbia and Alberta in International Perspective." *Choices*. Montreal: Institute for Research on Public Policy, 13: 2.

MacIvor, Heather 2006. *Parameters of Power: Canada's Political Institutions*. Toronto: Thomson/Nelson.

Mahon, Rianne 2006. "Varieties of Liberalism: Canadian Social Policy from the 'Golden Age' to the Present." Paper presented at the conference *Multi-Pillar Systems of Social Safety Nets*, Seoul, South Korea, November 24.

Mahon, Rianne and Susan Phillips 2002. "Dual-Earning Families Caught in a Liberal Welfare Regime? The Politics of Child Care Policy in Canada." In *Child Care Policy at the Crossroads: Gender and Welfare State Restructuring*, eds. Sonya Michel and Rianne Mahon. New York: Routledge, 191–218.

Maioni, Antonia 2008. "Health Care." In *Canadian Federalism: Performance, Effectiveness, and Legitimacy*, 2nd edition, eds. Herman Bakvis and Grace Skogstad. Don Mills, ON: Oxford, 161–181.

McKeen, Wendy and Ann Porter 2003. "Politics and Transformation: Welfare State Restructuring in Canada," In *Changing Canada: Political Economy As Transformation*, eds. Wallace Clement and Leah Vosko. Montreal and Kingston, ON: McGill-Queen's University Press, 109–134.

Noël, Alain, France St-Hilaire and Sarah Fortin 2003. "Learning from the SUFA Experience." In *Forging the Canadian Social Union: SUFA and Beyond*, eds. Alain Noël et al. Montreal: Institute for Research in Public Policy, 1–29.

Phillips, Susan 1989. "Rock-a-Bye, Brian: The National Strategy on Child Care." In *How Ottawa Spends 1989-90: The Buck Stops Where?* ed. K. Graham. Ottawa: Carleton University Press, 165–208.

Simeon, Richard 1976. "Studying Public Policy." *Canadian Journal of Political Science*, 9: 4: 548–580.

Skogstad, Grace 2005. "Policy Networks and Policy Communities: Conceptual Evolution and Governing Realities." Paper presented at the *Annual Meeting of the Canadian Political Science Association*, University of Western Ontario, London, ON, June 2.

Taylor, Malcom G. 1987. *Health Insurance and Canadian Public Policy: The Seven Decisions that Created the Canadian Health Insurance System and Their Outcomes*, 2nd edition. Montreal and Kingston, ON: McGill-Queen's University Press.

Titmuss, Richard M. 1968. *Commitment to Welfare*. New York: Pantheon Books.

Chapter 5

The Practitioner's Perspective: Canada is a Journey, Not a Destination

Maryantonett Flumian

The journey begins

Almost one hundred and fifty years ago, a group of men came together to begin the journey towards creating Canada. Canada was to be greater than the sum of its parts. Driven by many considerations, they had a mutual respect for their history, law, convention and personal experience. They put aside more parochial interests and differences to find the commonality and sustainability of their dream. Their accomplishments, with us today, speak to their leadership and vision.

Federalism is by definition the coming together to create a unity. That unity, to be successful, must reflect the challenges, differences and realities facing it. All are 'made different' by the effort. All agreed that they were creating a new nation—Canada, derived from two histories and traditions—shared and inextricably joined into the future. No provision was made for its dissolution; that thought was probably inconceivable to those great builders. In creating Canada, they came together to give life to a modern country that recognized their individual context and a structure that would speak for Canadians with one voice on the international and domestic stage.

Achieving collective outcomes

Building towards the collective outcome, they created a national government to consider, first and foremost, the interests of Canada. A new government was created to play the overarching role in how all Canadians would be treated in this collective. Like great builders, our forefathers recognized dynamic tensions and built into the system enough checks and balances to give shape to this common future. The duty to work things out on behalf of citizens—from all parts of the country—was key to the effective working of a national government and its constituent parts in the new federation. All governments are 'given' a voice. The national government has a particular duty and interest in recognizing and developing the national expression of that voice.

In casting their eyes to the future, these men were also undoubtedly comforted by the fact that British tradition recognized the evolving nature of constitutional convention. This is essential to the concept of evolving governance and its institutional capacity to continuously search for the modern expression of the original intent. It also allows for developments in unforeseen areas. Indeed, without this concept, our governmental institutions and their interactions with each other and citizens would be forever frozen in time, incapable of rising to future challenges and opportunities.

In their time, and to the best of their abilities, the founders also looked hard into the future and tried to outline and define the areas in which each level of government would be paramount. The notions of exclusive and shared jurisdictions also evolved, but government and its administration is not cut and dry. Nor should it be. Context in life and in the conduct of government matters.

Context matters

Context is how citizens actually relate to government. Context is both a function of where people live and their circumstances. They may live in Alberta, Ontario or Quebec, and they might be unemployed and seeking work in their own communities. They may live and work in Winnipeg, Manitoba, but export all of their production to the United States or Slovakia. They may study in London, England but need medical care in Sudbury, Ontario. They may vacation in Mexico, live in Rimouski, Quebec and have all their identity documents and money stolen while abroad. They may live in Port-aux-Basques, Newfoundland, work in Fort McMurray, Alberta and commute monthly. They may also have been born, grown up, work, retire and die in Nunavut. Context is essential to understanding how government plays a role in the life of citizens.

The crafters of the federation allowed for enough checks and balances to safeguard modes of legitimate expression and dissent. Over one hundred years later, the Charter of Rights and Freedoms has enshrined space for this individual expression. This has created even greater need for government to explain decisions about the greater good in the context of the individual. Yet debates continue using the paradigms of the past, with the result that citizens are badly served by their governments. Governments, by and large, are constrained by structures that no longer serve them—bureaucracies that were designed and equipped to support those outdated rigid structures and by sclerotic processes that clog the achievement of outcomes towards the 21st century expression of "Peace, Order and Good Government".

Openness, transparency, collaboration and participation

In academic discourse and literature, little account is taken of this reality. Instead of continuing our journey in search of a modern expression of Canada, too much effort and energy goes into the dialectic of 'to centralize or not to centralize'. That is not the pertinent framework for evolving the discourse, or for that matter, for day to day interaction with citizens. The federal government must have a view about the health and welfare of the country and its citizens. It must be in a position to do what was originally intended. Therefore, the discussion must move on from this sterile debate and focus on the new paradigm of governance in a federal state.

In today's world, governance has become a highly diffused phenomenon. In western democracies, it is more difficult than ever to achieve progress by dictating behaviour. The will of citizens, the provinces, the federal government, not for profit groups, business and labour must all take into account that openness, transparency, collaboration and participation are the characteristics of the ecosystem of governance. Traditional lines are blurred.

In this ecosystem, knowledge, information, talent and energy are moved, shaped and channeled in new ways across and outside the boundaries of government. In this open system, old style hierarchies are anachronistic. Structures are less relevant. This ecosystem is energized by collaboration. The single biggest driver is strong leadership, which must lead and oversee the transition in this far more distributed governance regime. Strong leadership seeks to enable two things: coherence and collaboration. Coherence provides the common context and values for interpretation and belonging. While the role of the state is certainly undergoing profound change, it is not clear where it will land. What is clear is that this more distributed, and even personalized nature of change, cries out for coherence to give it meaning in a national context. Collaboration, by definition, includes the will of the governed—directly and through existing governmental and institutional structures. However, these structures must now be reflective of an openness and transparency unheard of heretofore. Transparency must apply to information that fuels collaboration, to the need for different behaviours, to the evidence and where it leads decision makers, and finally, in the arrangements that support them.

In this paradigm, the leadership of the national government should be expressed and defined where the national interest needs a national 'voice'. In this reality, power—in and of itself—does not secure more power, public attitudes, or the best outcome. Our 'national voice' has changed over time to include a much larger and diverse group of players than the original men who came together to form our country. This does not change the intent of their outcome. It calls out for a modern re-statement of national coherence.

The need for greater collaboration in achieving better outcomes has led to a desire for greater citizen participation. While governments are still experimenting with what this participation means, a few things are now evident. The electoral process is no longer the primary means for citizen expression. Governments at all levels are struggling with what this means to their traditional view of consultation and engagement with 'representative' groups. In the recent past, governments preferred to deal with these 'representative' groups because they aggregated citizen response. The pervasive use of technology and its increasing ability to personalize interactions is making it very difficult for governments to find the equilibrium now between the needs and expectations of individuals, organization and structure. It is these features of the new governance ecosystem that are disassembling the old ideas of how government and governance actually work. In the process, they are also reinforcing the futility of looking at the debate from the standpoint of old paradigms. Once again context is key, and coherent expression in this transition is key to adapting to new realities.

Citizens' needs and expectations can change overnight. In a time of crisis governments can respond overnight. No one who has witnessed the last year on the global and Canadian federal landscape could have missed the reaction of the current government led by Prime Minister Harper to the plight of unemployed Canadians. In the mixed constitutional domain of labour market policy and programming, the federal government recognized the expression of the 'national' voice, and moved quickly to increase coverage, duration and expenditures under the flagship federal program, employment insurance, without protracted negotiations. The leadership, flexibility and the lack of ideology—demonstrated in a very compressed time period—were amazing to behold.

In the real world, social and economic 'powers'; the use of the federal spending power; and the openness and immediacy of citizen reactions all lead to the government becoming extremely responsive to the citizens it serves. The speed and collaboration with which the existing infrastructure program was launched is an example of the Harper government recognizing the current crisis and anticipating where the expanded role of government was required. This was not the time for discussions on the role of the federal spending power—indeed, it was left to the editorial press to raise this commentary. In the conventional wisdom, the traditional lines of jurisdiction have become blurred; the need for strong national leadership has not. The airtight world of purists does not translate well into this reality.

Coherence is key

A main tool of federalism is the national government's spending power. Strong national leadership spearheading coordinated action was needed to fight the recession of 2009. The national government acted to assist the adaptation of a whole nation in the midst of fundamental change—a change redistributing relative power and position between regions and individual Canadians. The national government acted strongly and opportunistically to help redefine the shape of the Canadian economy.

These examples are illustrative of how ideology, tradition and approaches can be altered overnight. Being constrained by the old discussions of "who is in charge" are truly guideposts from a different era. Furthermore, over the last fifteen years, there are at least three areas in the administration of national issues where thinking and doing have evolved into new models for redefining collaboration in the national interest. The needs of the country have enabled innovation in the structures, roles and responsibilities of our evolving institutions. The three areas are: tax administration and collection; delivering citizen-centred service; and securities regulation. In all three areas, it is looking beyond the legacy model of 'who is in charge' and understanding the evolving ecosystem that has enabled innovation.

These three examples speak to the evolutionary characteristics of a model of federalism that fits the times. Future directions are declared, debated and implemented. They evolve most rapidly in areas where leadership focuses on clear outcomes. The centralization versus decentralization debate is not an issue. The big issues that face Canadians—such as dealing with the environment, climate change, health and economic renewal—all need strong and collaborative models of leadership to position Canada for the rest of the 21st century. Only the national government can express the needed coherence that will allow for the ensuing expression of personalization and the pressures for asymmetry. Only the national government is in a position to lead the public discourse that contributes to the meaning and relationships of all the parts into a meaning for the whole. Coherence requires connection for all its parts. It is the essential organizing factor in a world of experimentation, asymmetry and personalization. It is the way to flourish and prosper while modernizing the nation state. Coherence is the glue that binds.

While the search for an overall, coherent vision of Canada's place in the 21st century continues to elude our national government, over the last ten years Canada has witnessed some success in implementing modern expressions of the potential of federalism led by a strong national government in a highly distributed world. Governments are by and large recognizing the new realities. They are, however, struggling with what to do. Nevertheless, some significant attempts are being made to reflect the new world that is still emerging. In the process, at least three emerging examples are worth exploring. These three examples are the Canada Revenue Agency; new arrangements in the domain of service delivery as expressed by Service Canada and provincial service delivery initiatives; and the area of securities regulation. Each reveals aspects of the new realities, the need for coherence, different governance arrangements and different 'delivery' arrangements.

Canada Revenue Agency

In creating what would become the Canada Revenue Agency, the government stated that it had three objectives:

- to deliver programs and services in a more effective and efficient manner through greater autonomy and flexibility;
- to improve services and reduce the cost of revenue administration and compliance by working with the provinces to eliminate overlap and duplication; and
- to strengthen the effectiveness of the federation and contribute to national unity by establishing the agency as an organization that provides Canadians with services that are both federal and provincial in nature.

On February 17, 1999, Minister of National Revenue Herb Dhaliwal, in an appearance before the Senate Standing Committee on National Finance, spoke about the creation of the new agency.

> The Canada Customs and Revenue Agency will infuse new flexibility and simplicity into the tax process. That means lower administrative costs and reduced overlap and duplication for Canadian small businesses. I also spoke with business owners and executives whose companies depend on easy access to international markets. The new agency would respond to this need by streamlining the customs services... In creating the new Canada Customs and Revenue Agency, we want to forge new partnerships with the provinces and territories. We want to give provincial governments the options they need to better serve Canadians. We want them to have a greater say in tax administration. That is why we have ensured in this legislation their right to nominate 11 of the 15 positions on the agency's board of management (Canada 1999a).

As Minister Dhaliwal was addressing the shape and structure of the new governance model, he based his view

of future success entirely on a new partnership with provincial governments.

> I wish to emphasize that the participation of the prov-
> inces and the territories in this new system is completely
> voluntary. The provinces and territories will maintain
> control over their tax policy, while the new agency will
> create new options to administer these policies. Nobody
> ever said that partnership is easy. There are no simple
> answers or quick fixes. Partnership turns on consensus
> and accommodation. It rests on a delicate balance of give
> and take. We intend to work closely with the provinces
> and territories to find that balance. Canadians want their
> governments to work together for their citizens. They do
> not want us to build parallel systems across the country
> (Ibid.).

Federal provincial cooperation, through a reordering of
'who does what', was seen as a main feature of this new
administrative arrangement.

> We want to build a vehicle where we can work with the
> provinces to create a single tax administration. We cur-
> rently collect about 50 per cent of the taxes for the prov-
> inces. However, there is a tremendous opportunity to do
> more. For example, in British Columbia there is a corpo-
> rate capital tax. When people fill out their corporate tax
> returns, there is no reason why they could not do that
> at the same time…These policies create new options that
> did not exist. They will reduce administrative costs and
> also reduce compliance costs (Ibid.).

In November 1999 when the Canada Customs and Revenue Agency (CCRA) was established, it incorporated a number of features that would assist the creation of an agency
befitting this truly national endeavour. The *Canada Customs
and Revenue Agency Act* (CCRA Act) provided mechanisms
to govern CCRA's relationship with the provinces and territories, including a role for them in nominating members

of the agency board of management; provisions for annual reports and meetings with the provincial and territorial revenue ministries; and service management framework agreements (Canada 2003a).

Over time the CCRA became the Canada Revenue Agency (CRA).[1] In implementing its general mandate, CRA has developed an approach to partnerships that extends to CRA's relationships with federal government departments, provinces, other countries, business groups, the voluntary sector and others. CRA has been working to advance its partner relationships with the provinces and territories by adding new programs, data exchanges, and business number arrangements all with improved accountability. In the early years, progress in working with provinces was slow. In its 2002–2003 annual report, the agency stated that "recent federal-provincial issues have made it somewhat more challenging to build new partnership arrangements, and that progress has been slower than planned. Nonetheless, CRA has positioned itself to offer more programs with its partners in the coming years" (Ibid.). Four years after its creation, the CRA was a key service provider to federal departments, provincial and territorial governments, and First Nations, with over sixty agreements for joint program delivery (Ibid.).

In 2004, in preparation for the mandated five year review of the new agency, the Public Policy Forum undertook a review for CRA on its relationship with the provinces and territories. At the heart of the assessment was a series of interviews conducted with the thirteen provincial and territorial governments. The Public Policy Forum interviewed senior tax officials from all thirteen provincial and territorial administrations. The interviews were designed to elicit feedback on CRA legislation and administrative arrangements; impact on provincial and territorial programs and administrative arrangements; definition and objectives of the relationship between CRA and the provinces and territories; satisfaction with the current state of CRA's relationship with the provinces and territories; dynamics of change; and the potential for growth.

The review confirmed that the mindset of CRA towards the provinces had changed.

> The CRA structure makes it much more accountable to the provinces. The status given to provinces within CRA (role in appointments to the board of management, annual report to and meeting with the provincial governments) has led to a significant improvement in the relationship between CRA and the provinces. Whereas provinces used to deal mostly with the Department of Finance on revenue matters, they now have a more direct and effective relationship with CRA (Public Policy Forum 2004).

The interviews found that there had been a general maturing of provincial capacity to develop tax policy and, in that sense, serve as a client for CRA's services. Provinces were now more likely to communicate among themselves and coordinate their tax policies.

Provincial officials were strongly of the opinion that it was both possible and desirable to continue with efforts aimed at further integration in tax administration across Canada. Major increases in the integration of tax administration improvements would require a quantum leap in benefits to the provinces. The prospect that provinces would hand over administration of their remaining tax systems was considered to be very low unless substantial and meaningful benefits could be clearly demonstrated.

All governments emphasized the importance, depth and strength of existing relationships with CRA. The parliamentary review of the CCRA Act, coinciding with the development of a new generation of tax collection agreements, offered a timely opportunity for reflection on the relationship. "It was generally agreed that here has been significant progress in the relationship over the first five years, representing a maturing of capacity and understanding on all sides" (Ibid.).

The provinces and territories highlighted several positive areas both in relationship and the services provided by CRA:

- services to taxpayers (tax services offices, call centres, electronic services);

- personal income tax and HST (harmonized sales tax) collection were well established;
- business number, workers compensation remittances;
- collaboration on areas of common interest (monitoring, compliance, taxpayer education, underground economy);
- CRA corporate capacity, economies of scale; and
- working relations and responsiveness of local and regional CRA offices.

The Public Policy Forum review also offered a starting point for judging future prospects in the already extensive range of services and relationships that CRA was managing.

1. *Service relationships*: where CRA acts on behalf of a province or territory, underpinned by some sort of contractual arrangement—this encompasses CRA's revenue collection and tax expenditure activities and related work. The profile of these relationships varies from province to province, but taken together they represent the bulk of CRA's work on behalf of other jurisdictions.

2. *Partnerships*: where CRA and all provinces have a common interest (including parallel or complementary taxes on the same groups such as small and medium business, measures to promote voluntary compliance, measures to address the underground economy, taxpayer education).

3. *Data collection:* where the provinces attached growing importance to data from CRA relating both to tax collection on their behalf and more generally. Data are used to meet a variety of needs—tracking provincial revenue streams and monitoring CRA performance are the core uses, but data are increasingly important for fiscal, economic and social policy development and for general government management purposes. For smaller and less wealthy provinces there is also a critical link between tax revenue

data and the calculation of equalization payments to the provinces.

Already in the first phase of CRA's life, a different model of the future was evolving. Indeed, on March 10, 1999 during the proceedings of the Senate Standing Committee on National Finance, Garth Whyte, representing the Canadian Federation of Independent Business, stated:

> As trust builds between the provinces and the federal government and as people start seeing the agency work, we believe that you will see more and more harmonization. Referring back to the Nova Scotia example where the revenue agency will collect workers compensation premiums, it will still appear as the Nova Scotia government, but it will make it much easier for our members on remittance schedules. They can pay on a monthly basis instead of having to project it for one year. We hear that Newfoundland may be going in that direction also. With the child tax credit, again, people in B.C. assume that they are remitting to the B.C. government but it is being collected by the revenue agency. As long as it sticks to the principles that are being put in place and there is accountability, we see a removal of an extra layer in many tax jurisdictions of the compliance burden, which can be quite positive (Canada 1999b).

As the CRA evolved, the relationship between federal, provincial and territorial governments has deepened and matured. The model is supple enough to allow for Revenue Québec to administer the goods and services tax and harmonized sales tax (GST/HST) in Quebec for both levels of government, and Revenue Québec receives and processes the applications for GST/HST registration for all persons carrying on a commercial activity in Quebec.

Based on all of this experience, in October 2006 a significant step was taken by the federal and Ontario governments to increase harmonization of the tax systems in Canada, reduce compliance costs for businesses, and reduce admin-

istration costs for governments with the signing of the agreement to transfer the administration of Ontario corporate tax
to the CRA. As of February 2008, Ontario corporations began
making a single installment payment for the 2009 taxation
year, thereby reducing their administrative costs.

The Ontario Minister of Revenue, in speaking to the
boards of trade and chambers of commerce from across
Ontario said:

> Ontario corporations have already started to see the bene-
> fits of the integrated system. Federal and provincial audits,
> rulings, objections and appeals for all pre-2009 taxation
> years have been combined thanks to an agreement signed
> between the Government of Ontario and the Government
> of Canada. This move will save Ontario business an esti-
> mated $100 million a year in administrative costs and an
> additional $90 million from reduced Ontario corporate
> income taxes through the move to a harmonized tax base
> for the 2009 taxation year (Canada 2008a).

In part because of this experience, on March 26, 2009, the
Ontario government decided to proceed towards the implementation of the harmonized sales tax. Beginning July 1,
2010, CRA will collect this tax for Ontario. The harmonization will see a shift from taxing inputs to taxing consump-
tion. In this fashion, the Ontario government has learned
from the experiences of the four Atlantic provinces, which
had moved to harmonize their sales tax in 1996.

Recent developments on tax collection continue to under-
lie the commitment of two levels of government to the original objectives set for the creation of CRA. On July 23, 2009,
British Columbia announced its intention to harmonize its
provincial sales tax with the federal GST.

> This is the single biggest thing we can do to improve
> B.C.'s economy. This is an essential step to make our busi-
> nesses more competitive, encourage billions of dollars in
> new investment, lower costs on productivity and reduce
> administrative costs to B.C. taxpayers and businesses.

Most importantly, this will create jobs and generate long-term economic growth that will in turn generate more revenue to sustain and improve crucial public services (Government of British Columbia 2009).

In adopting this approach, there is also a clear indication that the provinces are learning from each others' experience. "Evidence from the Atlantic provinces showed that the hidden tax is removed very quickly, with the majority of the savings passed through to consumers in the first year." said the Minister of Finance for British Columbia, Colin Hansen (Ibid.).

The federal government will provide British Columbia with CA\$ 1.6 billion in transitional funding in recognition of the improvement this change will make to business competitiveness in Canada. The full cost of administration will be borne by the federal government, saving the province an estimated CA\$ 30 million annually in administration costs. With this decision, the province can now move forward and work with industry to implement the new HST. Once fully implemented, the single sales tax will make British Columbia one of the most competitive jurisdictions in the industrialized world for new investments. The proposed changes are subject to approval by the governments of Canada and British Columbia.

The work of this national agency benefits clients and the citizens that are served by two levels of governments across the country—governments enjoy lower administration costs and more effective compliance; citizens receive more comprehensive and better-integrated benefits and services that are simpler for them to use. The CRA has come a long way in ten years in showing the potential for a model of national commitment to action in aid of citizens and businesses. It has taken strong leadership by the national government, and a spirit of innovation, experimentation and leadership on the part of provincial governments, to make progress and reshape the old consensus about who does what. In the process, citizens and businesses are better served and governments are more effective and efficient.

Improving service for Canadians

Over the past decade, the pursuit of citizen-centred service, combined with rapid advances in information and communication technologies, has stimulated innovative approaches to the organizational design of governments' service delivery systems. Service delivery organizations in Canada and elsewhere have taken a variety of organizational forms, thereby providing a range of models for adoption or adaptation.

Service Canada is building on over a decade of efforts, including extensive research and planning, to improve service in the Government of Canada. Among these efforts was Government On-Line (GOL), a six-year initiative (2000–06) aimed at promoting electronic service delivery by federal departments. In its final report, GOL announced that it had "succeeded in making the Canadian government the world's most connected country to its citizens" (Canada 2006). GOL delivered a number of online services and increased the confidence of Canadians in transacting online. It was a first step towards meeting the needs and expectations of Canadians and highlighted the need for more integrated and seamless service across all channels.

In the 2005 budget, the federal government announced its intention to create Service Canada and to give it responsibility for providing one-stop service through in-person, telephone, Internet and mail delivery channels. The budget noted that implementing this new model would involve "*one of the biggest single reforms ever in federal operations*" (Canada 2005, italics added for emphasis). In May 2005 the Treasury Board Secretariat approved the initial phase of an overall strategy for implementation and Service Canada officially opened its doors to the public on September 14, 2005.

Today, Service Canada employs over 18,000 employees to serve the country's 32 million citizens. It operates over 580 in-person points of service across the country and has taken over responsibility for the Government of Canada's one-stop telephone call centre (1-800-O CANADA) and the Government of Canada's Internet portal (www.canada. gc.ca). On an annual basis, Service Canada answers more

than 56 million telephone calls (over 80 percent of all calls
to the federal government, excluding those to the Canada
Revenue Agency) and handles more than 14 million unique
visits to its website. The pursuit of integrated service delivery (ISD) requires effective cross-agency and cross jurisdictional collaboration. Thus, Service Canada is working with
a growing number of federal departments, the majority of
provinces and community partners to bring services and
benefits together in a single service delivery network.

Service Canada and provincial service delivery organizations offer Canadians a new model for the delivery of
government services. Service Canada is a one-stop, multi-
channel, multi-jurisdictional initiative that is dedicated to
delivering seamless citizen-centred service. Its primary purpose is to bring together—and fit together—a wide range
of government programs and services from across federal
departments and other levels of government to provide citizens with integrated, easy-to-access, personalized service.
Service Canada is an ISD arrangement that responds to
the rising expectations of Canadians for improved service
delivery. It is also a response to the realization that the federal government cannot make substantial improvements in
the quality of its service delivery without a new partnership
model that engages other federal departments, provincial-
territorial governments, municipal governments, the not-
for-profit sector and business.

Service Canada aims not only to foster efficient, effective and accountable service delivery, but also to fulfill
the public service's traditional role of helping to sustain
and strengthen democratic institutions. The Citizens First
national surveys have found that Canadians' level of service
satisfaction appears to have a strong influence on their trust
and confidence in government (Citizens First 2003, 2005).

In the run-up to the creation of Service Canada—a close
cousin of Australia's Centrelink—most government officials believed there were no significant barriers to providing better service for citizens. To convince them of the need
for a holistic service experience, service advocates began
to map the multitude of programs and channels for ser-

vice delivery by population groupings. The picture demonstrated why it was so difficult to create a holistic experience for a typical family.

Figure 5.1 maps the major government departments
and discrete programs available to the disabled citizen of
Ontario. The lines describe actual communication channels—mail, in-person, phone, and Internet—that reinforce
government's silo approach to helping a disabled person
live a full life. Seeing this mapped out, it became clear to
service advocates that policy outcomes were getting lost in
implementation. In addition, this model is very expensive to
operate and, organizationally, it depends on linear change
happening sequentially in too many competing departments, agencies and levels of government.

**Figure 5.1   Finding government programs and services for
people with disabilities**

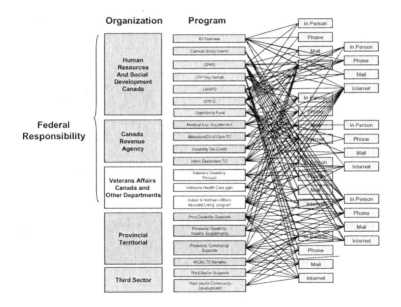

Source: Maryantonett Flumian, "Citizens as Prosumers; The Next Frontier
of Service Innovation." Syndicated research. nGenera insight, Government
2.0, October 2008. Available at the Institute On Governance, www.iog.
ca/publications.asp.

Citizen expectations and the Internet

The Internet has become a natural tool for building bridges between different agencies. Organizational structure became a more manageable problem because the 'restructuring' was now happening virtually. Powerful search engines available from Google, Yahoo and others are producing information from various sources in a coherent display. Governments began to bundle services together so that someone who needed a service, such as business registration, would be able to find everything in one place. These 'one-stop shops' began to evolve into organizations tasked with joining up services across government departments, coordinating information on behalf of citizens. In the case of Service New Brunswick, one of the first movers, this bundling took place only at the front-end offices where services were provided

Figure 5.2   The one-stop citizen-centered business model represents a significant shift from a . programmatic model

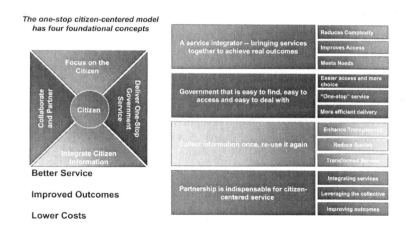

Source: Maryantonett Flumian, "Citizens as Prosumers; The Next Frontier of Service Innovation." Syndicated research. nGenera insight, Government 2.0, October 2008. Available at the Institute On Governance, www.iog. ca/publications.asp.

by an individual who could draw together information and applications to complete the one-stop transaction. It would take longer for the back-end legacy systems to catch up.

It was building on lessons from such world leaders as the UK government—especially the Department for Works and Pensions—Centrelink in Australia, and Singapore, that the Canadian government created a whole-of-government organization to deliver citizen-centred service.

The Hon. Joe Volpe, the federal minister who oversaw the creation of Service Canada, recalls:

> The amount of preparation we did to get ready was phenomenal. It took two years of research of global best practices in both the public and private sectors. The research included everything from call centre consolidation to information collection to integrating service to client segmentation to office design. After that, we developed proof of concepts for what might work in a Canadian context. Only after learning from those experiences did we begin to reshape our business practices and behaviors to reshape both our front-end service experience and our supporting back-end shared services and processes simultaneously. As a minister, I had to balance innovation and risk. But I knew we weren't going anywhere if we didn't risk something (Flumian 2008).

Four years of study, planning and proof of concepts preceded the 2005 launch of Service Canada. Significant effort went into preparing the workforce. Service Canada College, the first public sector training organization of its kind, was established to help introduce staff to best practices for enhancing the service experience and achieving better outcomes.

Once Service Canada was launched, it was lauded by citizens and politicians alike. Reg Alcock, then president of the Treasury Board—Canada's central agency for expenditure and management—said:

> I was blown away by how fast it scaled. Twenty-two thousand employees hit the ground running. The improvements were obvious almost immediately. To ensure its

success, we established a Committee of Cabinet to keep
driving implementation. We understood pressure from
the political level was necessary to get our departments
working together (Ibid.).

Service Canada created a citizen-centred business model
that broke the traditional program structure and instead
focused on developing, managing and delivering services
for citizens. It has successfully shifted away from an administrative compliance-based culture to a professional service
culture. It collaborated with other federal departments and
levels of government to develop integrated and seamless
services in partnership. It shifted to a more flexible and
responsive service delivery infrastructure, experimenting
with organizational structure, governance and culture to
allow services to be quickly introduced and changed.

Australia and Canada have shown that progress is possible through sustained leadership and learning by doing.
But accountability and culture issues have evolved into an
obsession with linking organizational structure to hard-
wired accountabilities—an overwhelming focus on 'Who's
in charge?' instead of 'What's the outcome?' Public ser-
vants hide behind 19th century models of organization and
structure of government, waiting for political processes
to resolve their perceived structural issues. Politicians are
seldom equipped to leap over these hurdles to innovation.
Without strong leadership focusing on the citizen, service
transformation gets stuck.

One clear example of progress that these levels of government were able to make is to be found in the highly complicated area of registering newborns.

Canada drew heavily from the progress made by the
Crossroads Bank in Belgium in its federated approach to
information management in its registry service for newborns. The registry is helping to create a cradle-to-grave
continuum for identity management. The pilot was aimed
at testing whether citizens would consent to sharing information if it contributed to more convenient and efficient

transactions. The benefits of such consent are numerous and can allow for multiple jurisdictions, with the appropriate protection, to serve citizens in a far more transparent fashion while reducing the overall costs to government.

In the past, registering a birth was time consuming, inefficient, and did little to enable collaboration or effective service delivery by government agencies. And yet it is with birth that the process of establishing a citizen's identity begins.

The process crossed departmental and jurisdictional boundaries. Historically, some of the process had to be undertaken in person and some had to be undertaken by mail. The application and issuance of documents had to follow a predetermined sequencing that is not entirely obvious to the citizen.

At a minimum, parents had to complete three separate paper applications to three different levels of government for birth registration, birth certificate, and a social insurance number (SIN) for their baby. After submitting the birth registration to the municipality, they had to wait to receive confirmation before they could apply for a birth certificate from their province. Then they had another wait for the birth certificate to arrive. Only after it arrived could they then apply to the federal government for the SIN.

As part of the Canadian government's inter-jurisdictional attempts to improve service delivery through more effective identity management, the Province of Ontario and Service Canada introduced the Newborn Registration Service—an innovation that enables parents to register their baby's birth and apply for the child's birth certificate and social insurance number all at the same time. Before parents leave the hospital they are provided with a birth information package which encourages them to do all this online, and without having to duplicate the required information. By streamlining the three application processes into one integrated online service, the newborn registration service has cut the time for processing important identity documents in half. Continuing improvements in the processes will result in enhanced speed of service, further cutting the processing time from months to weeks.

In addition to increasing operational efficiencies and speed of service, the newborn registration service offers parents the assurance that the privacy of their personal information is protected. The service has the advantage of enhancing the quality of data captured and maintained in provincial and federal registers. The electronic application process greatly reduces the number of errors that tend to plague paper-based processes with manual processing of documentation.

As confidence has grown as a result of this success, the parties are increasingly looking for ways to increase the members to the partnership. Programs and services under consideration include health cards, passports, child education savings grants, child tax benefits and child-care payments. The possibilities are endless.

In the process, two levels of government working together have also created the foundation for managing identity on a continuum that begins at birth and includes services and programs throughout one's life.

This was achieved by understanding that managing identity in a collaborative fashion would provide the backbone to 'joining up' services from many jurisdictions. The management of information was the key breakthrough. Understanding that each party had something that the other relied on—and trusting them to do their part for everyone—unlocked the door to a massive improvement in service.

Travelling down this road, governments are collectively striving to transform service for citizens. This path engages the citizen, empowers the network, changes the culture of government, and creates consistent standards and security for the holders and protectors of personal information. At the end of the day, it also does a better job of securing both individual identity and protecting the state—by managing individual identity along the entire continuum. It requires greater collaboration, consent and trust from all the parties—including citizens—and finds a better balance between all actors in the process.

The notion of 'partnership' or 'collaboration' has great potential in pursuit of the public interest and in the quest to modernize the public sector. Partnerships allow citizens to have a say in how government provides services and enables the participants themselves to take on more responsibilities. These arrangements permit all participants to combine their resources and bring about results more quickly and effectively than any partner could accomplish alone. Within and between governments, through horizontal integration among departments and vertical integration among governments, partnerships can provide an integrated approach to service. Where appropriate, partners from outside of government can also play a vital role in improving service delivery to citizens (Flumian 1999).

A forum of federal-provincial deputy ministers responsible for service delivery has been established. This forum can now build on the work of the last decade where much of the ground work has been laid. Service Canada, given the scope of its mandate and the numbers of Canadians it serves in all parts of the country, can easily collaborate with other levels of government to provide part of the new public infrastructure for integrated service.

The federal-provincial forum, with British Columbia and Service Canada as catalysts, can become an innovative, learning group in which officials at all levels, in individual jurisdictions or collectively, are continually working together to increase their capacity and understanding of ways to improve service to Canadians. These deputy ministers are able to model, for their organizations, the values and behaviours that reflect a service excellence culture. Their work, which is ongoing, had commissioned seminal works on a strategy for identity and management authentication across the country and on relevant statutes in provincial and federal jurisdictions related to information about the identification of individuals and inter-jurisdictional transfer.

The promise of Service Canada and a citizen-centred vision is ambitious, but it is achievable, and Canadians will be better served as the new reality materializes. Success builds on success. As of November 2009 all provinces and territories have now signed up to partner on initiatives like the newborn registration system. More partnerships will follow.

In the business world, the last few years have witnessed an explosion in the use of traditional collaboration. Today, books such as Don Tapscott's and Anthony Williams' *Wikinomics* chronicle the phenomenon of mass collaboration on an unprecedented scale (Tapscott and Williams 2006). Perhaps this phenomenon can spread to the public sector—different levels of the government being able to leverage each other's complementary capabilities, programs and proximity to their citizens to re-shape how governments work and interact.

The concept of citizen-centred service transforms the citizen into a co-innovator with government, and the new models of production based on community, collaboration and self-organization—rather than on hierarchy and control—provide the means to make it happen. Over the next few years it will be interesting to observe how federal-provincial fora will lead the way towards a renewed vision of government and a different engagement of citizens.

The securities regulator

Since the supervision of Canada's securities industry was not explicitly given to either the provincial or federal levels of government within the Canadian Constitution, the provinces and territories began to regulate securities under the "property and civil rights" clause of the *Constitution Act, 1867*. To this end, each province and territory has its own securities regulator (Canada 1867).

The idea for a common securities regulator first surfaced in a 1964 Royal Commission on Banking and Finance—the Porter Commission (Canada 1964). Few concrete steps had been taken towards this goal until the 1996 Speech from the Throne, when the federal government offered to work with any interested provinces towards the development of a Canadian securities commission.

In 1999 global pressures led to the consolidation of Canada's stock exchanges. The Vancouver, Alberta and Winnipeg stock exchanges merged into the Canadian Venture Exchange (later renamed TSX Venture Exchange), which was then acquired by the Toronto Stock Exchange (TSX) in 2001. Today, Canada has three major national exchanges.

Senior equities are traded on the TSX and junior equities are traded on the TSX Venture Exchange. The Bourse de Montréal is Canada's national derivatives exchange. Although securities trading was consolidated, regulation remained largely decentralized. Beginning in the 1990s, many began to suggest that the system was overly complex and inefficient. Issuers and dealers incurred significant compliance costs as a result of regulatory overlap and duplication. For example, a company trying to raise capital through an IPO (initial public offering) across Canada had to comply with the prospectus requirements of every province and territory in which its stock was going to be offered, and could thus be subject to the rules and requirements of thirteen different securities regulators. Companies were also forced to pay fees to every regulator with which they dealt. These costs were ultimately borne by the investor.

In March 2003, the federal government established the Wise Persons' Committee. Its mandate was to recommend a securities regulatory structure that supports competitiveness, innovation and growth in Canada's capital markets; responds to the requirements of regional capital markets and emerging public companies; and maintains investor confidence. The committee's December 2003 report, entitled *It's Time*, recommended that Canada adopt a single regulator administering a single set of laws across the country (Canada 2003b). This new structure would be cooperatively created and overseen by the federal, provincial and territorial governments.

The report acknowledged that Canada's existing system of thirteen provincial and territorial regulators had positive attributes, namely the proximity of regulators to capital market participants in each jurisdiction as well as its responsiveness to local and regional issues. According to the committee, however, the weaknesses of the system were serious and outweighed its strengths. It found that Canada suffered from inadequate enforcement and inconsistent investor protection. The system also contributed to slow policy development, regulatory complexities and needless duplication, inefficiencies and costs. The committee concluded that these weaknesses made Canada less competitive at a time of increasing global competition.

The Wise Persons' Committee supported fundamental change to Canada's regulator regime and believed that a single securities commission would be a considerable improvement on the existing system. The committee argued that the common model would:

- significantly strengthen enforcement through more efficient allocation of resources, better coordination and uniform investment protection across the country;
- facilitate better and more timely policy innovation and development;
- address the disproportionate regulatory burden the current system places on small and emerging companies;
- enhance the 'brand' of Canada's securities regulation internationally;
- eliminate additional compliance costs resulting from multiple regulators;
- ensure responsiveness to local and regional needs by consulting provinces, territories and capital market participants on the common regulator's governance structure, and by setting up regional offices;
- establish clear accountability and governance mechanisms; and
- simplify the current system by reducing the number of regulators from thirteen to one.

The committee's report proposed that reform begin with the federal government enacting a Canadian securities act that would provide a comprehensive scheme of capital market regulation for Canada. The new act would be administered by a single Canadian securities commission consisting of nine full-time, regionally representative commissioners. The report also proposed a securities policy ministerial committee made up of the federal Minister of Finance and provincial and territorial ministers responsible for securities regulation. This ministerial committee would provide a forum for policy and administrative input.

The structure would ensure responsiveness to Canada's capital markets and regions by locating the proposed commission's head office in the National Capital Region, and establish "strong, functionally-empowered regional offices" in Vancouver, Calgary, Winnipeg, Toronto, Montreal and Halifax. The federal government would set up capital market advisory committees that would allow issuers and investors (the 'users' of the system) to provide their input.

Provincial reaction to the idea of a common securities commission, however, was mixed. Generally, Canada's four largest provinces—Ontario, Quebec, British Columbia and Alberta—have led efforts at securities law reform. The Ontario Securities Commission (OSC) supported the idea of a single national commission, but Quebec's *Autorité des marchés financiers* opposed it. The Alberta and British Columbia commissions had strong reservations, expressing fears that centralizing securities policy would impose uniform rules that ignore the varying needs of each provincial capital market. Regardless of these differences, most industry stakeholders, regulators and governments canvassed by the Wise Persons' Committee agreed that change is needed. There is considerable support in the financial industry for a common securities commission. Both the Investment Dealers Association of Canada (which later became the IIROC) and the Canadian Bankers Association cited efficiency and a better match between markets and regulators as reasons for adopting a common regulator. The debate revolved around the nature and extent of the change.

Since the release of the committee's report, the federal government has, on a number of occasions, expressed renewed interest in establishing a single common securities regulator. Moreover, Ontario's government appointed a panel which released a report, entitled *Blueprint for a Canadian Securities Commission*, calling for a common securities regulator and legislation, and a single fee structure (Government of Ontario 2006).

Following the release of the Wise Persons' Committee report in 2003, provincial and territorial governments and securities regulators, with the exception of Ontario, have attempted to simplify and standardize their laws and requirements through a 'passport' system, with the objective of eliminating inefficiencies in the current regulatory regime and precluding the need for a common securities regulator. A passport system leaves the existing infrastructure of the thirteen regulators intact, but requires capital market participants to comply with the rules and decisions of a single jurisdiction (the 'primary regulator') regardless of where they undertake capital market activity in Canada. The decisions of the single regulator are recognized across all Canadian jurisdictions except Ontario.

All provinces and territories, with the exception of Ontario, have also signed the 2004 Provincial-Territorial Memorandum of Understanding Regarding Securities Regulation, which commits regulators to implement harmonized, streamlined securities legislation (Provincial-Territorial Securities Initiative 2004). Signatory governments have formed a Council of Ministers of Securities Regulation, consisting of ministers responsible for securities law for all passport provinces and territories, to help promote the passport system. Passport provinces and territories have collaborated primarily through the Canadian Securities Administrators (CSA), an informal body of provincial and territorial regulators that acts as a forum to coordinate and harmonize regulation of Canadian capital markets.

Through the CSA, initiatives have been introduced to begin to reduce duplication and overlap among securities commissions and to minimize compliance costs to market participants. Beginning in 2005, phase one of securities law reform was meant to provide interim legislation that would enable greater harmonization and streamlining of securities regulations across Canada. Phase two, which began to take effect in March 2008, has further harmonized prospectus requirements, continuous disclosure requirements and the registration of investment dealers or advisers. It also allows for a company to obtain a discretionary exemption from its principal regulator and to have that decision apply in all other passport jurisdictions. Phase two is now fully implemented (Canadian Securities Administrators 2008). While Ontario has remained outside the passport system, the CSA has attempted to implement interfaces for market participants that want to gain access to the capital markets in passport jurisdictions and also in Ontario. The OSC has participated in developing those interfaces.

The Wise Persons' Committee report and the threat of a common regulator have done much to motivate provinces and territories to harmonize securities laws. Despite the progress made under the passport system, inefficiencies persist.

A number of market participants wonder whether the passport system can ultimately be effective without the participation of Ontario, usually considered to be Canada's most important securities jurisdiction (Gowling Lafleur Henderson LLP 2008). While the passport system may reduce regulatory burdens, a company wishing to raise money across Canada may still be required to pay fees to thirteen jurisdictions, imposing relatively higher costs on market participants than would be the case with a single regulator (Ibid.). Some market participants believe that the passport system, which requires virtual unanimity among provinces and territories, will be slow to respond to new policy requirements as they arise.

Proponents have argued that the passport system will preserve the current system's strengths, while alleviating excessive regulation by enabling capital market participants to deal with only one regulator (Hyndman 2007). They assert that the system will be responsive, and that policy changes can be adopted in a timely manner by building on the existing regulatory structure.

Supporters of provincial regulation point to the passport system's ability to respond to regional needs. Different provinces and territories want to promote distinct corporate activities, and will encourage policies consistent with the needs in their markets. The Alberta market, for example, focuses on oil and gas issues, while British Columbia is a leading jurisdiction for mining and mineral exploration companies. In contrast, Ontario has generally focused on the needs of larger and more established corporations, often with a view to creating regulations compatible with those in the United States. There is a continuing concern that a common securities regulator might create laws and policies suitable for the dominant Ontario market to the detriment of Canada's regions. Discussions on regional needs can also be seen as evidence of broader policy differences regarding securities laws, particularly between principles-based regulation and rules-based regulation.[2]

Many provinces have an economic stake in securities regulation, and argue against the diminishment of their securities industry-related infrastructure. Issuers that wish to sell shares across Canada usually hire local accountants, lawyers, underwriters and other professionals. Provincial jurisdiction has created regional clusters of securities professionals, primarily in Vancouver, Calgary and Montreal. Some observers believe that a common securities regulator that is based in Ottawa or in Toronto would further consolidate Ontario's dominance of corporate finance in Canada.[3] Employees of provincial securities commissions who work on policy issues also fear that policy jobs will be relocated to the common regulator's Ottawa or Toronto office, leaving only enforcement to the regional offices.

As the passport system has progressed, the debate over a common securities regulator has shifted to the lack of harmonization of enforcement activities across Canada. Enforcement varies from jurisdiction to jurisdiction since the different commissions have different powers and sanctions. While investigations of breaches in securities laws in multiple jurisdictions are often undertaken by a lead regulator, this approach is not always taken, which may cause delays and gaps in enforcement. Some commentators believe that a common securities regulator is the only way of promoting timely enforcement of securities laws, and eliminating overlap and confusion over jurisdiction (Government of Ontario 2006).

However, while these discussions have proceeded at their own pace, global financial markets were undergoing a 'meltdown'. The credit crunch and the turbulence in financial markets in 2008 and 2009 have renewed enthusiasm among many for a common regulator. In February 2008, the federal Minister of Finance announced that the government would appoint an expert panel on securities regulation (Canada 2008b). In the November 2008 Speech from the Throne, the government stated its intention to proceed with a common securities regulator.

In a speech to the Vancouver Board of Trade, the Hon. Tom Hockin, chair of the Expert Panel on Securities Regulation, explained the work that had been undertaken in this way.

> Our work really had its genesis in the 2007 federal budget, where the Government unveiled its capital markets plan, aimed at creating an entrepreneurial advantage for Canada and a more strongly linked national economy with fewer barriers between provinces.

> Following a meeting on June 19th with his provincial and territorial counterparts, the Minister of Finance, Jim Flaherty, announced that the Government of Canada would form a third-party Expert Panel on Securities Regulation to advise ministers.

> And, on February 21st, 2008 we began our work. We started by beefing up our own capacity – bringing in renowned experts to advise us, establishing a legal advisory committee to provide counsel on specific issues, and commissioning research papers on specific topics. We held extensive meetings with more than 100 stakeholders, receiving over 70 written submissions and consulting with experts from the United Kingdom and the United States (Hockin 2009).

At the same time, he reflected on what the panel had heard.

> As a panel, we heard some really very powerful stories about people who had lost their life savings either because

of inappropriate advice or outright fraud. That's troubling enough. But what's worse is that a person's chances of receiving redress varied dramatically depending on where they happened to live. And that's simply not good enough. We need to give Canadians the assurance of better and equal opportunity for redress no matter whether they live in Vancouver or High River or Halifax.

From market participants, we heard concern about 13 different regulators, administering 13 sets of rules and levying 13 sets of fees. From consumers we heard many – far too many – stories about enforcement that seemed weak and their efforts to get their money back that seemed to take forever. Many complained of the difficulty of even starting the complaint process or of trying to navigate through a web of provincial authorities and national organizations.

My friends, if a basic purpose of security regulation is to protect consumers, it's clear that Canada's system isn't doing the job.

From a macroeconomic perspective, we hear concerns about systemic risk – risks that affect the financial markets as a whole. If the current economic crisis has demonstrated anything, it's that systemic risk is no longer just a banking issue – or responsibility – it's increasingly showing up in capital markets as well (Ibid.).

On the matter of the structure that should guide securities regulation in Canada, Hockin said:

Now, on the issue of structure – whether Canada should have a single national securities regulator or continue with something like the current passport system – our conclusion is clear: it's time for a single, national regulator. Here's why.

While steady, incremental progress has been made with the development of the passport system, we heard again and again that it simply doesn't go far enough or fast enough. Not in today's interconnected capital markets. Not when investors can move money around the world so easily. Not when Canada is competing for investment with other developed countries – every one of which does have a national securities regulator (Ibid.).

On the issue of Canada's standing in the global community, he said:

> The lack of a national securities regulator brings other problems for Canada and B.C. It limits Canada's ability to speak with one voice in international fora. And it raises wider concerns about systemic risk because there is no national entity accountable for the stability of our national capital markets.
>
> While the Bank of Canada and the Office of the Superintendent of Financial Institutions are responsible – and accountable – for providing stability to their parts of the financial system, there is no national equivalent responsible for the stability of our capital markets (Ibid.).

In January 2009, the expert panel released draft common securities legislation and a report on the future of securities regulation in Canada, which are likely to form the basis of any move towards a common regulator (Canada 2009). The report's central recommendation was that a single securities regulator should administer a single securities act for Canada. In addition, the report recommended:

- a more principles-based approach to securities regulation in order to reduce compliance costs, strengthen enforcement actions and give Canada a competitive advantage;
- the establishment of an independent panel representing small reporting issuers to streamline reporting requirements and reduce compliance costs for smaller companies;

- an exploration by the common securities regulator of risk-based securities regulation and tailored regulation to the size of public companies and the sector in which they operate;
- the establishment of an independent adjudicative tribunal at the federal level; and
- the establishment of an investor compensation fund to protect investors.

Following the release of the report, one of the holdout provinces, British Columbia, said that it would support the initiative—and it would appear that all provinces and territories with the exceptions of Quebec, Manitoba and Alberta have now endorsed the concept of federal legislation in the area. While the federal government has promised that participation in a single securities regulator will be voluntary, federal legislation may render the passport system redundant. In the event that the federal government enacts legislation with the support of the remaining provinces and territories, it remains to be seen whether Quebec, Manitoba and Alberta would be able to operate outside a single regulator system. The Hon. Tom Hockin, however, said:

> I think it's time to give investors a stronger voice, with better enforcement and quicker response. It's time to create a common securities regulator, applying one set of principles, one set of rules and one set of fees. It's time to cut the costs of compliance and give Canadians a system that is nimble enough to respond to rapidly changing markets (Ibid.).

By proceeding in this fashion, the federal government, in concert with most provinces, is responding to international and domestic economic and financial realities. Furthermore, despite provincial 'responsibility' for securities regulation, it is felt by many that the federal government could very likely assert jurisdiction over capital markets. This course of action was clearly examined by the Wise Persons' Committee in 2003. It consulted with constitutional experts who found that pursuant to its power to legislate in respect to the regulation of trade, the federal government had the constitutional authority to pass comprehensive legislation regulating all capital market activity in Canada.

The Wise Persons' Committee found that provincial-territorial cooperation would facilitate the process but that, in the absence of agreement and invoking the doctrine of federal paramountcy, the federal government could create a single common regulator. This matter has never been tested in the courts. Earlier this year, Quebec said it would ask for a reference from the Quebec Court of Appeal on this matter. On October 16, 2009, the federal government moved to seek the opinion of the Supreme Court of Canada on this very matter. The federal government believes it has the constitutional authority and will submit draft legislation to the Supreme Court by the spring of 2010.

> "The government strongly believes that Parliament has the constitutional authority to enact a comprehensive Federal Securities Act and is initiating preparatory steps in that direction," said Justice Minister Rob Nicholson. "In coming to this view, the government is supported by many of Canada's foremost constitutional experts. However, for greater certainty, we will be asking the Supreme Court for its opinion, which is why we are proceeding with this reference."
>
> Nicholson said the government will submit a draft of the *Federal Securities Act* to the court sometime before the spring of 2010. Lawyers said the Supreme Court could take up to a year after that to provide its opinion (Akin 2009).

Conclusion

These three examples—developments in the administration of tax, the provision of service and securities regulation—cast the role of governments, including the federal government, in an evolutionary light. In these areas of administration, the paradigm for the 'new normal' has been reset. The operating frameworks and mindsets are fundamentally changed. The case is clearly made for a model of federalism that is evolutionary in finding the modern expression of the founding intent that the whole is greater than the sum of its parts. Sterile debates about 'centralization versus decentralization' have lost their currency. Progress is arrived at opportunistically.

We can learn much about the character of the federation by how it responds when it is confronted by crisis. Faced with the most severe economic crisis since the 1930s, leadership has fallen to central governments. The recent crisis has shifted the locus of decision making. Collaboration, coordination and coherence are key elements of the 'new normal', both domestically and internationally. All levels of government needed to work together—and they did. The need for economic stimulus put the incentive on collaboration. Further looming issues such as climate change and the environment will provide the next promising example in a world where citizens are no longer passive consumers of what governments provide. Citizens will demand better and different outcomes. Information will fuel common purpose and collaboration. Collaboration, domestically and internationally, will lead to innovation on a wider scale than previously imagined. This echo system is energized by collaboration. Strong leadership speaking on behalf of all Canadians must provide a common context and values for interpretation and belonging.

If there is one major shortcoming in the role of the national government in the last twenty years, it is that it has failed to articulate that common coherent vision that will power the Canadian journey in the 21st century. The three examples—developed over the same timeframe—speak to a spirit of innovation that is primarily managerial with overtones of a new evolving vision for the federation. The time, however, has long since passed for this restatement. The Canadian federation was not created to be prescriptive. Rather, the original men who came together had faith that future generations, bound by history, tradition, law and a desire to achieve "Peace, Order and Good Government", would continue to evolve the ways for a modern day expression of the journey that is Canada.

Endnotes

[1] A further change was introduced in the December 12, 2003 reorganization of the federal government when Customs and border-related activities of CCRA were transferred to the new Canada Border Services Agency. The balance of CCRA—centered on its tax collection activities—was renamed the Canada Revenue Agency (CRA).

[2] Some jurisdictions, most notably British Columbia, want principles-based regulation, while Ontario has traditionally believed in rules-based regulation, which is the approach taken in the United States. Under principles-based securities laws, regulatory outcomes are enforced through the development of overarching principles governing market conduct, and businesses are given relatively more freedom to develop their own internal compliance systems to achieve those outcomes. Under the rules-based approach, businesses are required to follow a strict body of rules, and liability for wrongdoing is centred on compliance with the rules. Under the principles-based approach, regulators are supposed to work closely with businesses, while the rules-based approach is thought to rely on a more adversarial relationship (Canada 1964: 17).

[3] The Wise Persons Committee's report recommended that a common securities regulator be based in the National Capital Region with regional offices across Canada. Draft legislation released by a federally appointed expert panel on securities regulation left the location of the head office to be determined at a future date (*Draft Securities Act*, Section 20, www.expertpanel.ca/eng/reports/index.php). In its commentary on the draft act, the expert panel stated that the legislation "contemplates that the location of the head office would be specified in the implementing legislation [the expert panel has indicated that the decision as to location will likely reflect negotiations with participating jurisdictions] and that the commission would maintain regional offices and district offices across Canada [the expert panel has recommended the establishment of regional offices in major financial centres and smaller local offices]" (Canada 2009).

References

Akin, David 2009. "Feds seek court ruling on national securities regulator." Canwest News Service, October 16. http://news.globaltv.com/money/Feds+seek+court+ruling+national+securities+regulator/ [consulted March 27, 2010].

Canada 1876. *Constitution Act, 1867*. Section 92 (13). Ottawa.

_____1964. Royal Commission on Banking and Finance (Porter Commission). *Report of the Royal Commission on Banking and Finance, 1964*. Ottawa.

_____1999a (February 17). Senate Committee on National Finance. *Proceedings of the Standing Senate Committee on National Finance, Issue 23—Evidence*. Ottawa.

_____1999b (March 10). Senate Committee on National Finance. *Proceedings of the Standing Senate Committee on National Finance, Issue 27—Evidence*. Ottawa.

_____2003a. Canada Revenue Agency. *CCRA Annual Report to Parliament 2002–2003*. Ottawa.

_____2003b (December 2003). Wise Persons' Committee. *It's Time*. www.wise-averties.ca/reports/WPC%20Final.pdf [consulted March 27, 2010].

_____2005. Department of Finance. *Budget 2005*. Ottawa: Department of Finance, 13. www.fin.gc.ca/budget05/bp/bpc1-eng.asp [accessed April 5, 2010].

_____2006. Government On-Line. *Final Report*. Ottawa. www.gol.ged.gc.ca/rpt2006/rpt/rpt04_e .asp [no longer available, April 5, 2010].

_____2008a. Canada Revenue Agency. "Corporate tax harmonization will save Ontario business up to $190 million a year." News release, May 2. Oshawa, ON. www.cra-arc.gc.ca/nwsnm/rlss/2008/m05/nr080502-eng.html [consulted April 29, 2010].

_____2008b. Department of Finance. "Government of Canada Appoints Expert Panel to Review Securities Regulation." News release, February 21. Ottawa: Department of Finance. www.fin.gc.ca/n08/08-018-eng .asp. [consulted March 27, 2010].

_____2009. Expert Panel on Securities Regulation. *Creating an Advantage in Global Capital Markets—Final Report and Recommendations*, January. www.expertpanel.ca/eng/documents/Expert_Panel_Commentary.pdf. [consulted March 27, 2010].

Canadian Securities Administrators 2008 (January 25). "Securities Passport System Implemented: Regulators Introduce Streamlined Review Policies for Passport Jurisdictions and Ontario." News release. Vancouver.

Citizens First 2003. Institute for Citizen-Centred Service. www.iccs-isac. org/en/cf [accessed April 5, 2010].

Citizens First 2005. Institute for Citizen-Centred Service. www.iccs-isac. org/en/cf [accessed April 5, 2010].

Flumian, Maryantonett 1999. "Redesigning Government around the Citizen: The creation of Nunavut." In *Collaborative Government: Is There a Canadian Way?* eds. Susan Delacourt and Donald G. Lenihan. Toronto: Institute of Public Administration of Canada, 6: 92–98.

Flumian, Maryantonett 2007 (April). "Service Canada As Innovation." *Optimumonline*, 37: 1: 43–50.

Flumian, Maryantonett, Amanda Coe, and Kenneth Kernaghan 2007. "Transforming Service to Canadians: the Service Canada Model." *International Review of Administrative Sciences*, 73: 4: 557–568.

Flumian, Maryantonett 2008 (October). "Citizens as Prosumers: The Next Frontier of Service Innovation." Syndicated research. nGenera Insight™–Government 2.0. Available at Institute On Governance, www.iog.ca/publications .asp.

Government of British Columbia 2009 (July 23). Office of the Premier and Ministry of Finance. "Harmonized Sales Tax to Boost Investment, Job Creation." News release. Victoria, BC.

Government of Ontario 2006 (June 7). Crawford Panel on a Single Canadian Securities Regulator. *Blueprint for a Canadian Securities Commission.* Final paper. www.crawfordpanel.ca/Crawford_Panel_final_paper.pdf [consulted March 27, 2010].

Gowling Lafleur Henderson LLP 2008 (March). "Singing the Passport Blues: Perfect Harmony Eludes Provincial Securities Harmonization Efforts." *MarketCaps@Gowlings*, 4: 6: 14.

Hockin, Hon. Tom 2009 (January 12). Expert Panel on Securities Regulation. Speech to the Vancouver Board of Trade. Vancouver. www.expertpanel. ca/eng/media/speech.2009-01-12.001.html [consulted March 27, 2010].

Hyndman, Doug 2007 (September 19). "Separating Fact from Fiction: Canadian Securities Regulation in the 21st Century." Speech to the Economic Club of Toronto. British Columbia Securities Commission.

Inter-jurisdictional Identity Management and Authentication Task Force 2007 (July). "A Pan-Canadian Strategy for Identity Management and Authentication." Final Report. www.cio/gov.bc.ca/local/cio/idim/documents/idma_executive_summary.pdf [accessed April 29, 2010].

Jordan, Cally 2008. "Political Prisoner: A Securities Regulator For Canada—Again?" Social Science Research Network, http://ssrn.com/abstract=1143516 [consulted March 27, 2010].

Kitching, Andrew 2009. "Securities Regulation: Calls for a Single Regulator." Ottawa: Library of Parliament PRB 08-38E.

Provincial-Territorial Securities Initiative 2004 (September 20). "Securities Reform—Provinces and Territories Agree to Implement Passport System." News release. Calgary.

Public Policy Forum 2004 (October). *Public Policy Forum Assessment of Canada Revenue Agency Relationship with Provinces and Territories: External Perspectives—Summary Report*. Ottawa: Public Policy Forum.

Smart, Michael 2007 (July). *Lessons in Harmony: What Experience in the Atlantic Provinces Shows About the Benefits of a Harmonized Sales Tax*. Toronto: C.D. Howe Institute, Commentary, No. 253.

Tapscott, Don and Anthony D. Williams 2006. *Wikinomics: How Mass Collaboration Changes Everything*. London UK: Portfolio.

Chapter 6

The Great Green North? Canada's Bad Environmental Record and How the Feds Can Fix It

Inger Weibust

Canada's environmental policy is broken and only federal government action can fix it. Since the late 1970s, the federal government has limited its role in Canadian environmental policy, particularly for regulation. The federal government no longer promulgates environmental regulations. It long ago gave up enforcing the few regulations it has, having delegated that responsibility to the provinces with almost no oversight. It has deferred entirely to interprovincial cooperative processes in setting national standards. The federal government has made strenuous efforts to avoid offending the provinces. In environmental policy, it has pursued impotence, choosing *not* to exercise even those powers the Supreme Court has already said it has.

On the whole, the Canadian environmental policy system has emphasized process to the detriment of performance and outcomes. The decentralization and fragmentation of the Canadian system has had the effect of making it less transparent, which in turn has made it difficult for anyone—particularly NGOs and citizens—to get an accurate picture of environmental performance in Canada. Only recently have data become available to show trends across Canada over time. The data which became available in the late 1990s does not paint a pretty picture. On most dimensions of environmental protection Canada performs poorly compared to the United States and European Union policies.

This chapter will make the case for the necessity of stronger federal action by exposing the weaknesses of the existing decentralized and cooperative system, as well as its lackluster performance in protecting Canada's environment. The chapter has six sections. The first section highlights how decentralized environmental standard setting is in Canada and points to the dominant role of the Canadian Council of Ministers of the Environment (CCME). The second section describes the CCME standard-setting process and its consequences for environmental protection in regulating dioxin and ambient air quality. The third section discusses the difficulties Canada has in implementing international environmental treaties, focusing on species at risk and climate change. The fourth section discusses the federal government's constitutional powers for acting on the environment. The fifth section makes recommendations for how the federal government could act to improve environmental quality. The sixth section concludes by arguing that the system which has been in place for over three decades is not up to the task and the federal government needs to assume greater responsibility for this policy.

Canada's system of environmental governance emphasizes:

- provincial autonomy;
- minimal federal involvement in standard setting;
- intergovernmental cooperation, with federal and provincial governments as equals;
- non-binding accords;
- guidelines, not enforceable regulations;
- a lack of transparency about regulations and their enforcement; and
- closed door negotiation between industry and provincial governments.

The Canadian environmental policy making system is very decentralized in comparison to the United States. In the United States, since the early 1970s, the federal government has set minimum national standards. State environmental protection agencies (EPAs) can set more stringent standards and are responsible for implementation. If the state EPAs performance is deemed inadequate, the federal EPA can take over the agency (Lowry 1992).

The Canadian environmental policy-making system is actually more decentralized than that of the European Union (EU). Individual provinces have more discretion than European Union member states and the federal government plays a more circumscribed role than the European Commission. The European Commission has set more EU-wide standards than the Canadian federal government has set national standards for Canada. These European Union standards are binding upon European Union members and must be transposed into member state legislation. Failure to properly implement a European Union directive in national legislation can often result in legal action through the European Court of Justice.

There are no equivalent provisions in Canadian law for the federal government to act on behalf of a province if a province is failing to protect the environment. Canada has few federal environmental laws and the enforcement of those laws and regulations has mostly been delegated to the provinces. The Office of the Auditor-General found that the federal government had exercised very little oversight to determine whether these regulations were, in fact, being enforced appropriately (Canada 1999)

The focal point of Canadian environmental policy making is the Canadian Council of Ministers of the Environment (CCME). The CCME is supposed to secure some of the benefits of centralization—such as economies of scale, consistency, transparency—without centralization. As a governance arrangement, the CCME can be compared to other institutions for intergovernmental cooperation within federations, as well as governance arrangements within international regimes. In general the CCME process is quite similar to international cooperation where decisions are made by consensus and the sovereignty of members is of great importance. As an institution, the CCME does very little to constrain the autonomy of its members.

The CCME process is slow; the standards it produces are few and low.

A comparative study of intergovernmental arrangements (IGAs) between sub-national units within federations found that most Canadian IGAs—for example, on social policy—showed low levels of institutionalization. In particular, Canadian IGAs lacked the key features of the highly institutionalized IGAs found in some other federations such as majority decision making and the capacity/willingness to draft legally binding agreements (Bolleyer 2007). In comparison to other IGAs in Canada, the Canadian IGA on the environment—the CCME—showed a medium level of institutionalization.

The CCME was characterized at this level of institutionalization because, since the 1980s, it has had a large and well resourced secretariat. Given this high level of administrative capacity, the study's author found it striking that this secretariat's role is limited to facilitating information exchange (Ibid.). Based on interviews with CCME officials, Nicole Bolleyer concluded that protection of provincial autonomy was a major priority in CCME activities, not facilitating interprovincial cooperation.

In contrast to the Canadian provinces, the Swiss cantons have actively pursued inter-cantonal cooperation with the explicit purpose of *discouraging* federal encroachment. Cantons were not concerned about the loss of individual autonomy that follows from such a cooperative approach because they saw horizontal cooperation as strengthening the hand of cantons collectively *vis à vis* the Swiss federal government (Bolleyer 2006). Perhaps this pragmatic stance has failed to emerge in Canadian IGAs because federal encroachment seems unlikely.

The CCME can also be compared to governance arrangements found in international regimes. Edward Miles, Arild Underdal and a team of researchers undertook a large scale study of effectiveness in thirteen international environmental regimes. Among their explanatory variables was the level of collaboration. They found that greater regime effectiveness was positively associated with higher levels of collaboration in the regime.

Arild Underdal set out the following typology to characterize varying levels of collaboration:

0. joint deliberation, but no joint action;
1. coordination of action on the basis of tacit understanding;
2. coordination of action on the basis of explicitly formulated standards, but with national action implemented on a unilateral basis and no centralized appraisal of effectiveness;
3. the same as Level 2 but with centralized appraisal of effectiveness;
4. coordinated planning combined with unilateral implementation, including centralized appraisal of effectiveness; and
5. coordination through fully integrated planning and implementation, including centralized appraisal of effectiveness (Underdal 2002).

Applying this typology, the CCME would be an example of Level 2 collaboration. Thus, even as a form of cooperative (not hierarchical) governance, the CCME is relatively weak. Also, extrapolating from the findings of Miles and others with regard to international regimes, we would predict modest effectiveness for the CCME.

A 1995 study of the CCME's effectiveness found little evidence that the CCME has had an independent effect on improving environmental quality (Hillyard 1995). The CCME emphasized harmonious relations among governments. The study found that the CCME voluntarily limited its ambit, ignoring some areas of environmental policy and producing strictly voluntary codes of practice and guidelines in all other areas (Ibid.).

Despite the stated aim of developing national strategies, the CCME's guidelines do not result in consistent policies across Canada. The provinces do not necessarily implement the CCME recommendations that they themselves helped negotiate. Rather, provincial governments pick and choose which guidelines to adopt, if any. Even its deliberate efforts at harmonization have not been oriented towards producing consistent national rules.

In November 1993, the CCME's council of ministers announced that harmonization would be the CCME's top priority over the next few years. Harmonization appeared to mean different things to the provinces and the federal government, however. Federal bureaucrats wanted the harmonization initiative to create minimum national standards through interprovincial cooperation. One of the stated objectives was:

> ...to develop and implement consistent environmental measures in all jurisdictions, including policies, standards, objectives, legislation and regulations (CCME 1998: 1).

However, the final outcome, the 1998 Canada-Wide Accord on Environmental Harmonization (Harmonization Accord), fell well short of this goal.

The provinces and industry argued that the rationale for the accord should be the elimination of duplication and overlap (Ibid.). In 1978, the provincial premiers had identified overlapping federal and provincial environmental regulation as a problem and requested a study. The resulting study on regulation, covering several industries, found no evidence of overlap or duplication (Thompson 1980). Subsequently, a 1997 report to the House of Commons Standing Committee on Environment and Sustainable Development noted that no evidence of duplication or overlap was provided (Canada 1997). The former president of *Conseil patronal de l'environnement du Québec* (Quebec Business Council on the Environment), Michael Cloghesy, cited federal and provincial environmental impact assessment processes as one example of duplication and overlap.

The House of Commons Standing Committee heard testimony from political scientists and environmental groups who argued that the primary goal of the accord was turf protection, not environmental protection. The main objective was keeping the federal government out of provincial areas of jurisdiction—and limiting its jurisdiction. For example,

both the second and fourth objectives of the accord emphasize having only one level of jurisdiction of government
responsible for any particular role and eliminating overlap. Environmental groups and other NGOs were strongly
opposed to the accord; industry representatives were far
more positive about it in their testimony before the committee.

The final harmonization accord resembles an international treaty.[1] Any government may withdraw from the
accord with six months notice. The accord's provisions
are vague and un-constraining. The accord contained sub-
agreements on setting Canada-wide standards (CWS) and
inspection (replaced in 2001 by a sub-agreement on inspec-
tions and enforcement). The 2001 sub-agreement focuses on
clarifying lines of responsibility and the administration of
delegated enforcement, rather than any clear commitment
that the signatories will be held accountable to the public
for enforcing their regulations. It provides for information
sharing with other jurisdictions but does not mandate public transparency.

The province of Quebec never signed the harmonization
accord and hence does not sign on to any Canada-wide standards. Quebec has, however, indicated that it will behave
in a manner 'consistent with the standards' (CCME 2000a).
Given that many of the standards involve action plans
unique to each province, it is not clear what this means. Furthermore, any province may withdraw from a Canada-wide
standard upon three months notice. There is no indication
of what, if any, penalty is incurred by withdrawing *without*
three months notice.

The harmonization accord was accompanied by a work
plan for negotiating CWS in a variety of areas. Compared
with the regulatory frameworks of the United States or the
European Union (which cover hundreds or thousands of
substances for dozens of sectors), the number of pollutants
and industrial sectors addressed is very limited—fewer than
ten pollutants for a handful of sectors. Nonetheless, the process of negotiating Canada-wide standards has been slow.
In 1998, the harmonization accord identified nine CWS to be

negotiated. As of 2009, approximately thirteen Canada-wide standards had been concluded. A few are ambient standards; others are targets for emissions cuts. A few CWS are emissions standards for industrial sources, primarily covering dioxide or mercury emissions from a particular sector.

This section will examine a few of the Canada-wide standards that have been published to date. The resulting CWS are not particularly stringent. There is no requirement that these standards be adopted in provincial legislation nor that they be enforced. Thus, although the standards ostensibly serve the function of 'national standards', they are not equivalent to the binding minimum standards found in US or EU regulations. The focus here will be on two ambient air CWS—ozone and particulate—and also the CWS for dioxin from waste incineration.

The scope of the Canada-wide standards for ambient air quality is quite limited in international comparison. There are two CWS for ambient air quality: ozone and particulate matter (PM2.5). The US *Clean Air Act* set ambient air quality standards in 1970 and these have been revised repeatedly since. As of 2008, the United States has six ambient quality standards: carbon monoxide; lead; nitrogen dioxide; particulate matter (PM10) and (PM2.5); and ozone. The World Health Organization published six ambient standards in 1987, including sulphur dioxide—not found in the US standards. Between 1980 and 1992, the European Union set four ambient air quality standards: sulphur dioxide; nitrogen dioxide; lead; and ozone.

The Canada-wide standards for ozone and PM2.5 are approximately as stringent as the US standards. The Canada-wide standard for ground level ozone, set in 2008, is 65 ppb (averaged over eight hours), which is in line with the recommendations made to the US EPA by a scientific advisory panel in 2007. The CWS is more stringent than the new 75 ppb standard the EPA announced in 2008, which replaced a standard of 84 ppb (Wald 2008). The more stringent standards were recommended because higher levels of ground level ozone are associated with increased death rates among the elderly and those with lung diseases.

However, while the numerical values of the US and Canadian ambient standards are similar, their policy consequences are very different. Ambient standards by themselves are unenforceable; they only have an effect in conjunction with other measures, such as regulations or taxes, that *limit the emissions causing* ambient standards to be exceeded. The OECD's (Organisation for Economic Co-operation and Development) 2004 review of Canada's environmental performance noted that, under the Canada-wide standards, there are no penalties for noncompliance nor any plans for distinguishing between areas that meet ambient standards and those that do not yet meet them (OECD 2004).

In contrast, the United States distinguishes between 'attainment' areas, generally in compliance with ambient standards, and 'non-attainment' areas, which exceed ambient limits. The US EPA has policies tailored to air quality 'non-attainment' counties to improve air quality, as well as policies to prevent 'attainment' counties from slipping into 'non-attainment' status. In particular, non-attainment counties face federal restrictions on new highways and industries (Wald 2008). Thus tightening the ambient standard increased the number of non-attainment counties to 345. The EPA estimated that bringing these counties into attainment would cost US$ 8.8 billion (Ibid.).

As noted earlier, while emissions limits for specific substances number in the hundreds in US and EU regulations, they are rare in Canadian federal or national standards. One such class of substances is dioxins. Under the *Canadian Environmental Protection Act, 1999*, dioxins are designated for 'virtual elimination' from the environment, because they are carcinogenic and highly toxic.

In the 1990s, the burning of waste was identified as a major source of dioxin emissions to the air. Although Canada has made progress in reducing dioxins, these efforts have been hamstrung by the CCME's unanimity requirement. In 2000 the CCME announced plans for a Canada-wide standard for dioxin, which the provinces would be responsible for implementing. That year the CCME announced a numeric emissions limit for municipal solid waste (MSW) incinerators,

80 pg I-TEQ/m^3 (or 0.08 ng) (CCME 2000b). Existing municipal solid waste incinerators were to meet the standard by
2006.

However, one of Canada's largest remaining sources of
dioxin emissions to the air was *explicitly excluded* from this
standard (CCME 2000c). Investments were made to achieve
marginal improvements in dioxin emissions from modern
MSW incinerators. Meanwhile, in the province of Newfoundland and Labrador, as of 1999, forty-five teepee or
conical waste combusters continued to operate. These very
low-technology, low-temperature, combustion plants are
not much more advanced than the open burning of garbage.
They result in very high levels of dioxin emissions for each
unit of garbage burned (CCME 1999).[2] They also contribute
to mercury emissions.

The justification for excluding the teepee burners was
that it was impossible for these burners to meet the Canada-
wide standard.

Although Newfoundland and Labrador is not very pop-
ulous—about 500,000 inhabitants—its teepee burners produced *more* dioxin than the nine large MSW incinerators
in the rest of Canada combined (75 g TEQ/year versus 67
g TEQ/year) (UNEP 1999). This discrepancy became even
greater because 62 of those 67 g TEQ/year came from a single incinerator in Quebec. Once this source in Quebec was
modernized, emissions from *all* Canadian MSW incinerators
fell to 7 g TEQ/year in 1999. From then on emissions from
the teepee burners were *ten times* those of the all the MSW
incinerators in the rest of Canada. As of 1999 Newfoundland teepee burners were thought to account for forty-two
percent of total Canadian dioxin emissions to the air, even
though they burn a tiny fraction of the waste of the modern
MSW incinerators (CCME 1999).

In a 2000 statement addressing the Canada-wide standard, the government of Newfoundland and Labrador
pledged to 'review' the use of conical waste combusters
(CCME 2000c). In the 2004 CCME final agreement, the conical waste combusters were to be phased out by December
31, 2008. As of April 2008, a majority of those forty-five

conical waste incinerators (twenty-five) were still operating (*The Northern Pen* 2008: A14). In October 2008, the municipal affairs minister acknowledged that only three or four of the remaining twenty-five incinerators would be closed by 2009 (Brautigam 2008). Extensions would be granted 'on a case-by-case basis' for the still operating incinerators (CBC 2008).

What effect has the Canada-wide standard setting process had? In international comparison, Canada has been slow to regulate dioxin emissions from MSW incineration (Weibust 2005). For example, the United States and the European Union set binding emissions limits on dioxin from incinerators in 1992 and 2000 respectively. The European Union had set minimum combustion temperatures for new and existing incinerators in 1989, which would be expected to limit dioxin emissions.

From the dioxin example, it is difficult to conclude that the Canada-wide standard caused the government of Newfoundland and Labrador to act on dioxin emissions any sooner than it would have *absent* the Canada-wide standard. Eight years after the CCME dioxin standard had been negotiated (in 2000), this source of dioxin continued to pollute, unabated and unregulated. The outcome of the CWS process was that the dioxin source that was most polluting by weight of garbage, and eventually, by total dioxin emissions, was regulated last. Furthermore, since the 2008 deadline has come and gone, there is no longer any specific end in sight for these highly polluting incinerators.

With the benefit of hindsight, it seems unrealistic to expect small municipalities in Canada's poorest province to solve their waste management problems without external assistance, both technical and financial. Given Newfoundland's rockiness, land-filling waste has never really been an option. Burning garbage seemed relatively 'green' compared to the alternative of throwing the garbage into the sea.

Unfortunately, Canada's decentralized and cooperative system of environmental management is not conducive to generating financial assistance. In general, we don't observe transfers of wealth between sub-units in highly decentralized federal systems. For example, the Canadian system of equalization payments is a federal program. The province and smaller municipalities of Newfoundland and Labrador would have had a good case for demanding financial assistance from the federal government, had the federal government imposed minimum national standards on incineration, rather than relying upon the CCME process.

It might be argued that the regulation of dioxins from incineration is an outlier—that on the whole, Canadian environmental policy adequately protects the environment. A comparison with other countries suggests this view is inaccurate. In the past the bleakness of the picture has been obscured by a lack of information. However, in the last ten years, information has emerged to show that Canada's environmental record is poor in comparison with other OECD countries.

As the details of Canada's environmental quality come into focus we can conclude that our decentralized governance structure leads to several negative outcomes. First, it produces a limited number of regulations, which are not particularly stringent and are not consistently enforced. Canada lags behind other OECD member countries in terms of levels of environmental protection, innovation in policy tools and addressing emerging problems. Furthermore, we have been unable to comply with the international treaties we have signed on to.

While the OECD is tactful to a fault and discourages using its analyses for ranking, several aspects of Canadian environmental protection performed poorly in a comparative context in the OECD's 2004 performance review. Canada performs poorly in terms of environmental quality and also lags behind other OECD countries in using effective and innovative tools for managing the environment. The report noted the very limited use of market mechanisms, such as cap and trade or taxes, in addressing environmental problems, as well as the failure to metre and price water provided to consumers.

For example, the 2004 OECD *Environmental Performance Review* observed that levels of "emissions of traditional air pollutants in Canada remain very high compared with most OECD countries" (OECD 2004: 33). Both per capita and also per unit of GDP (gross domestic product), emissions of traditional air pollutants—for example, SO_x, NO_x and VOCs—in Canada were among the highest in any OECD country. Canada's largest source of SO_x emissions was industry, with almost half of industrial emissions coming from nonferrous mining and smelting (Ibid., 36). Canadian sulphur dioxide emissions per unit of GDP were twice the OECD average and thirty percent higher than US levels (Ibid., 37). The report indicated that Canadian economic activity is relatively pollution intensive compared to the United States and the other OECD countries. This is consistent with earlier findings comparing the pollution intensity of Canadian facilities and corresponding American ones (Olewiler and Dawson 1998).

Furthermore, Canada has done especially poorly in limiting greenhouse gas emissions (GHGs); our per capita emissions are among the highest in the developed world. Oil producing states—particularly those in the Middle East—have the highest per capita emissions. The GHG intensity of Canada's economy is greater than that of other OECD countries. In the 1997 Kyoto Protocol, Canada committed to reducing GHG emissions by six percent (by 2008–2012), over the 1990 baseline. However, between 1990 and 2005, Canada's GHG emissions increased twenty-five percent. As a result, Canadian annual emissions are thirty-three percent greater than Canada's Kyoto target (Canada 2007a). Even though Canada ratified the Kyoto Accord and the United States did not, Canadian GHG emissions since 1990 have grown faster than US emissions.

Although the federal government has clear constitutional authority in negotiating and concluding international agreements, it is powerless to implement some of them, environmental treaties in particular. The question of provincial implementation of and compliance with international treaties arose not long after Canada asserted autonomous treaty making powers. Canada was a signatory to the *Treaty of Versailles* in 1919, portions of which insisted upon the ratification of International Labour Organization (ILO) Conventions as they were created. To meet this requirement, the Canadian federal government passed laws in the 1930s to implement ILO conventions on wages and working hours. The provinces challenged these laws, arguing they were outside federal jurisdiction.

Canada's highest court at the time, the Judicial Committee of the Privy Council in the United Kingdom agreed. In 1937 it found the federal laws to be *ultra vires* federal jurisdiction, in Canada versus Ontario (the Labour Conventions Case [1937]). The justices pointed out that, according to British law, ratified treaties do not have the force of law and depend upon legislative action for their implementation. In a federal system, this means that the federal government must secure the cooperation of provincial legislatures in order to implement international treaties in areas of provincial jurisdiction.

The judges employed the metaphor of a ship's 'watertight compartments' to describe federal-provincial relations:

> ...while the ship of state now sails on larger ventures and into foreign waters, she still retains the watertight compartments which are an essential part of her original structure (Canada v Ontario 1937).

As a result of the decision, the federal Canadian Parliament had the power to implement treaties that had been negotiated while Canada was part of the Empire, *but not* the power to implement international treaties Canada negotiated on her own behalf.

The consequences of this limited power to implement can be clearly seen in the case of the 1987 United Nations Convention on Biodiversity (CBD). Canada was very active in the negotiation of the CBD and, in 1992, was the first industrialized nation to ratify the treaty. The secretariat of the CBD has been located in Montreal since 1996. Despite Canada's prominent role in this treaty it has failed to implement, and hence comply with, it. The most serious failure in implementation, and hence compliance, is the lack of nation-wide legal protection for endangered species. Article 8 (k) of the CBD obliges signatories to use legislation and/or other regulatory provisions to protect species and populations that are threatened, developing or maintaining those provisions as necessary. The CBD does not permit any reservations to the treaty.

Canada is anomalous among the OECD countries in having no national endangered species legislation. The 2002 federal *Species at Risk Act* (SARA) only offers protection for a small percentage of Canadian endangered species: those on federal lands. Several Canadian provinces have no endangered species legislation (Table 6.1). Provincial governments are concerned that legal protection of endangered species and their habitat would limit economic development, particularly natural resource development. In 1998 the World Wildlife Fund gave Canada an 'F' for its record in implementing the convention (Le Prestre and Stoett 2001).

Even those provinces that have endangered species legislation are not necessarily proactive in protecting biological diversity. A puzzling result of shared jurisdiction on this issue is that a provincial government's list of endangered species within its territory does not match, and can be shorter than, the relevant portions of the Canadian national list of endangered species. The final decision to list a species as endangered is made by provincial politicians, not scientists:

> ...[t]he majority of legislation related to protected areas is discretionary. Under provincial/territorial endangered species legislation, where such exists, the decision to list a species as endangered rests at the political level (Gauthier and Wiken 2001: 57).

In contrast, the national list is drawn up by scientific experts in the Committee on the Status of Endangered Wildlife in Canada (COSEWIC). Only Nova Scotia's legislation automatically includes any species listed by COSEWIC that is native to the province in the provincial species-at-risk list (Boardman, Clarke and Beazley 2001).

Ontario's environmental commissioner noted that "the list of endangered species on the Ontario portion of COSEWIC is not consistent with the species 'threatened with

extinction' listed in Ontario's *Endangered Species Act* [ESA]."
The commissioner concluded by asking: "How can the
Ministry of Natural Resources (MNR) justify longstanding
discrepancies between the *ESA* list and the COSEWIC list,
especially since MNR is a member of COSEWIC?" Ontario
listed twenty-four 'threatened' species, whereas the corresponding number listed under COSEWIC was forty-three,
almost twice as many (Government of Ontario 2000).

Table 6.1   Legislation on endangered species in Canada

	Endangered species or species at risk legislation
Government of Canada	*Species at Risk Act*
British Columbia	*Wildlife Act* but no specific endangered species legislation
Alberta	*Wildlife Act* but no specific endangered species legislation
Saskatchewan	Wild Species at Risk regulation
Manitoba	Yes
Ontario	Yes
Quebec	Yes
New Brunswick	Yes
Nova Scotia	Yes
PEI	*Wildlife Conservation Act*
Newfoundland	*Endangered Species Act*
Yukon	*Yukon Wildlife Act* Species at Risk legislation in development since 1998. As of 2009, final draft is in preparation.
Northwest Territories	*Species at Risk* (NWT) *Act*
Nunavut	*Wildlife Act* but no specific endangered species legislation

Sources: Nature Canada, www.cnf.ca/species/report/pdf.html 2004.
Government of the Northwest Territories, www.nwtwildlife.rwed.gov.
nt.ca/legislation/pdfs/Species%20At%20Risk.pdf, 2003 [consulted March
30, 2010].
Government of the Yukon, www.environmentyukon.gov.yk.ca/pdf/pwsar.
php [accessed April 5, 2010].

At the international level the consequences of our internal fragmentation are particularly acute for the climate file. Both the CCME as well as the Council of the Federation, in which the federal government does not participate, have placed climate change on their agendas. Climate change was on the agenda when the Council of the Federation met in the summer 2008. The provincial and territorial governments were unable to reach any substantive agreement (Laghi, Howlett and Séguin 2008). In 2009 the CCME indicated that they would build on the work begun in the Council of the Federation. The CCME website, which is usually full of reports and publications, has virtually no content on climate change. Climate change is listed as a subcategory of air pollution. There is no evidence of any work plan on the file. The only material presented is scientific research on the impacts of climate change.

This should not surprise us. Given the very substantial discrepancies of interests between the provinces, it would be remarkable if they could reach agreement on reducing greenhouse gas emissions. Both Alberta and Saskatchewan contain oils sands, which are the fastest growing source of Canadian greenhouse gas emissions. On the other side of the dispute are Quebec and Manitoba, with comparatively low per capita emissions and a wealth of hydroelectric resources.

The result of this fragmentation and paralysis within Canada is that several governments are looking to the United States for leadership. During the presidency of George W. Bush in the United States, individual provinces were seeking closer ties with regional groups of US governors cooperating on climate change. It is anticipated that, if the United States decides to implement a cap and trade system, one of the two regional schemes may serve as the kernel for a nationwide system: the Western Climate Initiative and the Regional Greenhouse Gas Initiative (RGGI). Thus, there may be advantages to joining an American regional scheme early.

The provinces of British Columbia, Manitoba, Ontario and Quebec are partners in the Western Climate Initiative, which has been spearheaded by the government of California. Saskatchewan has observer status in the initiative. Lest this sound overly amicable, the governments of Alberta and Saskatchewan have registered their strenuous objections to a cap and trade scheme within the Western Climate Initiative. The state of New York spearheaded the RGGI. Ontario, Quebec and New Brunswick have observer status within this group.

Upon the election of President Barack Obama, Prime Minister Harper showed almost unseemly haste in proposing joint Canada–US action on climate change. The assumption is that the Prime Minister hoped to obtain some kind of exemption for oil from the tar sands, in exchange for letting the United States set the terms of continental climate policy.

Globe and Mail columnist Jeffrey Simpson characterized the Prime Minister's initiative thus:

> By offering a pact, the Harper government is acknowledging what has been obvious to any serious observer of Canadian affairs for a very long time - that because Canada cannot get its own act together on climate change, we must ask the Americans to save us from our incoherence. Put another way, with provinces running off in all directions and the Harper government unwilling to even try to craft a national policy, only by joining a U.S. system and imposing that system on ourselves can Canada achieve domestic coherence. It's a sad way for a sovereign country to behave, but such is the nature of Canadian federalism these days, the yawning gaps among the provinces and the disinclination of the national government to be a national government (Simpson 2008: A23).

As we have seen, Simpson's description fits most of Canadian environmental policy, not just climate change.

With the possible exception of internal trade, it is difficult to imagine a policy field where the federal government has been more 'hands off' in exercising its power than in the environment. When we observe that the federal government has vacated a policy field, this decision is often attributed to constitutional factors. Although the environment is an area of shared jurisdiction, lack of constitutional authority is not a sufficient explanation for federal timidity. As with other policy issues, the federal government has powers under the Constitution it has chosen not to use (DiGiacomo 2010). Some of these powers have been used and upheld by Supreme Court decisions. The extent of other powers has not been tested.

Table 2 shows heads of power which are relevant to environmental policy making (Lucas 1987). The federal government's powers pertaining to the environment can be divided into the conceptual and functional powers (Gibson 1973). Conceptual powers include Peace, Order and Good Government (POGG); trade and commerce; taxing and spending; criminal law; and the declaratory power. The declaratory power permits the federal government to declare that particular public works are for the general benefit of Canada or two or more provinces. The functional powers arise from federal responsibilities for: sea coast and inland fisheries; navigation and shipping; canals; harbours; rivers and lake improvements; federal lands; and federal works and undertakings.

The functional federal power over fisheries has formed the primary basis for federal regulations on water pollution. The first *Fisheries Act* was passed in 1868. In the early 1970s a small number of regulations were promulgated under the *Fisheries Act* to limit emissions to water from selected industries: pulp and paper; metal mining; petroleum refining; meat and poultry processing; potato processing; and chloralkali mercury plants. While still theoretically in force, these regulations have not been relevant for some time. The federal government soon delegated enforcement of the regulations to the provinces, with little oversight of that enforcement. Furthermore, these regulations have not been updated since they were introduced almost four decades ago.

The federal government has periodically used its spending power to protect the environment. The 1990 Green Plan of the federal government is perhaps the best known example. The scope of federal spending on environmental protections has been relatively modest compared to other

Table 6.2   Heads of power under the Canadian Constitution pertinent to environmental policy

Heads of legislative power and areas of jurisdiction	Relevant section of Constitution	Whose jurisdiction?	
		Federal	Provincial
Residual powers not enumerated in s. 91 and s. 92		x	
Federal lands		x	
Treaty making	originally s. 132 of *BNA*	x	
"Extra-provincial works and undertakings"	s. 92 (10) (a)	x	
"Works for the general advantage of Canada"	s. 92 (10) (c)	x	
International trade and commerce	s. 91 (2)	x	
Interprovincial trade and commerce	s. 91 (3)	x	
Spending power		x	
Residual power to make laws for "peace, order and good government"	s. 91 (29)	x	
Sea coast and inland fisheries	s. 91 (12)	x	
Agriculture		x	x
Direct taxation	s. 92 (2) s. 91 (3)	x	x
Indirect taxation	s. 91 (3)	x	
Indirect taxation of natural resources			x
Statistics		x	
Navigation and shipping	s. 91 (10)	x	
Criminal law (including protection of public health)	s. 91 (27)	x	
Administration of civil and criminal justice	s. 92 (15)		x

Nuclear energy		x	
Local works and undertakings	s. 92 (10)		x
Municipal government			x
All matters of a merely local or private nature	s. 92 (16)		x
Property and civil rights	s. 92 (13)		x
Forestry	s. 92 (5)		x
Mining	s. 109		x

Source: Alastair R. Lucas, 1987. *Natural Resource and Environmental Management: A Jurisdictional Primer*, page 33.

countries, particularly in the area of wastewater treatment. Prior to 2000 the federal government had only one program to finance sewage treatment plant construction. Between 1961 and 1972, a federal government agency made over two thousand loans (totalling CA\$ 627.6 million) for sewage treatment plant construction. The US federal government, in contrast, spent billions of dollars in grants for sewage treatment plant construction, beginning during the Great Depression and continuing through the 1990s. In order to help newly acceded European Union members implement the 1991 Urban Wastewater Treatment Directive, the European Union projected spending of at least € 500 million per annum for environmental investments between 2000–2006 (European Union 2001).

The Canadian trend was partially reversed in 2000, when the Canadian federal government announced the Infrastructure Canada program. Between 2000 and 2007 the federal government spent CA\$ 960 million on wastewater treatment infrastructure, which was matched by provincial and municipal spending for a total of CA\$ 2.88 billion resulting from the new federal initiative (CCME 2007). Given the scale of the problem, however, these were relatively modest sums. For example, the city of Ottawa, which already has a sewage treatment facility, budgeted CA\$ 200 million for water and wastewater infrastructure construction costs between 2003 and 2021 (City of Ottawa 2007). The 2004 OECD performance review estimated that if current trends continued it would take another twenty years for Canada to build the necessary wastewater infrastructure, noting that it would be a challenge to make the necessary investments while also improving drinking water infrastructure (OECD 2004).

More recently, the Building Canada Fund has identified wastewater treatment and the provision of clean drinking water as priority infrastructure projects. One of the goals of the infrastructure funding for clean drinking water is to increase the number of households with access to water that meets or exceeds the *Guidelines for Canadian Drinking Water Quality*. There are a broad range of other projects, including tourism and highway construction that are also eligible for these funds, however. Thus, while the federal government has exercised its spending power for the environment, it could do much more to fund green infrastructure spending.

While the federal government has a large number of enumerated powers, it also has residual powers under the Peace, Order and Good Government clause (POGG). As a result of Ontario versus Canada and the Distillers and Brewers' Association of Ontario (the Local Prohibition case) [1896], the federal government's ability under POGG to override provincial governments in local matters is subject to a test of 'national concern'.[3] In a subsequent decision Canada v. Alberta (the Board of Commerce case) [1922], the Judicial Committee ruled that POGG was an emergency power, an interpretation which held sway until the 1970s (DiGiacomo 2010).

This very narrow interpretation of POGG came to an end in 1988. That year, in R. v Crown Zellerbach [1988], the Supreme Court of Canada upheld the federal government's *Coastal Dumping Act*. In a four to three decision, the Court ruled that the federal government had the authority to regulate the dumping of wastes into coastal waters on the basis of POGG. The Court found that coastal water pollution met the criteria of 'national concern', subject to several specific tests. Several scholars predicted that this decision would open the door to dramatic centralization and unilateral federal action on environmental policy (DiGiacomo

2010). However, two decades hence, these predictions have not come to pass.

The Supreme Court has also found that the federal government has other powers in legislating on the environment. In 1997 the Supreme Court determined that the federal government could use its criminal law power in environmental protection. In R. v Hydro-Québec [1997], the court upheld the federal government's authority to regulate toxic substances under *Canadian Environmental Protection Act* (CEPA), on the basis of the criminal law power. In this decision Justice Gerald La Forest, who was among the three dissenting judges in the Crown Zellerbach decision, strongly endorsed the federal government's authority to use criminal sanctions in addressing environmental problems. According to constitutional law expert Peter Hogg, R. v Hydro-Québec "emphatically reinforced" the trend to use the criminal law power as the basis for extensive regulation, which "goes well beyond the prohibiting and penalizing of harmful conduct." Hogg went on to argue that the criminal law power could form the basis for federal action on greenhouse gas emissions (Hogg 2008).

Lastly, as noted above, the federal government's treaty power has been interpreted by the courts in such a way as to severely constrain it. This appears to be one instance where the federal government's scope for action actually is limited by the Constitution, or at least the reigning interpretation of it. Other federal systems have encountered this problem. In Australia, the High Court expanded the Commonwealth's power to implement treaties at the expense of state and territorial power in matters such as economic development.

The expansion of Australian Commonwealth power in order to ensure compliance with international treaties was derived from "an expansive interpretation to…the external affairs power" by Australia's High Court (Lynch and Galligan 1996: 210). One centralist judge argued that, without a greater federal external affairs power, "Australia would be an international cripple unable to participate fully in the emerging world order" (Ravenhill 1990: 89). To support their argument, the centralists noted Australia's poor record in ratifying treaties where the consent of the states had been deemed necessary. By 1982, Australia had ratified only forty-three of one hundred fifty-eight ILO treaties (Ibid., 90). By 2008, Canada had ratified thirty of the ILO's one hundred eighty-five conventions. Australia's expanded external affairs power has been used to implement international environmental agreements, sometimes in politically unpopular ways (Marlin 1996). For Canada to move in a similar direction, the decades old Labour Conventions case would have to be repudiated.

Let us take stock for a moment. The existing Canadian system produces limited measures on a limited number of pollutants and, compared to other OECD countries, has performed poorly in protecting environmental quality in Canada. The measures in place are often guidelines, not legally enforceable rules. Even where measures are regulations little is known about their actual enforcement. The federal government almost certainly has more powers to act on the environment than it has been willing to use.

What then is to be done? At a minimum, there is a need for a fresh perspective. The existing cooperative system, which has been in place for over three decades now, is not delivering environmental protection. This doesn't reflect a defect of Canadian character—there is no evidence that any jurisdiction has been able to adequately protect its environment with a wholly decentralized or cooperative approach (Weibust 2009).

What should the federal government do? The strongest response would be for the federal government to set minimum national standards or minimum national taxes on pollutants. This would be analogous to what the US federal government has done since the 1970s and what the European Commission does for the European Union member states. In the European Union and the United States, the resulting minimum standards have been substantially above the lowest common denominator of existing state or national standards.

The Canadian federal government has, in the past, shown very little stomach for setting minimum national environmental standards (Harrison 1996). In periods of perceived environmental crisis, such as the early 1970s or early 1990s, the federal government has taken action, by setting national standards for some industries, such as the standards under the federal *Fisheries Act*. After 1979, the federal government retreated from standard setting and attempted (unsuccessfully) to get the provinces to cooperate in creating binding minimum national standards.

Minimum standards create a floor; provinces can set more stringent standards but they cannot set lower standards. This solves the problem of standards that remain 'stuck at the bottom' because different jurisdictions fear comparative disadvantage from raising their standards. In an analysis of US state level environmental standards, William Lowry found that states were more likely to be ambitious in setting standards if there was a federal minimum standard (Lowry 1992). National floor standards would also make the Canadian environmental regulatory system far more transparent than it is at present.

There are several possible objections to this approach. Some would argue that the federal government might do a worse job than the provinces. If, however, the standards establish floors, they cannot be worse than provincial standards already in place. For protection to be reduced under minimum national standards two conditions would have to apply. First, the minimum federal standards would have to be weaker than at least some of the existing provincial standards. Second, for protection to deteriorate provinces with higher standards would have to relax their standards to the level of the new federal standard.

This would be very unlikely to occur. Since provinces currently have complete discretion in their standard setting, there is no reason why they should make their standards less stringent if there is a federal floor standard. If federal standards were set too low they would be ineffective but this could not, by itself, cause a deterioration of environmental protection.

The opposite objection would be that the federal government might set standards that are too stringent. There is little empirical evidence to support concerns on this point. On the rare occasions when the Canadian government has stepped into the breach, as with regulations under the *Fisheries Act*, its standards, while more stringent than provincial ones, were not particularly ambitious. For example, the standards were attainable with existing technology.

Another objection would be that minimum standards focused on reducing end-of-pipe emissions are an outdated approach, which should be replaced by a focus on pollution prevention. In a similar vein, one might object that minimum standards would be a drag on flexibility and innovation. However, if maximum discretion gave rise to maximum innovation, we should observe significant innovation in provincial environmental policy. The provinces have largely had *carte blanche* in determining their environmental policies for decades.

Kathryn Harrison and Barry Rabe, who have studied Canadian environmental regulations, found that the approaches taken by the provinces have not been effective or innovative. Harrison found that environmental regulators in Canada have been flexible to a fault (Harrison 1995). In Canada, 'flexible' has meant 'toothless'. She notes that those countries that have successfully combined flexibility with improvements in environmental quality have retained a credible threat of applying more stringent regulation.

Barry Rabe compared state and provincial environmental policies, looking for pollution prevention and other signs of policy innovation (Rabe 1998). He found that provincial policies were conspicuously lacking in innovation, compared to the states he studied. Provincial standards were very traditional in nature, remaining stuck in the 1960s. Regulations were 'end-of-pipe' standards, with separate standards for air and water. Rabe found that provincial governments did not use pollution prevention economic instruments nor integrated pollution permitting, which holistically cover emissions to air, water and soil.

From the perspective of improving environmental protection, there are no compelling arguments against minimum national standards. They remain rare in Canada, however, because of the provincial hostility to such measures and the federal government's reluctance to pick a fight with the provinces over the environment. In the past, this reluctance has only been overcome if the public perceives the environment to be in crisis (Harrison 1996).

The federal government could also pick its battles, by focusing on issues most closely related to public health and safety, such as drinking water quality. It would surprise many Canadians to know that Canada has no national standards for drinking water quality. Since 1968 there have been national guidelines developed by the CCME, however, there is no requirement that the guidelines be incorporated into provincial legislation or that they be enforced.

Despite the extensive involvement of all provinces in this standard setting process, only a minority of provinces have adopted the Canadian guidelines in legally binding provincial standards. In 1972 Alberta became the first to adopt, incorporating the guidelines into binding regulations. Quebec adopted its own binding standards in 1984. In 2002 the Ontario government replaced its non-binding provincial drinking water objectives with binding standards for drinking water quality. This change was made after polluted drinking water in Walkerton, Ontario sickened 2,300 people and killed seven (Hill and Harrison 2006).

As of 2006, thirty-eight years after the first guidelines were published, only Nova Scotia, Ontario, Quebec and Alberta had adopted most or all of the voluntary guidelines into their provincial standards (Hill et al. 2007). There was significant variation across the other jurisdictions, even though the cooperative standard setting process had been in place for twenty years. Even where binding standards have been put in place, it is difficult to reach any conclusions about enforcement because of a lack of data.

What role could the federal government take on, assuming its traditional reluctance remains? It could focus on information provision and 'carrots', particularly in improving water and sanitation infrastructure. It has a unique role to play in collecting and disseminating information about environmental quality in Canada, and particularly information about environmental regulation and enforcement in Canada. There are economies of scale in collecting and disseminating this kind of information. Even if the provinces were willing to provide the information, there is no guarantee it would be presented in a comparable format to facilitate comparison and benchmarking.

In its periodic reviews of environmental policy, the OECD found that Canadian environmental policy suffered serious gaps in information about environmental quality. There are very few indicators which provide a national snapshot and even fewer which provide information on patterns over time. It is not possible to determine whether policies are working in the absence of trend data.

Species at risk are one example where it would be very useful for the federal government to provide a snapshot of conditions across Canada. There is a national list of species at risk, identified by province. This list is created by scientists in COSEWIC solely on the basis of scientific information and traditional knowledge, not economic factors. Species at risk only receive protection if the provincial governments—and sometimes, the federal government—identify species which are subject to protection. Thus individual provinces maintain their own lists of species subject to protection within their province.

These provincial lists determine which species are covered by provincial initiatives. It is very difficult to know how many of the species on the COSEWIC list are also found on provincial lists. In 2000, the Ontario environment commissioner compared the two lists for Ontario and questioned the persistent discrepancy between the two. Why did the provincial list not include all the species on the COSEWIC list which were considered at risk in Ontario?

In general, there is a serious lack of information necessary for benchmarking and measuring changes in performance. It is very difficult to determine what regulations apply to different facilities across Canada. The pulp sector is probably the only one where data on permits for different facilities has been collected. The CCME has shown no inclination to collect or circulate information which would enable interprovincial or international comparisons. The information gap is particularly acute with regard to regulatory enforcement. There is little information available which the public or interested groups could use to hold provincial regulators accountable (Harrison 1995).

There is some evidence to support government initiatives based on mandatory information disclosure. The federal government's most extensive program of this type is the NPRI (National Pollutant Release Inventory), which required firms to disclose toxic emissions. Since 1997 this database has made it possible, for the first time, to quantify toxic emissions to air, water and soil, by industry. It thus became possible to determine the extent of pollution by factory, as well as permitting the tracking of trends in pollution. In general, per facility emissions have fallen where PRTRs (pollutant release and transfer register) have been introduced. There is debate as to whether these reductions have been caused by PRTRs or whether they simply reflect reductions in emissions caused by more traditional regulatory means (Harrison and Antweiler 2003). In any case, emissions from US facilities were lower than Canadian facilities and emissions by source in the United States have fallen more sharply than in Canada (Olewiler and Dawson 1998).

The federal government could also follow the example of the United States, the European Union and Switzerland by providing substantial funding for wastewater treatment infrastructure, in combination with minimum standards for sewage treatment. Although Canada has been making progress in this area there are still major Canadian cities, such as Victoria, which have no sewage treatment. Many cites in Canada would fail to meet the minimum standards for sewage treatment which apply in the United States and the European Union. In the United States, the *Federal Water Pollution Control Act* (Clean Water Act) of 1972 required that all existing sewage treatment plants provide a minimum of secondary treatment by 1977. The European Union's Urban Waste Water Treatment Directive (91/271/EEC), which dates from 1991, requires that all cities with greater than ten thousand people subject all their sewage to secondary treatment.

Canada is unusual in having no minimum national standards for sewage treatment. In September 2007, the federal Minister of the Environment John Baird announced that the federal government would propose regulations in 2008 to establish minimum national standards for sewage treatment (Canada 2007b). He stated that these standards, which would apply to 4,600 wastewater collection systems across Canada, would bring Canadian standards in line with those of the European Union. A consultation exercise on federal standards was concluded in January 2008.

On February 19, 2009 the CCME announced its Canada-wide Strategy for the Management of Municipal Wastewater Effluent, which had been in development for five years. This effort emerged from a CCME working group created in 1995 to address municipal wastewater treatment. The Canada-wide strategy set out national performance standards for three water quality parameters which will apply to approximately 3,500 facilities across Canada. The CCME indicates that these national standards are equivalent to secondary sewage treatment, the minimum standard of treatment required by the United States and the European Union—although the 1991 EU directive covers more than three parameters.

As of February 2009, the federal government had not promulgated regulations in this area. It is not clear what impact the CCME strategy will have on the proposed federal regulations; it might pre-empt them. The CCME backgrounder states that the federal government will negotiate bilateral agreements with the provinces and territories (CCME 2009).

It is also not clear how compliance with these national performance standards will be ensured. The backgrounder to the strategy states: "It is expected that jurisdictions will incorporate the key elements of the Strategy into their respective regulatory frameworks" (Ibid.). That sounds rather weak for a measure that is intended to set a national minimum for performance. Furthermore, although the CCME document sets out timelines for compliance with the standards—ten years for high risk facilities, up to thirty years for low risk facilities—there is no mention of any consequences for failure to comply. The thirty year timeline (2039) would bring Canadian facilities into compliance over sixty years after the 1977 deadline the US EPA set to implement its 1972 standard of secondary wastewater treatment. Given the spotty record of the implementation of existing CCME guidelines, it is difficult to see why these standards should have a different fate without any concrete incentives for compliance.

The recent example of wastewater treatment appears to reprise past patterns of federal behaviour. In a period of heightened environmental consciousness, the federal government proposed minimum national standards. However, having let the interprovincial cooperative process run its course, the federal government appears likely to retreat once again, conceding the field to the provinces. As in the past, the CCME process has been slow and the resulting standards are low. Given the poor past record of this approach, it seems unlikely that it will bring Canadian environmental quality standards into line with those in the United States and the European Union. This is particularly true since those jurisdictions are moving forward with higher standards for treatment and addressing a broader range of pollutants.

The reluctance of the federal government to set minimum national standards does not establish that such measures would be ineffective. In the United States and the European Union, mandatory minimum standards have been important in producing substantial improvements in environmental quality, often quite quickly. In contrast, the Canadian approach, with its overwhelming focus on the executive federalism process rather than environmental outcomes, has little to recommend it as a strategy for responsive and effective environmental protection.

The system is beset by problems which only the federal government can solve. The strongest response would be for the federal government to set floor standards for emissions or minimum taxes for pollutants. Failing that, the federal government could play a crucial role in mandating information disclosure about environmental permits and their enforcement. This relatively less intrusive approach would strengthen the ability of civil society to monitor environmental outcomes and could compensate for Canadian governments' reluctance to take action.

Endnotes

1   It is actually probably weaker because, unlike the accord, international treaties are binding, in the sense that signatories are obliged to comply—even if noncompliance goes unpunished.
2   Whereas modern MSW incinerators operate at temperatures of at least 800°C (1470°F), teepee burners operate at far lower temperatures. In 2006, a man was rescued after spending about five minutes in an operating teepee burner that he had fallen into: "I wasn't going to burn to death. I was going to cook" (Brautigam 2008).
3   This decision was made by the Judicial Committee of the Privy Council (UK), which was Canada's highest court at the time.

References

Boardman, Robert, Amelia Clarke and Karen Beazley 2001. "The prospects for Canada's species at risk." In *Politics of the Wild: Canada and Endangered Species*, eds. Karen Beazley and Robert Boardman. Don Mills, ON: Oxford University Press, 217–234.

Bolleyer, Nicole 2006. "The Internal Life of Sub-national Governments, Interdepartmental Spill-over and the Organizational Convergence of Intergovernmental Relations." Paper presented at the DVPW Kongress. Münster Germany, September 26.

Bolleyer, Nicole 2007. *Internal Government Dynamics and the Nature of Intergovernmental Relations*. Ph. D. dissertation. Florence, Italy: European University Institute, 231–232.

Brautigam, Tara 2008 (October 26). "NL Struggles to Close 'Industrial Age' Incinerators." http://cnews.canoe.ca/CNEWS/Politics/2008/10/26/7211476-cp.html [consulted March 30, 2010].

Canada 1997. House of Commons Standing Committee on Environment and Sustainable Development. *Harmonization and Environmental Protection: An Analysis of the Harmonization Initiative of the Canadian Council of Ministers of the Environment*. Ottawa: House of Commons. http://cmte.

parl.gc.ca/cmte/CommitteePublication.aspx?SourceId=36163 [consulted March 30, 2010].

_____1999. Office of the Auditor-General of Canada. "Chapter 5. Streamlining Environmental Protection through Federal–Provincial Agreements: Are They Working?" Report of the Commissioner of the Environment and Sustainable Development. www.oag-bvg.gc.ca/internet/English/parl_cesd_199905_e_1141.html [consulted March 30, 2010].

_____2007a. Environment Canada. *Canadian Environmental Sustainability Indicators: Highlights.* Catalogue no. 16-252-XIE, 3.

_____2007b (September 24). Environment Canada "Government of Canada Takes Action to Combat Dumping of Raw Sewage and Upgrade Sewage Treatment." News release. www.ec.gc.ca/default. asp?lang=En&n=714D9AAE-1&news=FA83843D-2731-4CA1-8750-C75F380B572A [consulted March 30, 2010].

Canada v Alberta (Board of Commerce Case) A. C. 283 (1922).

Canada v Ontario (Labour Conventions Case) A. C. 326 (1937).

Canadian Council of Ministers of the Environment (CCME) 1994. Annual Report. Winnipeg, MB: CCME, 93–94.

_____1998. "A Canada–Wide Accord on Environmental Harmonization." www.ccme.ca/assets/pdf/accord_harmonization_e.pdf [consulted March 30, 2010].

_____1999. "Socio–Economic Analysis for Dioxins and Furans: Summary by Priority Sector." Winnipeg, MB: CCME.

_____2000a. "Environment Ministers Meet at Kananaskis." www. ccme.ca/about/communiques/2000.html?item=4 [consulted March 30, 2010].

_____2000b (June 6). "Canada-wide Standards for Dioxins and Furans." Winnipeg, MB: CCME.

_____2000c (June 6). "Initial Set of Actions. Dioxins and Furans Canada-wide Standards. Emissions from Incinerators and Coastal Pulp and Paper Boilers." Winnipeg, MB: CCME.

_____2007. *Canada-wide Strategy for the Management of Municipal Wastewater Effluent: DRAFT.* Winnipeg, MB: CCME. www.ccme.ca/assets/pdf/mwwe_cda_wide_strategy_consultation_e.pdf [consulted March 30, 2010].

_____2009. "Backgrounder: Canada-wide Strategy for the Management of Municipal Wastewater Effluent." www.ccme.ca/assets/pdf/mwwe_backgrounder_feb_17_final_en.pdf [consulted March 30, 2010].

CBC 2008 (October 15). "Garbage Incinerators to Get Extension, Minister Says".). www.cbc.ca/canada/newfoundland-labrador/story/2008/10/15/teepee-extensions.html [consulted March 30, 2010].

City of Ottawa 2007. "Ottawa 20/20: Infrastructure Masterplan." www. ottawa.ca/city_services/planningzoning/2020/imp/annex1_en.shtml [consulted March 30, 2010].

DiGiacomo, Gordon 2010. *The Impact of a Constitutional Abeyance on the Assertion of Federal Power.* Ph. D. dissertation. Ottawa: Carleton University.

European Union 2001. European Commission. DG Environment. "The Challenge of Environmental Financing in the Candidate Countries." COM (2001) 304.

Gauthier, David and Ed Wiken 2001. "Avoiding the Endangerment of Species: The Importance of Habitats and Ecosystems." In *Politics of the Wild: Canada and Endangered Species,* eds. Karen Beazley and Robert Boardman. Don Mills, ON: Oxford University Press, 49–74.

Gibson, Dale 1973. "Constitutional Jurisdiction over Environmental Management in Canada." *University of Toronto Law Journal,* 23: 1: 54–87.

Government of Ontario 2000. Environmental Commission of Ontario. *Changing Perspectives: Annual Report 1999-2000.* www.eco.on.ca/english/publicat/ar1999.pdf [consulted March 30, 2010]

Government of the Northwest Territories 2009 (January). www.nwtwildlife.rwed.gov.nt.ca/legislation/pdfs/Species%20At%20Risk.pdf [consulted March 30, 2010].

Government of the Yukon 2009 (January). www.environmentyukon.gov. yk.ca/speciesatrisk.php [consulted March 30, 2010].

Harrison, Kathryn 1995. "Is Co-operation the Answer? Canadian Environmental Enforcement in Comparative Context." *Journal of Policy Analysis and Management,* 14: 2, 221–44.

Harrison, Kathryn 1996. *Passing the Buck: Federalism and Canadian Environmental Policy.* Vancouver, BC: University of British Columbia Press.

Harrison, Kathryn and Werner Antweiler 2003. "Incentives for Pollution Abatement: Regulation, Regulatory Threats and Non-Governmental Pressures." *Journal of Policy Analysis and Management,* 22: 3: 361–382.

Hill, Carey and Kathryn Harrison 2006. "Intergovernmental Regulation and Municipal Drinking Water." In *Rules, Rules, Rules, Rules: Multilevel Regulatory Governance,* eds. G. Bruce Doern and Robert Johnson. Toronto: University of Toronto Press, 234.

Hill, Carey et al. 2007. "A Survey of Water Governance Legislation and Policies in the Provinces and Territories." In *Eau Canada: The Future of Canada's Water,* ed. Karen Bakker. Vancouver, BC: University of British Columbia Press, 369–392.

Hillyard, Dwight S. 1995. "From Tomorrow to Today: The Canadian Council of Ministers of the Environment and Canadian Environmental Policy." Master's thesis. Windsor, ON: University of Windsor.

Hogg, Peter W. 2008 (August). "A Question of Parliamentary Power: Criminal Law and the Control of Greenhouse Gas Emissions." *C.D. Howe Institute Backgrounder*. Toronto: C. D. Howe Institute, 114.

Laghi, Brian, Karen Howlett and Rhéal Séguin 2008 (July 15). "Premiers See No Hope for Deal on Green Plan." *Globe and Mail*. www.theglobeandmail.com/servlet/story/RTGAM.20080715.wpreems16/BNStory/National/home [consulted March 30, 2010].

Le Prestre, Philippe and Peter J. Stoett 2001. "International Initiatives, Commitments and Disappointments: Canada, CITES and the CBD." In *Politics of the Wild: Canada and Endangered Species*, eds. Karen Beazley and Robert Boardman. Don Mills, ON: Oxford University Press, 190–216.

Lowry, William R. 1992. *The Dimensions of Federalism: State Governments and Pollution Control Policies*. Durham, NC: Duke University Press.

Lucas, Alastair R. 1987. "Natural Resources and Environmental Management: A Jurisdictional Primer." In *Environmental Protection and the Canadian Constitution: Proceedings of the Canadian Symposium on Jurisdiction and Responsibility for the Environment*, ed. Donna Tingley. Edmonton AB: Environmental Law Center, 33.

Lynch, Georgina and Brian Galligan 1996. "Environmental Policymaking in Australia: The Role of the Courts." In *Federalism and the Environment: Environmental policymaking in Australia, Canada and the United States*, eds. Kenneth M. Holland, F. L. Morton and Brian Galligan. Westport CT: Greenwood Press, 205–224.

Marlin, Richard 1996. "The External Affairs Power and Environmental Protection in Australia." *Federal Law Review*, 24: 71–92.

OECD 2004 (Organisation for Economic Co-operation and Development). *Environmental Performance Reviews: Canada*. Paris: OECD.

Olewiler, Nancy and K. Dawson 1998. "Analysis of National Pollution Release Inventory Data On Toxic Emissions by Industry." Working paper 97–16, prepared for the Technical Committee on Business Taxation. Ottawa: Government of Canada, Department of Finance.

Ontario v Canada and the Distillers and Brewers' Association of Ontario (Local Prohibition Case) A. C. 348 (1896).

R. v Crown Zellerbach 1 S.C.R. 401 (1988).

R. v Hydro-Québec 3 S.C.R. 213 (1997).

Rabe, Barry G. 1998. "Federalism and Entrepreneurship: Explaining American and Canadian Innovation in Pollution Prevention and Regulatory Integration." *Policy Studies Journal*, 27: 2: 288–306.

Ravenhill, John 1990. "Australia." In *Federalism and International Relations: The Role of Sub-national Units*, eds. Hans J. Michelmann and Panayotis Soldatos. Oxford, UK: Clarendon Press, 77–123.

Simpson, Jeffrey. 2008 (November 12). "Little New for Obama in Ottawa's Energy 'Offer'." *Globe and Mail*, A23.

The Northern Pen 2008 (May 5). "NLEIA approves of planned incinerator shutdown". St. Anthony, NL, 29: 19: A14.

Thompson, Andrew R. 1980. *Environmental Regulation in Canada: An Assessment of the Regulatory Process*. Vancouver: Westwater Research Center, University of British Columbia.

Underdal, Arild 2002. "One Question, Two Answers." In *Environmental Regime Effectiveness*, eds. Edward L. Miles et al. Cambridge MA: MIT Press, 3–46.

UNEP 1999. United Nations Environment Programme. "Dioxin and Furan Inventories." Geneva: UNEP Chemicals, 66.

Wald, Matthew L. 2008 (March 13). "Environmental Agency Tightens Smog Standards." *New York Times*. www.nytimes.com/2008/03/13/Washington/13enviro.html?hp [consulted March 30, 2010].

Weibust, Inger 2005. "A (Slow) Burning Issue: Convergence in National Regulation of Dioxins from Incineration." *Policy and Society*, 24: 2: 46–73.

Weibust, Inger 2009. *Green Leviathans*. Aldershot, UK: Ashgate Publishing.

The Federal Government Is Not Simply One Government Among Many

Gordon DiGiacomo

The chapters in this book have tried to show how and why the federal government has transformed itself from a government of the people to a government of the provinces. On internal trade, child care, the environment and several other policy areas not discussed in this book, the federal government has shown a degree of submissiveness that must leave many Canadian citizens totally perplexed about what is happening to their national government. Unfortunately, both of the major political parties appear to have embraced this approach. The collaborative federalism of former Prime Minister Jean Chrétien and the open federalism of current Prime Minister Stephen Harper are indistinguishable and converged around the same idea—greater provincialization for Canada. Lurking in the background is the wish of virtually every member of the Quebec intellectual establishment—constitutionally entrenched, open-ended asymmetrical federalism. Further, there is no indication that the transformation of Canadian federalism has run its course.

The analysis of the Agreement on Internal Trade presented by Gordon DiGiacomo in the first chapter concludes that its ineffectiveness has to do with the collaborative federalism model that was used to bring it about. This type of decision making, "where the federal government plays the role of equal partner as opposed to guardian and protector of the national interest, is problematic because the provincial participants have little incentive to make anything other than painless, inconsequential demands on each other". Without a government actor—that is, the federal government—to insist that the provinces deal seriously with the issue, the negotiators arrived at an agreement that has almost no defenders.

In chapter two, Michael Behiels's careful analysis of asymmetrical federalism leads him to conclude that, while a limited number of informal asymmetrical legislative and administrative arrangements are not likely to disrupt the stability of federations, formal, constitutionally entrenched asymmetries can "threaten the long-term viability of the federation." He writes: "Major conflicts invariably emerge in federations when specific political elites, backed by sizeable constituencies, demand constitutional recognition of asymmetry entailing additional powers for well-defined national communities with sub-states of their own". He, therefore, calls upon citizens and their leaders to ensure that formal and informal asymmetries are counterbalanced by informal and formal symmetries.

In the comprehensive analysis of open federalism in chapter three, the author Brooke Jeffrey observes that the Harper government's apparent determination to decentralize power within the Canadian federation is at odds with the direction taken by virtually every other western democracy in light of current social issues and concerns. She is impelled to conclude further that the likelihood of developing new social architecture, or even of maintaining current programs, is slim. This suggests that open federalism would inevitably "lead to a patchwork set of programs providing wildly unequal services". She agrees with *National Post* columnist Andrew Coyne who said that such a development would lead to the "ebbing attachment" of citizens to the idea of Canada.

This idea—about citizens' sense of attachment to the national government, the relationship between that government and citizens, and the impact of federal retrenchment on the relationship—is the subject of recent research by two American scholars, Suzanne Mettler and Andrew Milstein. They contend that political scientists have neglected the impact of state-building processes and the creation of specific policies on the lives of individuals and the ways in which they relate to government. After tracing the reach of American federal programs over the past several decades, they suggest that the relationship between government and citizens may shape "the formation of civic identities, attitudes about government, and political interests or preferences, as well as rates of participation in politics" (Mettler and Milstein 2007: 128). Elaborating, the authors write:

> The form taken by governing arrangements across time is likely to shape citizens' attitudes about and levels of support for government generally and for particular policies. Perhaps most significant, distinct regimes may mobilize citizens to participate to varying degrees, in different ways, and for diverse purposes (Ibid., 110).

They refer to "the stunning levels of political participation of those who came of age during the New Deal and World War II" (Ibid., 129). This, of course, was a time of active federal government involvement in the lives of Americans. Their research leads them to hypothesize that there is a link between the coverage and benefit levels of government programs and the levels of political participation. "Citizens' experiences as beneficiaries might affect their trust and confidence in government, their perceptions of their own political efficacy, and the extent to which government is responsive to them" (Ibid., 130).

What does this imply in our context? Simply that provincialization may carry with it certain political effects having to do with the attitude of Canadians toward their national government. This would not be an inconsequential development, especially in a country with a secessionist movement and provincial governments too eager to pursue their own particular interests at the expense of national solidarity.

Cheryl Collier's comparative analysis of the introduction of universal health care and universal child care, presented in chapter four, comes to the conclusion that, given the current policy context, universal child care is not likely to become a reality in the near future. One reason is related to the 'ideational landscape'. Another is set out by Collier this way:

> Both child care policy directions introduced by the Conservative government—the UCCB [Universal Child Care Benefit] and the Child Care Spaces Initiative (CCSI)—are examples of a move away from traditional intergovernmental discussion on the child care file in favour of lone federal government action in areas of sole federal jurisdiction. The UCCB in fact is not truly a "child care" policy in anything but in name alone as the taxable transfer of $100 per month/per child for children under six years of age can conceivably be spent on anything parents desire.

In other words, the Harper government's reluctance to use the federal spending power—stemming from a desire not to offend mainly Quebec—is one of the two factors inhibiting the emergence of a national child-care program.

Provincial governments of Quebec have long opposed the use of the federal spending power. At least since 1950, they have denounced the power and federal prerogative to resort to conditional grants. The most recent expression of this opposition was contained in the report of the Quebec Commission on Fiscal Imbalance which called upon the federal government to vacate the tax field now occupied by the federal goods and services tax. Further, the commission expressed doubt as to the constitutionality of the power—a view vigorously argued by Professor Andrée Lajoie.

And yet, no provincial government, including that of Quebec, has taken the issue to the Supreme Court of Canada. One reason may be that in a number of cases lower courts have affirmed the constitutionality of the power. Further, Supreme Court justices, in *obiter dicta*, appear to have acknowledged the constitutionality of the power. Legal scholar, David Yudin, has written of "an unspoken judicial consensus" in support of the constitutionality of the power (Yudin 2002: 481). Similarly, Andrew Petter, who had expressed doubt about the constitutionality of the power in a well-known article for the *Canadian Bar Review* in 1989, recently agreed that the consensus appears to be 'in' (Petter 2008).

So, notwithstanding the historic importance of the federal spending power to Canada's economic and social development, and notwithstanding the apparent judicial consensus that exists in support of the power, the federal government nevertheless seems determined to circumscribe it.

It is worth affirming here that there is nothing 'un-federal' about the federal government's spending power. Contrary to the argument of some, the spending power does not offend the 'federal principle'. In the United States, the federal spending power is a broad one and has been strongly upheld by the courts. Indeed, former US Supreme Court Chief Justice, William Rehnquist, wrote: "[O]bjectives not thought to be within Article 1's 'enumerated legislative fields' may nevertheless be attained through the use of the spending power and the conditional grant of funds" (Sky 2003: 345). The central government of Australia also has a spending power. Section 96 of the Australian Constitution provides that the Commonwealth government "may grant financial assistance to any State on such terms and conditions as the Parliament thinks fit." Jurisprudence has upheld a broad interpretation of this power. Are we to conclude from this that the US and Australian constitutions—and the Canadian—so offend the federal principle that they are not really federal states? Of course not.

In her chapter, Maryantonett Flumian suggests that the 'centralization versus decentralization' debate is not really pertinent in today's world. The simple fact is that in the new context "The federal government must have a view of about the health and welfare of the country and its citizens. It must be in a position to do what was originally intended." The particular job of the national government is to ensure coherence in policy development and policy delivery. Flumian looks at a number of examples to analyze how the federal government acted to provide coherence and to ensure collaboration in the interests of Canadian citizens. She concludes by observing that "We can learn much about the character of the federation by how it responds when it is confronted by crisis". When the economic crisis hit Canada, there was no question but that the leadership necessary to address it had to come from the central government, not from a federal-provincial conference or committee of provincial premiers. To be sure, collaboration was necessary, but leading the country out of the quagmire was most definitely Ottawa's job.

Federal environmental policy is the subject of the final chapter. At the time of writing, Quebec Premier Jean Charest was in the media to publicly criticize the Harper government's inaction on climate change and to urge Ottawa to get into the game. In other words, the premier of Canada's most committed autonomy-seeking province felt so frustrated by federal inaction that even he was impelled to speak out. It would be hard to deny that if there is a consensus on anything in this country it is that Ottawa is not lacking in the constitutional powers but rather the political will to develop and implement an environmental policy appropriate to the 21st century.

In the final chapter, Inger Weibust does a masterful job analyzing the federal stance on the environment. She answers her own question "What should the federal government do?" with the following:

> The strongest response would be for the federal government to set minimum national standards or minimum national taxes on pollutants. This would be analogous to what the American federal government has done since the 1970s and what the European Commission does for the European Union member states.

Acknowledging that Ottawa has shown little stomach for setting minimum national environmental standards, Weibust nevertheless argues:

> From the perspective of improving environmental protection, there are no compelling arguments against minimum national standards. They remain rare in Canada,

however, because of the provincial hostility to such measures and the federal government's reluctance to pick a fight with the provinces over the environment. In the past, this reluctance has only been overcome if the public perceives the environment to be in crisis (Weibust, see chapter 6 in this book, page 241).

Weibust recommends that Ottawa pick its battles when setting standards by focusing on issues most closely related to public health and safety, such as drinking water quality. "It would surprise many Canadians," she writes, "to know that Canada has no national standards for drinking water quality." Surprise indeed!

So what can be done to stiffen the federal government's backbone? How can the federal government get off the path of deference and knee-jerk subservience? Only an initial step will be proposed here; that is, that federal officials, political and bureaucratic, take their nation-building role and nation-building powers more seriously. Further, they can change their perception of how they see themselves. The federal government is not just one government among many. It is the government of all Canadians. As former Prime Minister Pierre Trudeau put it: "We [the members of Parliament] are the only group of men and women in this country who can speak for every Canadian. We are the only group, the only assembly in this country, which can speak for the whole nation, which can express the national will and the national interest" (McRoberts 2001: 702). After all, "when there is a conflict of interest, not of laws, which will be judged by the courts, the citizens must be convinced that there is a national government which will speak for the national interest and will ensure that it does prevail" (Ibid.). It is time for the MPs who believe in the value and potential of the federal government to find their voice.

All parts of the Government of Canada can try to understand federal powers, not as tradeable assets to be used as bargaining chips with the provinces or as gifts to attract Quebec nationalists, but as powerful tools to pursue great national objectives and to link the federal government with citizens. With this conception of federal powers in mind, federal representatives can confidently speak to citizens in all of the provinces and territories of Ottawa's role in enhancing national solidarity; in constructing a competitive, green economy; in protecting citizens' rights; in securing the economic union; in environmental protection; in reducing economic inequality; in re-building health care; in building child care; and in pursuing internationally the values that Canadians espouse.

La Presse journalist Lysiane Gagnon is reported to have once said that, around Quebec tables, when the discussion turns to politics, it is the federalists who fall silent. This observation can be applied to the federal government and federal officials. At the national dinner table, when difficult issues arise, it is the occupant of the federal chair who shrinks.

And it must end. When issues of national concern arise, Ottawa must resist the urge to stay silent, to defer—or worse, to devolve its own powers to the sub-national units. If Ottawa must work with the provinces on a national matter, it must assert that it is there as the government of all Canadians. It is not just another government at the table. The federal and provincial governments do not have equality of status; the federal government is the lead government and it should act accordingly. Among other things, it must no longer govern as though antagonizing Alberta or Quebec was the thing to be most avoided. When Ottawa negotiates with the sub-national governments, its bargaining strategy must include getting something concrete from the provinces that will advance the national interest. The federal government should no longer negotiate as if its only objective is intergovernmental peace.

While the founders of this country may have been ambivalent about the idea of a sovereign, fully independent Canada, they came together on a Constitution that, above all, featured a dominant central government. They proposed a hierarchical relationship between the government of all Canadians and the governments of some Canadians. It is time for Ottawa to reclaim this position. Equally important, it must ceaselessly engage with citizens and explain why it is taking a leadership role on the environment; why it will no longer tolerate internal trade barriers; why it will demand accountability from provinces that receive huge federal transfers; why it will assert its right to be fully involved in labour force training; why there will be one securities regulator for all provinces and territories; why it will not fetter its spending power; and why it, and only it, will speak for Canadians at meetings of the United Nations and of any other international organization.

Political competition enlivens democracies. They do not benefit when one of the major players voluntarily withdraws from the competition.

References

Harrison 1996. *Passing the Buck: Federalism and Canadian Environmental Policy.* Vancouver, BC: University of British Columbia Press.

McRoberts, Kenneth 2001. "Canada and the Multinational State." *Canadian Journal of Political Science,* 34: 4: 681–713.

Mettler, Suzanne and Andrew Milstein 2007 (Spring). "American Political Development from Citizens' Perspective: Tracking Federal Government's Presence in Individual Lives over Time." *Studies in American Political Development,* 21: 110–130.

Petter, Andrew 2008. "The Myth of the Federal Spending Power Revisited." *Queen's Law Journal,* 34: 1: 163–173.

Sky, Theodore 2003. *To Provide For the General Welfare: A History of the Federal Spending Power.* Newark: University of Delaware Press.

Yudin, David 2002. "The Federal Spending Power in Canada, Australia and the United States." *National Journal of Constitutional Law,* 13: 3: 437–484.

Index

Governance Series Publications

14. Tom Brzustowski 2008
    The Way Ahead — Meeting Canada's Productivity Challenge
13. Jeffrey Roy 2007
    Business and Government in Canada
12. N. Brown and L. Cardinal (eds.) 2007
    Managing Diversity — Practices of Citizenship
11. Ruth Hubbard and Gilles Paquet 2007
    Gomery's Blinders and Canadian Federalism
10. Emmanuel Brunet-Jailly (ed.) 2007
    Borderlands — Comparing Border Security in North America and Europe
9. Christian Rouillard, E. Montpetit, I. Fortier, and A.G. Gagnon 2006
    Reengineering the State — Toward an Impoverishment of Quebec Governance
8. Jeffrey Roy 2006
    E-Government in Canada
7. Gilles Paquet 2005
    The New Geo-Governance — A Baroque Approach
6. C. Andrew, M. Gattinger, M.S. Jeannotte, and W. Straw (eds.) 2005
    Accounting for Culture — Thinking Through Cultural Citizenship
5. P. Boyer, L. Cardinal, and D. Headon (eds.) 2004
    From Subjects to Citizens — A Hundred Years of Citizenship in Australia and Canada
4. Linda Cardinal and D. Headon (eds.) 2002
    Shaping Nations — Constitutionalism and Society in Australia and Canada
3. Linda Cardinal et Caroline Andrew (dir.) 2001
    La démocratie à l'épreuve de la gouvernance
2. Gilles Paquet 1999
    Governance Through Social Learning
1. David McInnes 1999, 2005
    Taking It to the Hill — The Complete Guide to Appearing Before Parliamentary Committees